God's Gift of Sexuality

Leader's Guide
Revised Edition

God's Gift of Sexuality

A Study for Young People in the Presbyterian Church (U.S.A.)

Leader's Guide
Revised Edition

Writers
Janet Bartosch
Woody Berry
Eleanor Cammer
Janet Ollila Colberg
Carol Hunter-Geboy
Diane Maodush-Pitzer
Paul M. Thompson
Rebecca Voelkel-Haugen
Linda Woodard

Editor
Mary Lee Talbot

Editor for Revised Edition
David M. Dobson

Witherspoon Press
Louisville, Kentucky

Editor: Mary Lee Talbot
Editor for Revised Edition: David M. Dobson
Editorial Assistants: Connie Ellis and Ruth Ann Burks
Art Director: Anthony Feltner
Cover Design: Anthony Feltner
Illustrations: Bud Hixson

Revised edition

Published by Witherspoon Press, a Ministry of the General Assembly Council, Congregational Ministries Division, Presbyterian Church (U.S.A.), Louisville, Kentucky

PRINTED IN THE UNITED STATES OF AMERICA

98 99 00 01 02 03 04 05 06 07 — 10 9 8 7 6 5 4 3 2 1

Web site address: http://www.pcusa.org/pcusa/witherspoon

ISBN 1-57895-059-7

Contents

Preface to the Revised Edition

The numbers are staggering.

In the nine years since this course was introduced, nearly eight million teenage Americans became pregnant. More than twenty million teens acquired some type of sexually transmitted infection. And more than 500,000 cases of AIDS were diagnosed; many of those diagnosed most likely acquired the disease as teens.

We live in a culture that constantly bombards its young people with confusing messages about sex and sexuality. Sex is everywhere: in the advertisements aimed at our children, in the television shows and movies they watch, in the music they listen to. But the media and popular culture can't be blamed for everything. We as parents and educators have to take some responsibility for too often standing on the sidelines as the numbers grow: by age 15, one in four girls and one in three boys are sexually active; by age 20, four out of five young Americans have had sexual intercourse; HIV/AIDS is increasing in the heterosexual population, especially among young women; and the number of teen pregnancies shows no signs of decreasing.

But there is reason for hope. AIDS awareness and education has improved dramatically in the 1990s; sex education is now the rule rather than the exception in our public schools; ratings systems are helping parents decide what is appropriate for their children to watch on television; and after a public outcry, a prominent fashion company was forced to cancel advertisements featuring youth in sexually suggestive situations.

The Presbyterian Church (U.S.A.) has not stood by silently either. This course for youth and older youth was created in response to a mandate from the General Assembly. And in 1996, a sexuality education curriculum for elementary-age children and their parents was produced, also in response to a General Assembly mandate.

There are the numbers, but there is also hope. This course is part of that hope.

Preface to the First Edition

This course is a response to an action of the 195th General Assembly (1984) of the Presbyterian Church (U.S.A.) and a response to all who are concerned for young people today. The former Youth and Young Adult Staff Team and Third World Women's Coordinating Committee of the Program Agency began this project. It has been completed by the Education and Congregational Nurture Ministry Unit. Developmental money for *God's Gift of Sexuality* came from Presbyterian Women through the Women's Opportunity Giving Fund, which is one of the predecessors to the Creative Ministries projects of Presbyterian Women.

This course is made up of four sections: a leader's guide, a book for parents, a book for younger youth, and a book for older youth. It is designed to be used in church retreat settings. The course uses the Scripture and the church doctrine, as well as activities from a variety of sources, to help young people put sexuality into a Christian perspective.

In its development this course has doubly benefited from the wisdom of a task force and the willingness of fifty congregations in the Presbyterian Church (U.S.A.) to test the course with their young people and parents. Their help has been invaluable.

The task force, the authors, and the editor hope that this course will help the young people of our denomination to develop a healthy Christian attitude toward their sexuality.

Members of the Task Force on Sexuality

The Rev. Idalisa Fernandez, New York, New York
The Rev. Paul Thompson, Louisville, Kentucky
Dr. Eva Smith, Washington, D.C.
Elder Candida Flores, New York, New York
Elder Pamela Wagoner, Philadelphia, Pennsylvania
Nicole Brown, Atlanta, Georgia
Esther Velasquez, Compton, California
Joel Lee, San Francisco, California
Elizabeth Parrott Daniel, Wichita, Kansas
The Rev. Bernadine McRipley, Trenton, New Jersey
The Rev. Diane Maodush-Pitzer, Grand Rapids, Michigan

Staff

Maria Allen, Intern 1984–85
Lonna Lee, Intern 1987–88
Kris Thompson, Intern 1988–89
The Rev. Mary Lee Talbot
Elder Mildred Brown
The Rev. Janice Nessibou, D.Min.
Robert H. White, Jr., Synod of Mid-America

About the Writers

Janet Bartosch is a family nurse practitioner with a master's of science in nursing and a master's of education in community health. She has extensive clinical experience in women's health and has offered workshops for parents and teens on sexuality. She has published for professional journals, is currently employed as a medical software editor, and contracts her services as a nurse practitioner. She is the mother of two teenage boys.

The Rev. Woody Berry is pastor of Webster Presbyterian Church, Webster, Texas. He has served as an ordained minister for twenty years in congregations in Texas and Colorado and has been active in educational leadership events across the denomination. He received his bachelor's degree at the University of Texas and master of divinity and doctor of ministry degrees from Austin Presbyterian Theological Seminary. He was coauthor of the Presbyterian Church (U.S.A.) sexuality curriculum for children, *God's Plan for Growing Up,* as well as other church curricula. He has been married for more than twenty-five years to Jan Berry, and they have two teenage children, a daughter, Kennedy, and a son, Christopher.

Eleanor Cammer is a certified Presbyterian Christian educator for Vienna Presbyterian Church in Vienna, Virginia. She has an M.R.E. from Wesley Theological Seminary in Washington, D.C., and is also a certified Human Sexuality Educator. In 1996, she delivered a lecture on "The History of Sexuality," as part of the Smithsonian Lecture Series. She is married, with three daughters and six grandchildren.

Janet Ollila Colberg has worked as a high school nurse for twenty years in Helena, Montana. She and her husband Steve and son Josh are members of the First Presbyterian Church of Helena. Her son Jason and daughter-in-law Laura are active in the Presbyterian Church and Youth Fellowship in Seattle. Janet's master's degree is in counseling. She has written two books and several papers on youth health and sexuality issues, including the book *Red Light, Green Light: Preventing Teen Pregnancy.* She is the 1997–98 Montana School Nurse of the Year.

Carol Hunter-Geboy has her Ph.D. in developmental psychology and has taught sexuality education for more than twelve years. She has trained more than eight thousand people in thirty-five states to work with young people on issues of sexuality education. She has developed curricula for a variety of national organizations including the Salvation Army, Girls Clubs of America, and the Center for Population Options. She currently works for the American Red Cross on issues concerning sexuality.

The Rev. Diane Maodush-Pitzer is the founding director of Witness—a nonprofit ecumenical center of mentoring, advocacy, and support that works toward the transformation of the church through the witness of women so that men and women, as equal partners, may participate fully in the ministry of Jesus Christ. Ordained in the Reformed Church in America, Diane regularly lectures, teaches, and writes in the area of sexuality, education, and liturgy. Along with her husband, Diane is the parent of three young boys and lives in Grand Rapids, Michigan.

The Rev. Dr. Paul M. Thompson is an interim pastor in the Dallas area and is a licensed professional counselor in private practice. He has taught parenting and sexuality education courses for youth and adults in churches throughout the country for more than twenty years. He is the author of *The Giving Book,* a resource for youth ministry. Paul's wife Terri is a middle school principal, and they have four children.

The Rev. Rebecca Voelkel-Haugen is the pastor of Spirit of the Lakes United Church of Christ. Before that she was a program staff member at the Center for the Prevention of Sexual and Domestic Violence. She is coauthor of *Sexual Abuse Prevention: A Course of Study for Teenagers,* published by United Church Press. Rebecca lives with her partner Kris in Minneapolis.

The Rev. Linda Woodard is a pastor in Rome, Georgia. She has led courses on sexuality education at the Montreat Youth Conference and the Youth Triennium. She began teaching in this subject area through her work with the United Methodist Church sex education program.

About the Editors

David M. Dobson is an acquisitions editor for Bridge Resources and Witherspoon Press, two imprints of Curriculum Publishing, Presbyterian Church (U.S.A.). He is a member of the National Council of Churches Committee on Family Ministry and Human Sexuality. He and his wife Myriam, a Montessori educator, have two children and are members of Highland Presbyterian Church in Louisville, Kentucky.

The Rev. Mary Lee Talbot served on the Youth and Young Adult Staff Team of the Program Agency from 1981 to 1988. She is the writer and/or editor of a number of youth ministry resources. She received her Ph.D. from Columbia University Teachers College in New York City. Currently, she serves as director of Continuing Education and Special Events at Pittsburgh Theological Seminary.

I. Background Materials

Guidelines for Leaders

Criteria for a Good Leader

The leader of an educational program about sexuality is probably the most important variable in determining the success of the program. Thus, it is important for this person to be well trained. Many leaders who teach other topics well may be less effective in the area of sexuality. It takes a person with specific characteristics to teach sensitive subject matter. Some of these characteristics, such as comfort in using sexual terminology, can be developed with good training. Other more basic qualities, such as warmth and a sense of humor, cannot be taught. An effective educator in a sexuality program should

- believe in the importance of parents and young people communicating about sexuality.
- convey warmth and a sense of humor.
- know and understand the biblical and theological teachings about sexuality, especially Reformed/Presbyterian teachings.
- keep well-informed about sexual topics.
- continually explore his or her own attitudes about a variety of sexual issues.
- feel enthusiastic about teaching sexuality.
- discuss sexuality with adolescents comfortably.
- use sexual terminology comfortably.
- have good communication and group facilitation skills.
- be capable of using, and comfortable with, a variety of teaching techniques in the classroom.
- be familiar with the needs and sensitivities of adolescents.
- have experience with adolescents (as a parent, older sibling, aunt/uncle, teacher, etc.).

Underlying Assumptions and Values

Programs dealing with human sexuality cannot and should not be value-free. Instead, programs should be based on our understanding of biblical and theological teachings about sexuality. We have a set of values about sexuality that we want to convey to our children.

Some of the basic assumptions for this course are the following:

- At appropriate age levels, people need access to accurate information about the physical, psychological, social, and moral aspects of sexuality.
- More accurate information, clearer values, and enhanced skills will increase responsible decision making.
- Parents are the primary educators about sexuality of their children. Churches, schools, and other agencies function as partners with parents in providing education about sexuality.

Some values that should be stressed implicitly and explicitly throughout the course are the following:

- Recognize the worth and dignity of all individuals and treat all individuals with respect, regardless of their sex, race, religion, culture, or sexual orientation.

- To use pressure or physical force to make people do things against their will or values is wrong.

- To take unfair advantage of, or exploit, others is wrong.

- People are responsible for their own behavior and its consequences.

- Before making important decisions about sexuality and other matters, individuals need to weigh the current and future consequences for themselves, significant others, and society.

- Before making important decisions, individuals need to consider their responsibility to God and to consider the decision within a faith framework.

- Open communication is an important part of healthy relationships with others.

Maintaining a Constructive Learning Environment

1. Make your meeting room a special place. In as many ways as possible, establish an atmosphere in your room that encourages students to feel special, unique, inspired, and accepted. For example, one teacher brings in an instant camera on the first day of the program and takes pictures of all the students. She then places the pictures on the wall under a banner that says, "You are special." She tells her students that they are special—that most people in this country don't have this unique learning experience.

2. Develop a relationship with each student. Relate to each student as an individual. Know all students' names and use them during group discussions. Knowing the names of some students and not others can damage the self-esteem of the less-noticed students.

3. Outlaw put-downs. Make a strong statement about how you feel when you hear a put-down. Ask students to remember a time when they were unfairly criticized or teased. Ask them to draw on those feelings to understand how others might feel when they get put down.

4. Be yourself. Allow your own personality to influence the group atmosphere. You do not have to assume the stereotyped role of "The Successful Youth Leader." Although we have identified certain qualities that we think are important, to come across as an authentic human being with real emotions, a sense of humor, and strengths, as well as flaws and weaknesses, is most important. However, at the same time, do not bring your personal problems to class. Adolescents do not need to add their teacher's troubled home life or conflict with fellow teachers to their own burdens.

5. Facilitate discussion in a relaxed manner. Too often, educators get impatient after only seconds if students have not responded to a question. They immediately follow that question with another, then another. As a result, students can feel overwhelmed. Instead, ask a relevant question and give students a minute or so to think about their responses. Silence after a question is often the result of students' thinking or working up the courage to speak.

Some teachers take a minor point and go over it again and again. Don't beat a dead horse! Discuss a point thoroughly, but take the cue from the group when interest in the discussion is waning.

Ways to Encourage Participation

Invite young people to learn about themselves, their plans and dreams, and each other by creating an environment that fosters group activity and encourages participation:

- Select a quiet, private setting for instruction.

- Be aware that a comfortable learning environment invites active participation. You may need to rearrange seating or restructure your room so the feeling is one of informality rather than of a classroom.

- Demonstrate open, honest discussion and sharing about yourself.
- Reduce anxiety by telling young people in the group what they will be doing and what will be expected.
- Keep the size of the group small (fifteen to twenty) if possible.
- Communicate enthusiasm about this special opportunity to talk to one another about important topics. Point out how seldom we have a chance to talk about our feelings, especially about something as personal as relationships or sexuality.

Setting the Stage: Ground Rules

Establish ground rules for group behavior so that young people know their limits as members of the group. Examples of appropriate rules include the following:

- *Full participation:* Group members are expected to actively participate in activities and discussions. Participation may sometimes mean just listening, but everyone is encouraged to share his or her thoughts and feelings.
- *Right to "pass":* Everyone is encouraged to participate in each session, but if a question or activity makes a person feel too uncomfortable, he or she always has the right to say "I pass."
- *Nonjudgmental approach:* Members are expected to respect each other; put-downs and teasing are not allowed. It is okay to disagree with others, but not to make judgmental or negative remarks, call people names, or make fun of someone.
- *Confidentiality:* Confidentiality is required. Participants may not quote one another outside of this program. They should talk over sessions with family and friends but not identify specific individuals.
- *Appropriate sharing:* Members are not to bring in personal business of friends or family members and share it with the group. They may share stories or

experiences but should be careful not to use anyone's real name. Also, they are never to talk specifically in the group about their own sexual behavior.

- *Openness:* To be open and honest is important, but this does not mean sharing your own or other people's (family, neighbors, friends) personal or private lives. To discuss general situations is okay, but using names is not.
- *I-statements:* To preface personal feelings or values with "I," such as "I believe . . . " or "I feel . . . ," is best.
- *There are no "dumb" questions:* All questions will be answered, so it is all right to ask any question, no matter how silly it seems. A question box will be provided so questions can be asked anonymously.
- *Acceptance:* To feel embarrassed or uncomfortable when talking about sensitive topics like values or sexuality is all right.

You may choose to add more ground rules of your own.

Processing Activities

Processing simply means talking with the group about what they have experienced and learned as they participated in an activity. Processing allows you to assess and reinforce learning and may require that you repeat or summarize key points as you bring the group to closure. Asking the following questions may be useful during any of the activities in this program:

- Why? What was the objective or point of the activity?
- What did you learn?
- Do you still have any questions?
- Is anything unclear?
- How did you feel about the activity?
- Is anyone upset about anything we did or said? If you would rather talk privately, we can talk after this session.
- Have your feelings changed now that you have participated in the activity?

Seeking feedback from the group helps keep the young people interested and involved. You won't need to process each activity to the same extent, but do process any activity that seems to cause conflict or concern for the group or for any individual member.

Cultural Awareness

Every attempt has been made to make this course inclusive of the many cultural heritages within the community of faith. At the same time, there has been deliberate work to make this course not reflect any one cultural heritage. For this course to be effective, the leaders should be familiar with the different cultural heritages represented in the group and understand the critical role that these backgrounds play in transmitting values to youth. Such cultural awareness would include such things as the following:

Avoid stereotypes. Stereotyping does not allow for individuality, nor does it take into account the diversity existing within ethnic groups.

Be sensitive to verbal expression. Cultural background often plays a role in the willingness or reluctance of people to discuss openly topics they consider of a private nature. Do not push for participation.

Avoid preferential treatment. At the same time, avoid making special allowances that may be interpreted by others as preferential treatment. Ensure that both genders have equal opportunity for questions, answers, and discussion.

Provide role models. Describe appropriate role models whenever possible during discussions.

Watch for cultural friction. Often there is friction between particular cultural under-standings and the values of the predominant community in which you live. Such issues as single parenting, birth control, and abstinence may be regarded differently by various cultures. Be sensitive to cultural understandings.

Be sensitive to family patterns. The course has several opportunities for parental involvement. Family patterns vary. Because of this, the definition of *family* used in this resource is those who love and care for us. When involving parents, be aware that the term *parents* may mean only one parent, grandparents, guardians, other family members, or foster parents. Adapt your language as necessary to include whatever configuration of family you may find in your community.

Recognizing and Reporting Abuse

Youth and children who have been or are being abused or harassed are often afraid to tell anyone. They may feel frightened, threatened, alone, and confused about what to do. In many cases, the offender is a family member or someone the young person knows, and therefore that may keep the victim silent. Sometimes the victim feels guilty about the abuse and feels it is his or her own fault. And there is also the fear of the response once someone is told about the abuse.

Because there are sessions in this resource that deal with harassment, rape, and abuse, and because of the trust that may grow between the young person and the leader(s), it is possible that he or she may break the silence and tell you of abuse or harassment. Here are some guidelines to help you in your response:

Support the youth. Allow the youth to tell what happened in his or her own words. Do not press for details. Simply listen and be caring and loving with the youth. Accept what the youth is telling you even if it is difficult for you to believe or accept. Comfort the youth by saying that it is good that you were told.

Remain calm and don't overreact. Even if the information angers or upsets you, stay with the youth and tell him or her that he or she is not to blame. The alleged abuser has done something wrong. Reassure the youth, because the divulging of a secret often produces anxiety. Let the youth know that you will do something to help.

Do not confront the suspected offender. That is not your responsibility, but rather the responsibility of someone trained to deal with abuse.

Report the alleged abuse, or encourage the youth to do so. This will be a very difficult decision to make. The process for reporting and investigating sexual abuse and assault varies for each state. In many states, anyone who works with children and suspects abuse is mandated to report it. As Christians, we have an ethical obligation to report suspected abuse; it is the best way that we have to stop the abuse and keep the youth safe. You do not have to be able to prove abuse; the investigation is the job of trained professionals. You do not have to give your name when reporting abuse, but it may help those investigating if you do. You are immune from liability for an unfounded report as long as it was made "in good faith."

Be prepared. One of the best things you can do for yourself is to be prepared and have a plan of action. Investigate the resources in your area.

Have the names and phone numbers of local rape crisis centers and child protective agencies on hand. See the Resources section in this guide for more materials to help you recognize and report abuse.

You are ready to begin. Remember how important the program can be to the futures of the young people in your group. Most important, think of the opportunity you have to help.

Good luck and enjoy.

A Reformed/Presbyterian Understanding of Sexuality

Our essential affirmation is that God is a God of love who comes to us, offering us the gift of a new and meaningful life through Jesus Christ. We know and understand who God is through Jesus and can best know Christ through Scripture and through its interpretation by the church. We believe that God has given us God's Spirit to enliven and empower us to be God's followers in the world. We believe that our lives are to be used in thanksgiving to God by loving God, one another, and ourselves.

Thus a Reformed/Presbyterian understanding of sexuality begins with a belief in a God of love who has created us as sexual beings to relate to one another in love. We believe in educating young people so they can learn about all aspects of sexuality, including the physical aspects, the emotional aspects, the beliefs and values we hold that inform our sexuality, and the appropriate ways to make decisions about our sexuality. All of this knowledge helps us live out our sexuality in love and thanksgiving to God.

We begin the explanation of our understanding of sexuality with the Bible. The Bible is our basic textbook because it describes God's faithfulness to us. Some things we need to remember about our biblical faith include the following:

1. We believe in a personal, transcendent God who is the self-sufficient Sovereign of all being. Based on God's attributes of justice, righteousness, holiness, and love, God determines what is right and just in creation.

2. Through the law in the Old and New Testaments, God has specified what is right and wrong. All of God's commands undergird and reinforce the objective moral universe. God holds us accountable as moral stewards of creation.

3. Men and women are unique as God's image bearers. Like God, we are personal, moral, and spiritual beings, capable of an intimate relationship with God and with other human beings.

4. Christian ethics founded on biblical principles will try to avoid the following dangers: legalism (belief that Scripture is merely a rule book containing moral proof texts); situationalism (belief that there are no moral absolutes but that situations dictate what is right and wrong); and intuitionism (belief that moral knowledge is an exclusively internal and subjective experience).

5. A biblical ethic on human sexuality needs to include the following precepts:

a. Norms or standards are revealed by God in Scripture. In every situation we must ask, What does the Bible teach?

b. Situations in history progress under God's guidance. In every situation we must ask, What would honor God?

c. Existential motivation is prompted by the Holy Spirit. In every situation we must ask, How do I (we) respond?

We are forgiven sinners, and, guided by the Holy Spirit, we can use our sexuality as God intended. Norms, context, and motivation are essential to moral Christian sexual activity.

This course is based on seven biblical and theological principles that provide the guidance and support for understanding our sexuality. These affirmations are the following:

1. God created us and gave us the gift of our sexuality.
2. God created us for life in community.
3. Our church is a community of love.
4. Our church is a community of responsibility.
5. Our church is a varied community.
6. Our church is a community of forgiveness.
7. God gives us responsibility for our own decisions.

Each of the foregoing theological affirmations is highlighted in this section. In standard Reformed/Presbyterian fashion, each affirmation begins with Scripture, is followed with a quotation from a theological document, and is then briefly explained in language meaningful to a young person. Use these affirmations to set the stage for understanding our sexuality, and post them in a prominent place to remind your young people of the strong and positive guidance the church provides for them. These theological affirmations have also been included in the guides for the young people to help them understand and apply these values and beliefs in their decision making about the use of their sexuality.

We have stated the theological affirmations in a positive way. Sexuality is a good and positive part of our lives as intended by God. In order for our sexuality to be a good part of our lives, it must be used responsibly.

To belong to the church means to share in the values of the church. On the one hand, we have boundaries; on the other hand, we must each make decisions for ourselves. Thus, within the community, there is room for us to move about. This freedom allows for the variety that exists within the Reformed/Presbyterian family.

The guiding principles that define our community are love, responsibility, and forgiveness. Within the boundaries of the church, there is freedom, but this freedom is bounded by love and responsibility. There is always the possibility of the irresponsible use of our sexuality. When this happens, we are still a part of the church and are called to confession and forgiveness within the bounds of the church.

We hope that young people in the Reformed/Presbyterian churches can grow to appreciate the wonderful gift of human sexuality God has given them and will be able to make a good, healthy, and hopeful affirmation about their own sexuality.

God Created Us and Gave Us the Gift of Our Sexuality

> Then God said, "Let us make humankind in our image, according to our likeness; and let them have dominion over . . . the earth." So God created humankind in [God's] image, in the image of God [God] created them; male and female [God] created them. . . . God saw everything that [God] had made, and indeed, it was very good.
>
> (Gen. 1:26, 27, 31a)

> For we are what [God] has made us, created in Christ Jesus for good works.
>
> (Eph. 2:10)

> God made human beings male and female for their mutual help and comfort and joy. We recognize that our creation as sexual beings is part of God's loving purpose for us. God intends all people . . . to affirm each other as males and females with joy, freedom, and responsibility.
>
> ("A Declaration of Faith,"
> ch. 2, lines 80–84, 87–88)

> God has created . . . male and female and given them a life which proceeds from birth to death in a succession of generations and in a wide complex of social relations. . . . Life is a gift to be received with gratitude and a task to be pursued with courage.
>
> (The Confession of 1967, 9.17)

God created us and called us very good. God did not create us as spirits. God did not create us as bodies. Instead, God created us as total persons—body and spirit. And this entire creation, God called very good.

Not only did God create us, but God created us to be God's very own image in the world. All that we are—including our bodies, including our sexuality—is God's gift to us.

Our sexuality is our way of being male or female in the world. Our sexuality is basic and affects our thoughts, feelings, and actions. Because our sexuality is called good by God, because it is God's gift to us, and because we are made in the image of God, we can feel good about our sexuality.

God Created Us for Life in Community

> Owe no one anything, except to love one another; for the one who loves another has fulfilled the law. The commandments, "You shall not commit adultery; You shall not murder; You shall not steal; You shall not covet"; and any other commandment, are summed up in this word, "Love your neighbor as yourself." Love does no wrong to a neighbor; therefore, love is the fulfilling of the law.
>
> (Rom. 13:8–10)

> God made us for life in community.
>
> ("A Declaration of Faith," ch. 2, line 61)

> The new life takes shape in a community in which men and women know that God loves them and accepts them in spite of what they are.
>
> (The Confession of 1967, 9.22)

God created us to be together. From the very beginning, God's purpose was for us to be together—with God and with one another.

One word to define this togetherness is "relationship." A *relationship* is how we describe the connection between two people. The connection might be the result of birth; we have particular relationships with our parents and brothers and sisters. The connection might be the result of feelings and commitments; we have particular relationships with acquaintances, friends, and partners. God creates us with a basic need to form relationships with others. Our relationships are answers to the loneliness we feel, and they give our lives meaning.

Another word to define this togetherness that God has in mind for us is "community." A *community* is a group of people who join together with one another. You are a part of many communities—your neighborhood, your town or city, your own particular group of friends, your church. God created us to be together in communities, which can give meaning and identity to our lives.

The very heart of what it means to be in the image of God is to be in community—joined with God and with one another. When we gather in God's name, we are God's community, the church, in the world. In the church we learn to be who God created us to be. We find our true identity with God and one another in the church.

Our Church Is a Community of Love

> Beloved, let us love one another, because love is from God; everyone who loves is born of God and knows God. Whoever does not love does not know God, for God is love. . . . Beloved, since God loved us so much, we also ought to love one another. No one has ever seen God; if we love one another, God lives in us, and God's love is perfected in us.
>
> (1 John 4:7–8; 11–12)

> And one of them, a lawyer, asked [Jesus] a question to test him. "Teacher, which commandment in the law is the greatest?" He said to him, " 'You shall love the Lord your God with all your heart, and with all your soul, and with all your mind.' This is the greatest and first commandment. And a second is like it: 'You shall love your neighbor as yourself.' On these two commandments hang all the law and the prophets."
>
> (Matt. 22:35–40)

> Q. 42. What is the sum of the Ten Commandments?

A. The sum of the Ten Commandments is: to love the Lord our God with all our heart, with all our soul, with all our strength, and with all our mind; and our neighbor as ourselves.

(The Shorter Catechism, 7.042)

We are created to be in community, in relationship, with God and with one another. Above all else, God has loved us, does love us, and will love us faithfully. In the same way, we should love God and one another.

The summation of the law by Jesus—to love God and to love your neighbor as yourself—indicates that the love of oneself is included in the love of others. Clearly our sexual attitudes and relationships should be motivated by love both for our neighbors and for ourselves. Our sense of identity and our way of acting should affirm others as well as affirm ourselves and should respect others as well as respect ourselves. We are to be concerned for others' needs and feelings without discounting our own.

Because we are total persons, we express our maleness or femaleness in all our relationships. Physical intimacy progresses from the simple affirmation of a handshake or hug to the total intimacy of marriage. Different levels of physical intimacy are appropriate to different kinds and stages of relationships. Often in a relationship, we find ourselves asking what is appropriate. One way to determine the appropriateness of the physical expression of our sexuality is by evaluating the level of committed and faithful love in the relationship.

Our Church Is a Community of Responsibility

The fruit of the Spirit is love, joy, peace, patience, kindness, generosity, faithfulness, gentleness, and self-control.

(Gal. 5:22–23a)

[God] has told you . . . what is good; and what does the Lord require of you but to do justice, and to love kindness, and to walk humbly with your God?

(Micah 6:8)

We believe that we have been created to relate to God and each other in freedom and responsibility.

We may misuse our freedom and deny our responsibility by trying to live without God and other people or against God and other people.

Yet we are still bound to them for our life and well-being, and intended for free and responsible fellowship with them.

("A Declaration of Faith," ch. 2, lines 66–73)

The Church, as the household of God, is called to lead men [and women] out of this [sexual] alienation into the responsible freedom of the new life in Christ. Reconciled to God, each person has joy in and respect for his [or her] own humanity and that of other persons.

(The Confession of 1967, 9.47)

Sexuality is a good and positive part of our lives created by God. In order for our sexuality to continue to be a good part of our lives, it must be used responsibly. Some people define responsible sexuality by saying that certain actions are wrong and others are right and that responsible behavior is simply a matter of following these rules. At the other extreme, some say deciding for yourself what is right and wrong is an individual matter.

Our understanding of responsible sexuality is not found at these two extremes. We are a part of a community of faith. Joined together, we read and study God's Word, pray and listen for God's guidance for us, study the beliefs of our church in the past, and then, being guided by all this, we make statements together that express our beliefs. Presbyterians do take definite stands on issues. At the same time, we uphold the right of each person to maintain the dignity of his or her own conscience in the light of Scripture.

To belong to the church means to share in the values of the church. The guiding principle that defines the church is love. Within the boundaries of the church, there is freedom, but this freedom is bounded by love. We are free to use our sexuality, and yet we are limited in this freedom because of our commitment to God to live a life of love and obedience. We care about the effects of our actions on others as well as on ourselves. Therefore, our sexuality is to be expressed lovingly, responsibly, and obediently.

We know we are expressing our sexuality lovingly, responsibly, and obediently when we work for love and justice in the world. We also know that God's Spirit is present when there is love, joy, peace, patience, kindness, goodness, fidelity, gentleness, and self-control. We can be sure that we are acting responsibly when we keep God's Spirit as the guide of our lives.

Our Church Is a Varied Community

> For just as the body is one and has many members, and all the members of the body, though many, are one body, so it is with Christ. For in the one Spirit we were all baptized into one body—Jews or Greeks, slaves or free—and we are all made to drink of one Spirit. . . . Now you are the body of Christ and individually members of it.
>
> (1 Cor. 12:12–13, 27)

> There is no longer Jew or Greek, there is no longer slave or free, there is no longer male and female; for all of you are one in Christ Jesus.
>
> (Gal. 3:28)

> The young need to see in the church role models of both sexes who communicate by life, even more than by words, the goodness of our femaleness and maleness and the equal opportunity of both for service, responsibility, and authority in the life of the church. They need to see the varied responsible ways in which one can live out one's maleness and femaleness and be helped to affirm the goodness of their own sexuality.
>
> ("The Nature and Purpose of Human Sexuality," lines 469–475)

The many ways in which people choose to live out their relationships include casual acquaintances, friendship, and marriage. In all our relationships we are to relate to one another lovingly and responsibly.

Some people remain single all their lives. They have friendships and close loving relationships without necessarily having sexual intercourse. Sometimes people are widowed or divorced and must renew friendships and other relationships as a single person. Marriage is a covenant of love and responsibility in which a couple makes a commitment of faithfulness. Sexual intercourse is the ultimate expression of this mutual and lasting covenant. Some people choose to become parents, making commitments to love, protect, and support their children.

The ways we live out our relationships are influenced by many factors: our families, our friends, our early sexual experiences, and the sex education we receive. Other factors that influence us are the particular economic, racial, and ethnic group to which we belong and the community in which we live. Sometimes we live out our relationships in sexist ways—stereotyping males and females in particular ways and assigning them superior or inferior status simply because they are males or females. Sometimes we live out our relationships in racist ways—stereotyping particular groups of people simply because of their race or ethnicity. In our own church, we have held and sometimes still hold sexist and racist views. To avoid these views, we must embrace the diversity within our community and strive toward a good, positive, and healthy view of our sexuality as God has intended.

Whether we are children, youth, or adults; single, divorced, married, or widowed; male or female; heterosexual or homosexual; and whatever our economic status or racial/ethnic heritage, we are all loved by a God who is faithful and just.

Our Church Is a Community of Forgiveness

> Do not judge, and you will not be judged; do not condemn, and you will not be condemned. Forgive, and you will be forgiven; give, and it will be given to you. A good measure, pressed down, shaken together, running over, will be put into your lap; for the measure you give will be the measure you get back.
>
> (Luke 6:37–38)

When we fail each other as parents or partners, we are called to forgive each other as God forgives us and to accept the possibilities for renewal that God offers us in grace.

("A Declaration of Faith," ch. 2, lines 106–109)

The church comes under the judgment of God and invites rejection by [people] when it fails to lead men and women into the full meaning of life together, or withholds the compassion of Christ from those caught in the moral confusion of our time.

(The Confession of 1967, 9.47)

We have all misused our sexuality. There are times when we have not used our sexuality responsibly. There are times when we have not been grateful for the gift of our sexuality. There are times when we all have fallen short of the high calling God has for us, including the use of our sexuality. This is called sin. When this happens, we are still a part of the church and called to confession and forgiveness within the bounds of the church.

We can be grateful that the church is a community of forgiven people, not an exclusive circle of the morally pure. In our church, we can honestly acknowledge our sins. God's forgiveness makes such honesty possible and helps us to change our lives to reflect God's love. God's Holy Spirit enables us to change and guides us. Rather than rejection and condemnation because we have fallen short of God's intention and our own best aspirations, in the church we can experience forgiveness and receive help in living out our sexuality. We are then all the more willing to forgive the failings of others because we have experienced God's love in such abundance.

God Gives Us Responsibility for Our Own Decisions

I appeal to you therefore, brothers and sisters, by the mercies of God, to present your bodies as a living sacrifice, holy and acceptable to God, which is your spiritual worship. Do not be conformed to this world, but be transformed by the renewing of your minds, so that you may discern what is the will of God—what is good and acceptable and perfect.

(Rom. 12:1–2)

If the people of the church are to be given the resources to live out their lives responsibly as sexual beings, the enabling leadership of the church must . . . assist people in their problems of identity and moral choice. This assistance will, however, have deprived people of the chance to grow and of the need to wrestle with their own choices if it consists predominantly of handing out prescriptions and passing judgment. What is more, the counsel of the church will be sought more if people see in its stance not only a convinced perspective that orients its approach but also a willingness to recognize the complexity of sexual problems, the possibility of conscientious disagreement on moral decisions, and the opportunity for renewal of life for forgiven sinners.

("The Nature and Purpose of Human Sexuality," lines 689–700)

In our decision making, we are instructed by God's Word to us. We are to be influenced by our Christian beliefs. We are aware of other influences: what our friends believe, how we feel, and what we have learned about our sexuality. We need to learn to sort out those different factors, because some may be sexist, racist, or the result of pressures from others.

The guiding principles that define the church are love, responsibility, obedience, and forgiveness. Keeping these principles in mind and exploring their meanings within our community will lead us to make responsible decisions for our own lives.

To talk about how we make decisions for ourselves and how we communicate those decisions to others is important. Our decisions, based on love, responsibility, and forgiveness, are discovered in relationship with God, with one another, and with ourselves.

Guide for the Presbyterian Church (U.S.A.)

Each year the Presbyterian Church (U.S.A.) meets in a General Assembly of commissioners, comprised of clergy and elders, who gather to address the issues before the church. At these meetings, issues of moral and social concern are often discussed. The Assembly sometimes will appoint committees to study the issues and report back. The Assembly can then endorse these studies with recommended actions it believes should be taken.

These statements are then sent to the whole church. Their purpose is to speak to the church on the particular issues. They are meant as guides to help us in understanding the issues. They are meant to provoke our own thinking. They can help us understand and grow in our faith. These statements are not used as an official pronouncement of what Presbyterians believe. Although they are not binding on the conscience of any member of the Presbyterian Church (U.S.A.), they do help us understand the boundaries of our community.

This guide is compiled from the Scriptures and from several documents that have been endorsed as setting forth the understandings of recent General Assemblies. Included also are statements from *The Book of Confessions*. The guide is in the form of questions and answers that should be helpful to young people in the church. The guide is written in language meaningful to a layperson, so please refer to the original document as reprinted in the Minutes of the General Assembly for more thorough information or for issues of interpretation.

List of Topics for Definition and Discussion

Human Sexuality

Equality of Men and Women

Marriage

Procreation and Contraception

Infertility

Premarital Sex

Extramarital Sex

Sexual Abstinence

Masturbation

Divorce

Abortion

Homosexuality

Sexual Misconduct

Decision Making

Documents Cited

Document 1: The Second Helvetic Confession, from *The Book of Confessions*.

Document 2: The Confession of 1967, from *The Book of Confessions*.

Document 3: "Sexuality and the Human Community," a study document adopted by the 182nd General Assembly, PCUS (1970).

Document 4: "A Declaration of Faith," a study document adopted by the 117th General Assembly (1977) of the Presbyterian Church in the United States.

Document 5: "The Church and Homosexuality," a study document adopted by the 190th General Assembly, UPCUSA (1978), as reprinted in the Minutes of the 198th General Assembly PC(USA) (1986).

Document 6: "Homosexuality and the Church: A Position Paper," a study document adopted by the 119th General Assembly, PCUS (1979), as reprinted in the Minutes of the 198th General Assembly, PC(USA) (1986).

Document 7: "Marriage—A Theological Statement," a study document adopted by the 120th General Assembly, PCUS (1980).

Document 8: "The Nature and Purpose of Human Sexuality," a study document adopted by the 120th General Assembly, PCUS (1980).

Document 9: "The Covenant of Life and the Caring Community," a study document adopted by the 195th General Assembly, UPCUSA (1983).

Document 10: "Covenant and Creation: Theological Reflections on Contraception and Abortion," a study document adopted by the 195th General Assembly, UPCUSA (1983).

Document 11: Policy Statements and Recommendations of the 197th General Assembly (1985). Assembly Committee on Justice and the Rights of Persons.

Document 12: "A Brief Statement of Faith," from *The Book of Confessions*.

Document 13: Report of the Assembly Committee on General Assembly Council Review, adopted by the 206th General Assembly, PC(USA) (1994), as printed in the Minutes of the 206th General Assembly, pp. 86–90.

Document 14: "Do Justice, Love Mercy, Walk Humbly," report of the Special Committee on Problem Pregnancies and Abortion, adopted by the 204th General Assembly, PC(USA) (1992), as printed in the Minutes of the 204th General Assembly, pp. 357–377.

Document 15: Overture adopted by the 207th General Assembly, PC(USA) (1995), as printed in the Minutes of the 207th General Assembly, pp. 678–679.

Document 16: Resolution of the 205th General Assembly, PC(USA) (1993), as printed in the Minutes of the 205th General Assembly, pp. 118–119.

Document 17: Policy statement adopted by the 203rd General Assembly, PC(USA) (1991), as printed in the Minutes of the 203rd General Assembly, pp. 76–92.

Human Sexuality

Why Were We Created as Sexual Beings?

We were created as sexual beings so that we could be in relationships and community with one another and with God. Our sexuality allows for intimacy and allows us to be co-creators with God (Doc. 8, pp. 7, 11). See also Gen. 1:27–31; 2:18–25.

Were We Created as Sexual Beings for the Purpose of Procreation?

We are sexual beings, first, for the purpose of relating to one another, and second, for the purpose of procreation (Doc. 8, p. 7). See also Gen. 2:18–35.

In What Ways Should We Express Our Sexuality?

Our sexuality should be expressed in ways that are loving, self-expressive, creative, faithful, sensitive to the needs of others, honest, self-giving, socially responsible, joyful, and patient (Doc. 8, p. 11). See also Gen. 5:22–23.

When Do We Become Sexual Beings?

We are sexual beings from the moment of creation. No matter the age, state of development, or level of health, we are all sexual beings (Doc. 8, p. 3; Doc. 7, lines 79–88). See also Gen. 1:27–31.

What Is the Relationship between Sex and Love?

One's sexual attitudes and relationships should be motivated by unconditional care both for one's neighbor and oneself (Doc. 8, p. 10). See also Matt. 22:35–40; Luke 10:25–28; 1 Cor. 10:24–33.

What Is Our Church's Role in Developing Understanding of Sexuality?

First of all, the leadership of our church must be educated concerning sexuality. Second, we should not merely hand out prescriptions or pass judgment. Instead, we must recognize how complex our sexuality is, that we disagree in our understandings, and that there is always the need for forgiveness. Third, we should be clear about what we believe, but not speak as if we are sinless. Instead, we should see ourselves as fellow learners, trying to live responsibly with one another (Doc. 8, p. 18; Doc. 2, para. 9.47). See also Rom. 3:21–26.

Does Our Church Advocate Sex Education in the Schools?
We support sexuality education programs in families, churches, schools, and private and public agencies (Doc. 10, p. 60).

Equality of Men and Women

In the Genesis 2 Creation Story, Woman Is Created After Man. Does This Mean Woman Is Subordinate to Man?
No, woman is not subordinate, but rather, she completes Creation. She is created in equality and solidarity with man (Doc. 8, p. 7). See also Gen. 1:27–31; 2:18–25.

How Is the Equality of Men and Women Understood in Old Testament Times?
Male domination and male-centeredness were the norm, although there were exceptions, such as the following: (1) women took active roles in the liberation of the Hebrews from Egypt; (2) women assumed the role of judge; (3) Ruth and Naomi assumed roles different from those their culture prescribed; (4) the Song of Solomon celebrates the goodness of the sensual desire of a man and a woman for each other and presents the woman taking the initiative and being active in expressing her love (Doc. 8, p. 8). See also Ex. 1:15; 2:10; 15:20–21; Ruth 1—4; Judges 4—5; Song of Sol. 1—8.

What Was Jesus' Treatment of Women?
Jesus treated women as worthy human beings. Women were prominent among his followers. He freed women to assume roles and identities other than those the tradition prescribed (Doc. 8, p. 8). See also Mark 10:2–12; Luke 10:38–42; Matt. 5:27–28, 31–32.

How Did Paul Address This Issue?
Paul said that being baptized into Christ means that sexual distinctions are no longer important. This belief resulted in women's having significant places in leadership in local churches. In other passages, Paul's understanding of women shows much less belief in equality, but reflects the beliefs of the male-dominated culture of which he was a part (Doc. 8, p. 9). See also Gal. 3:23–29; 1 Cor. 11:2–16; 14:34–36.

What Does Our Church Say about Equality?
In sovereign love, God created the world good and makes everyone equally in God's image, male and female, of every race and people, to live as one community (Doc. 12, lines 29–32). See also Gen. 1:1—2:25; 5:1–32.

What Does Our Church Say about Equality in Church Life?
We affirm in the strongest possible terms that the body of Christ is made up of women and men. God calls both women and men to ministries in the life of the church. Any attempt to silence or marginalize any voices is not worthy of Christ's body (Doc. 13, p. 90).

Marriage

What Is Marriage?
A marriage is a covenant between a man and a woman in which they commit to live out their lives with each other. It is also an agreement that is licensed and regulated by the state (Doc. 7, pp. 7, 9, 12). See also Gen. 2:24–25.

What Is Christian Marriage?
A marriage is a Christian marriage when a couple make their covenant in the midst of a Christian community and when they acknowledge God's presence in their lives as they live out their relationship with each other. In a Christian marriage, a wife and husband promise to love and serve each other faithfully. God gives them the gift of sexual union as the sign of their mutual and lasting promise, as well as a means whereby they may share in creating new life (Doc. 7, pp. 9, 12; Doc. 4, lines 96–102). See also Mark 10:7–12; Gen. 2:24–25.

What Is God's Role in Marriage?

God established marriage. God preserves and guides all the relationships of life, and in marriage God works to increase love and faithfulness (Doc. 7, p. 9). See also Gen. 2:18–24.

Is It Necessary to Have a Wedding Ceremony to Have a Marriage?

A wedding ceremony is not necessary. Yet open acknowledgment of the covenant in the midst of the Christian community and seeking God's participation are needed. Some service akin to the wedding should be used (Doc. 7, p. 13).

How Should Married Couples Live?

A husband and wife are to love and care for each other in a relationship of equality (Doc. 7, p. 13). See also Mark 10:7–12; Eph. 5:21–23.

Procreation and Contraception

What Is the Purpose of Sexual Intercourse?

The primary purpose of sexual intercourse is to express love and intimate commitment. There does not need to be the intention to have children (Doc. 7, p. 14). See also Gen. 2:18–25.

Can a Marriage Be Fulfilled without Children?

A couple must decide this for themselves. It is quite possible that a couple might understand themselves and their gifts from God in such a way that their marriage could be fulfilled without children.

If married partners decide to become parents, their care for their children is intended to reflect God's love and discipline (Doc. 7, p. 14; Doc. 4, pp. 103–105).

What Does Our Church Believe about Contraception?

We believe any person who is physically capable of reproduction should have complete knowledge about contraceptives. We favor the general availability of contraceptive devices to persons who desire them. We consciously include the availability of contraceptives to unmarried persons in this recommendation (Doc. 3, p. 21; Doc. 10, p. 60).

Infertility

Does Our Church Support the Use of Medical Intervention in Cases of Infertility?

We affirm the use of drug and surgical therapies for problems that cause infertility (Doc. 9, p. 26).

Does Our Church Support Artificial Insemination?

We affirm the use of artificial insemination, with the husband as donor, as a responsible means of overcoming certain fertility problems (Doc. 9, p. 26).

Does Our Church Support Artificial Insemination by Donors other than the Husband?

We urge further study on the psychological, ethical, and legal ramifications for all parties, including the child, of using anonymous artificial insemination donors (Doc. 9, p. 26).

Does Our Church Support In Vitro Fertilization?

We affirm in vitro fertilization as a responsible alternative for couples for whom there is no other way to bear children, and oppose state or local legislation that would prohibit in vitro fertilization (Doc. 9, p. 26).

What Is Our Church's Position on Surrogate Motherhood?

We urge further study on the psychological, ethical, and legal ramifications for all parties, including the child (Doc. 9, p. 26).

Premarital Sex

What Is Premarital Sex?

Premarital sex means different things to different people. It can mean sexual intercourse that occurs as the result of a deliberate, thought-out act or just a spur-of-the-moment action. It could happen with an acquaintance, a friend, or a fiancée. It might occur during the course of a long-term relationship or on a casual date (Doc. 8, p. 16).

Should Teenagers Have Sexual Intercourse Before Marriage?

We believe it is best to postpone intercourse until marriage. If a teenage couple decides to have a sexual relationship, they have the responsibility to use effective contraception (Doc. 10, p. 51; Doc. 8, p. 16). See also Gen. 2:18–25.

What Does Our Church Believe about Premarital Sex?

We believe that total intimacy should happen in a relationship of total commitment, which marriage is intended to be. We advocate responsible behavior, understood as sexual expression that matches the seriousness and permanence of the relationship (Doc. 3, p. 29; Doc. 8, p. 16). See also Gen. 2:18–25.

If We Teach Young People about Contraception, Doesn't This Really Give Young People Permission to Engage in Sexual Intercourse?

No, young people should postpone sexual activity until marriage. Yet, in light of the number of teenage pregnancies that do occur, we would be failing in our ministry if we did not offer young people good contraceptive information (Doc. 10, p. 51).

Does Giving Young People Information about Contraception Lead to Greater Sexual Activity?

The most recent research shows that presentation of information about contraception serves both to delay the onset of sexual activity and to reduce its frequency (Doc. 10, p. 51).

What Options Does Our Church Offer a Pregnant Teenager Who Is Not Married?

The church offers the options of (1) marriage; (2) offering the child for adoption; (3) single parenthood; and (4) abortion (Doc. 10, pp. 50–51).

Extramarital Sex

What Is Extramarital Sex?

Extramarital sex is sexual intimacy with someone other than one's spouse. It is usually called adultery (Doc. 8, p. 17). See also Ex. 20:14.

What Does Jesus Teach about Extramarital Sex?

Jesus' teaching goes beyond the act to the state of the heart. Motivation and intent are the deciding factors. Evil that proceeds from the heart—

whether it be adultery, greed, envy, arrogance, or malice—defiles people (Doc. 8, p. 8). See also Matt. 5:27–28; 7:20–23.

What Is Our Church's Teaching about Extramarital Sex?

Marriage is an unconditional covenant to be faithful to each other. Sexual intercourse outside such love and commitment to lifelong fidelity is not in keeping with the biblical understanding of God's intention for humanity (Doc. 8, pp. 9, 17; Doc. 7, p. 12; Doc. 4, lines 89–95). See also Ex. 20:14.

Should Married Couples Restrict Their Relationships with Others?

We were created to be in relation with other people. A marriage relationship should not limit other relationships, except that sexual activity is reserved for the intimacy of marriage (Doc. 7, p. 12). See also Ex. 20:14.

Sexual Abstinence

What Is Sexual Abstinence or Celibacy?

These terms mean refraining from sexual activity (Doc. 7, p 10).

Does Our Church Advocate Celibacy?

We believe celibacy is not good in itself, any more than is sexual activity. It can be a good choice for some Christian people if, like any sexual choice, it is life-affirming, other-affirming, and joyous—not life-rejecting, self-enclosed, and desolate (Doc. 8, p. 15). See also Gal. 5:22–23.

Does Our Church Believe That It Is Better to Be Single or to Be Married?

God wills both marriage and singleness. Each is God's gift and gifts may differ (Doc. 7, p. 10). See also 1 Cor. 12.

Masturbation

Why Would Someone Masturbate?

People masturbate for many reasons: curiosity about how it feels, as a way of releasing tension, as a release that afterward keeps them from thinking about sex so much, as a substitute for sexual relations when they do not have a spouse, or just because it feels good to them (Doc. 8, p. 15).

Is Masturbation a Good or a Bad Thing to Do?

Masturbation can be good or bad, depending on the reason someone decides to masturbate (Doc. 8, p. 15).

What Would Be Bad about Masturbation?

It could be a way of focusing on yourself rather than on relationships with other people. It could be a way of constantly satisfying yourself rather than seeing sexuality as a way of satisfying someone else. It could be done out of fear of becoming involved with someone else (Doc. 8, p. 15).

What Would Be Good about Masturbation?

Because masturbation lessens the sexual drive, it can make a sexual relationship with someone else a freer choice rather than something to which one is driven by sexual urges. It can be a good choice for those who are not married. It can be a good choice for those who cannot have sexual relations with a spouse because of absence, disability, or illness (Doc. 8, p. 15).

What Does Our Church Believe about Masturbation?

Masturbation is a normal part of growing up. There should be no guilt or shame for engaging in masturbation. Although we believe our sexuality is to be shared with someone else, masturbation can be a good choice to make in some circumstances (Doc. 8, p. 15; Doc. 3, pp. 14, 15).

Divorce

What Was Jesus' Attitude toward Divorce?

Jesus saw marriage as a permanent, lifelong, intimate personal union. Jesus himself, however, recognized that there are things that break marriage apart. He therefore acknowledged divorce as a reality, but without approving it (Doc. 7, p. 11). See also Mark 10:7–12.

What Is Our Church's Attitude toward Divorce?

We seek first reconciliation and the healing of brokenness in the marriage. Divorce is seen as legitimate, on the grounds of adultery or desertion, or where a continuation of the legal union would endanger the physical, moral, or spiritual well-being of one or both of the partners or that of their children (Doc. 7, p. 11).

Can Ministers and Officers of the Church Be Divorced?

Yes, officers and ministers whose marriages end in divorce may continue in their ministerial office. They should be counseled, helped, and forgiven just like everyone else in our community (Doc. 7, p. 12).

Abortion

Can the Choice of Abortion Be a Responsible Christian Choice?

In the exceptional case in which a woman is pregnant and judges that it would be irresponsible to bring a child into the world, given the limitations of her situation, it can be an act of faithfulness before God to intervene in the natural process of pregnancy and terminate it. Abortion may be considered a responsible and morally acceptable choice within the Christian faith when serious genetic problems arise or when the resources are not adequate to care for a child appropriately (Doc. 10, p. 58; Doc. 9, p. 10; Doc. 10, p. 32; Doc. 14, pp. 367–368).

What Is Our Primary Guide in Decision Making?

We can trust in God's Spirit to guide us in our decisions. We are part of the community of faith, and we can be sure that the community will be here to help and sustain us in our decisions. Furthermore, the gospel reminds us again and again of God's grace, which brings us love, care, and forgiveness (Doc. 10, p. 58). See also Rom. 8.

Who Has the Responsibility for Deciding about Abortion?

Biblical faith emphasizes the need for personal moral choice. Each individual is ultimately accountable to God for individual moral choices. The choice for an abortion is to be made by the woman who is in the position to make the decision, and it is, above all, her responsibility (Doc. 10, pp. 58, 60; Doc. 14, pp. 367–368).

When Should a Decision about Abortion Be Made?

A decision about abortion should be made as early as possible, generally within the first three months of the pregnancy. Abortions in the second three months are an option for those who do not discover they are pregnant until then, or for those who discover grave genetic disorders, or for those who have not had access to medical care during the first three months (Doc. 10, p. 59).

Should Abortion Be Available to Anyone Who Chooses It?

Our church believes we have a responsibility to guarantee every woman the freedom to choose for herself. Abortion should be made available to all who desire and qualify for it, not just to those who can afford it (Doc. 10, p. 60; Doc. 14, pp. 367–68).

Should a Woman Feel Guilty for Considering an Abortion?

A woman who considers abortion and then decides to continue her pregnancy should never be made to feel guilty that she has thought about abortion. It is far better to give birth intentionally than to feel that the diagnosis of pregnancy constitutes an absolute obligation to bear a child. In most pregnancies, the question of abortion will never arise, but when it does, the choice of abortion can be an expression of responsibility before God (Doc. 9, p. 10; Doc. 10, p. 32).

Should Abortion Be Considered a Form of Birth Control?

Abortion is not and should not be used as a form of birth control. It should not be chosen as a convenience or to ease embarrassment. It is a very serious and far-reaching decision (Doc. 11, p. 80; Doc. 14, pp. 367–368).

What Does Our Church Believe the Public Policy on Abortion Should Be?

We believe in Christian freedom and responsibility so that individuals can make their own choices, rather than have the state make decisions for them. We believe in a public policy of elective abortion, regulated by the health code, not the criminal code (Doc. 10, p. 52; Doc. 14, pp. 367–368).

What Does Our Church Believe about Violence at Women's Health Clinics?

Our church condemns violence and threats of violence at women's health clinics, and encourages individuals to use language and images responsibly to avoid stimulating or encouraging violence or appearing to condone violent behavior (Doc. 15, pp. 678–679).

Are There Varieties of Beliefs about Abortion Within Our Church?

Yes, there is a great variety of beliefs, and those who hold these varying beliefs tend to hold them very strongly. It is for this reason that our church has been led to the conviction that the decision regarding abortion must remain with the individual, to be made on the basis of conscience and personal religious principles (Doc. 10, p. 60).

Homosexuality

Who Is Considered Homosexual?

Anyone who experiences repeated, intense attraction to a person or persons of the same sex is considered to be homosexual. Such a definition excludes the casual experimenter (Doc. 5, p. 971).

Are People Either Homosexual or Heterosexual?

It is believed that most people exist somewhere on a continuum that ranges from an exclusively heterosexual orientation to one that is exclusively homosexual (Doc. 5, p. 971).

Are People Created as Either Male or Female?

God created us male and female, but the process of creation is not finished, either chemically or psychologically, at birth. Our development process continues through adolescence, at the end of which we establish a comfortable identity with our given sexuality (Doc. 3, p. 17; Doc. 5, p. 972).

What Is Meant by "Gay" and "Lesbian"?

As used by the homosexual community, the words *gay* and *lesbian* are adjectives or nouns that refer to homosexual orientation, respectively, in a man and in a woman. Originally used by heterosexual persons as derogatory labels for homosexual persons, the terms have now been claimed by many homosexual persons as words that describe the full joy of their self-acceptance as homosexuals (Doc. 5, p. 977).

How Does Someone Become Heterosexual or Homosexual?

No one can say for sure why some people are heterosexual and some are homosexual. The majority of human beings develop a heterosexual orientation. Some people believe that homosexuality is determined biologically, while others believe that societal forces play a large role (Doc. 5, p. 972–974).

Do Gays and Lesbians Choose to Be Homosexual?

Most gay and lesbian adults have no awareness of having "chosen" homosexuality. In early adolescence, when fantasies of others focused on the opposite sex, theirs focused on the same sex. In later adolescence, when others enjoyed dating, they did not. In early adulthood, when others fell in and out of love with the opposite sex, they fell in and out of love with the same sex. Somehow, in some inexplicable way, something "different" had happened to them. Without knowing how or why, they believe they were created as homosexual (Doc. 5, p. 974).

What Is Homophobia?

Homophobia is contempt, hatred, or fear of people who are gay or lesbian (Doc. 5, p. 1021).

How Does Our Church View Homophobia?

We believe there can be no place within the Christian faith for homophobia. Persons who manifest homosexual behavior must be treated with the profound respect and pastoral tenderness due all people of God (Doc. 5, p. 1021).

Does Our Church Believe Gays and Lesbians Should Be Welcome in the Church?

We believe gay and lesbian persons are loved by Christ. We believe the church must turn from its fear and hatred to move toward the gay and lesbian community in love and to welcome gay and lesbian inquirers into our congregations (Doc. 5, p. 1021).

Do Gays and Lesbians Need to Change or Hide Their Behavior in Order to Become a Part of the Church?

We believe gays and lesbians should be free to be candid about their identity and convictions. There is room in the church for all who give honest affirmation to the vows required for membership in the church. Gay and lesbian persons who sincerely affirm, "Jesus Christ is my Lord and Savior" and "I intend to be his disciple, to obey his word, and to show his love" should not be excluded from membership (Doc. 5, p. 1021).

Can a Gay or Lesbian Person Be Ordained as an Officer or Minister in the Church?

Our church's present understanding is that persons who do not repent of homosexual practice cannot be officers or ministers (Doc. 5, p. 1022).

Can a Gay or Lesbian Person Who Does Not Act Out His/Her Homosexuality Be Ordained?

The repentant gay or lesbian person who finds the power of Christ redirecting his or her sexual desires toward a married heterosexual commitment, or who finds God's power to control his or her desires and to adopt a celibate lifestyle, can certainly be ordained, all other qualifications being met. Indeed, such candidates must be welcomed and made free to share their full identity (Doc. 5, p. 1022).

Can Any Committee of the Church Ask What a Person's Sexual Orientation Is?

No, it is up to the individual to take the initiative in declaring his or her sexual orientation (Doc. 5, p. 1022).

What Is Our Church's Understanding of Laws That Discriminate Against a Person on the Basis of Sexual Orientation?

We believe we should work to oppose laws that discriminate against persons on the basis of sexual orientation. In addition, we should initiate and support laws that prohibit discrimination against persons on the basis of sexual orientation (Doc. 5, pp. 1005, 1023; Doc. 16, pp. 118–119).

Is There Disagreement with This Understanding of Homosexuality within Our Church?

Yes, there are those within the church who believe that gays and lesbians should be ordained as officers and ministers. There are also those who believe that homosexuality is sinful. The stand of our church is to encourage all church members to continue dialogue within the church. We believe there is always the possibility for more light to break forth from God's Spirit to aid our understanding (Doc. 5, pp. 978, 1024).

Sexual Misconduct

What Is Our Church's Position on Sexual Misconduct?

Sexual misconduct is a misuse of authority and power that breaches Christian ethical principles by misusing a trust relationship to gain advantage over another for personal pleasure in an abusive, exploitive, and unjust manner. Sexual misconduct takes advantage of the vulnerability of children and persons who are less powerful to act for their own welfare. It violates the mandate to protect the vulnerable from harm (Doc. 17, pp. 76–92).

Decision Making

What Is Our Authority in Deciding Issues About Human Sexuality?

The Bible is our authority, as it is understood and interpreted within the church (Doc. 8, p. 7).

Does the Bible Have an Answer for Every Question about Sexuality?

The Bible primarily tells about God, God's community, and God's grace toward us. The Bible is not a catalog of infallible prescriptions concerning each moral problem we face (Doc. 8, p. 7).

Do People in Our Church Live Out Their Sexuality in the Way God Intended?

Like all people, we act from mixed motives and divided intentions. All of us fail in some ways (Doc. 8, p. 12).

Do All Members of Our Church Agree on How to Live Out Our Sexuality?

No, a variety of opinions exist on what constitutes responsible sexuality. Christians may behave in good conscience in ways that other conscientious Christians, in good conscience, neither approve of nor understand (Doc. 8, p. 12).

What, Then, Is the Role of Our Church in Human Sexuality?

Our church is a place where people experience forgiveness and help in living out their sexuality, rather than rejection and condemnation because they have fallen short of God's intention and their own best aspirations. The church is a community of forgiven sinners. When we fail each other as parents or partners, we are called to forgive each other as God forgives us and to accept the possibilities for renewal that God offers us in grace (Doc. 8, p. 12; Doc. 4, lines 106–109). See also Rom. 3:21–26; 8.

Sexuality Redefined

Many people find it difficult, at the outset of a discussion, to talk about sex and sexuality. As the leader you will want to acknowledge that some people in the group may be feeling embarrassed or uncomfortable. That is okay. You may want to tell the group that you sometimes get embarrassed, too, but that we can all learn to be more comfortable talking about sexuality. Practice will help. Point out that our feelings of comfort or discomfort with the topic of sexuality came from our family and friends, our religion and culture—and what they have taught us.

This course is based on a broad definition of sexuality, using a model that was developed by a social scientist at the University of Kansas.[1] A new and broader definition of sexuality is shown in Figure 1. Each interconnecting circle represents one aspect of our sexuality. In order to fully understand the term *sexuality* as it is used in the course, you will need to understand the concepts in each individual circle and what they include.

Sensuality is the need and ability to be aware of others, especially a sexual partner. Sensuality is that sexual part of ourselves that lets us feel good about our bodies—how they look and what they can do—and that allows us to enjoy the pleasure our bodies can give to us as well as to others. Sensuality includes several different aspects of our sexuality:

- Awareness of our physiology— understanding and appreciation of how and why our bodies function as they do.
- Body image—includes our feelings about how our bodies look and work; whether we feel satisfied or dissatisfied with our bodies.
- Attraction—an aspect of our sexuality (determined by the brain, our most powerful sex organ) that enables us to feel attracted to some people, but not to others.
- Satisfaction of skin hunger—our need to touch, to be held by, and to make contact with another person.
- Release of sexual tension—the unique human sexual response cycle that enables human beings to experience arousal, followed by a release of sexual tension through orgasm. Males and females experience this process differently.
- Importance of sensory expression—our ability to experience sensuality through our many senses, as well as through fantasy and memory. It has been demonstrated that sexual fantasies are normal and are generally unrelated to sexual behavior.

Intimacy is another aspect of sexuality that captures much of the richness found in our relationships with one another. Intimacy is the ability and need to experience emotional

1. Dennis M. Daily, "Sexual Expression and Aging," in *The Dynamics of Aging: Original Essays on the Processes and Experiences of Growing Old.* Edited by Forrest J. Berghorn, Donna E. Schaefer, et al. (Boulder, CO: Westview Press, 1981), pp. 311–330.

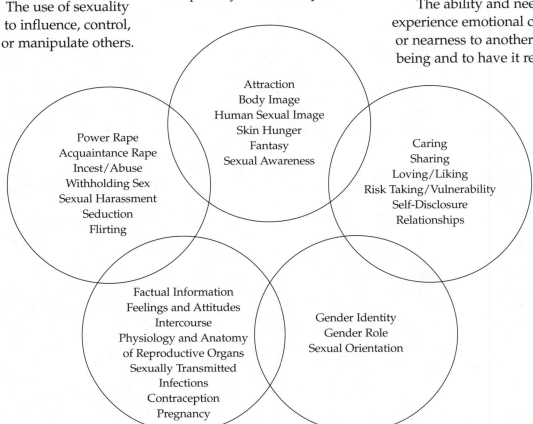

Sensuality
The need and ability to be aware of, in touch with, and accepting of your own body and the bodies of others—especially of a sexual partner.

Sexualism
The use of sexuality to influence, control, or manipulate others.

Sexual Intimacy
The ability and need to experience emotional closeness or nearness to another human being and to have it returned.

Attraction
Body Image
Human Sexual Image
Skin Hunger
Fantasy
Sexual Awareness

Power Rape
Acquaintance Rape
Incest/Abuse
Withholding Sex
Sexual Harassment
Seduction
Flirting

Caring
Sharing
Loving/Liking
Risk Taking/Vulnerability
Self-Disclosure
Relationships

Factual Information
Feelings and Attitudes
Intercourse
Physiology and Anatomy
of Reproductive Organs
Sexually Transmitted
Infections
Contraception
Pregnancy

Gender Identity
Gender Role
Sexual Orientation

Reproduction
Attitudes and behaviors related to producing children and the consequences to society and individuals that result.

Sexual Identity
The development of a sense of who one is sexually, including a sense of maleness and femaleness.

Figure 1

closeness or nearness to another human being and to have these feelings returned. Intimacy focuses on our closeness to others in emotional terms, whereas sensuality relates to our physical selves and physical closeness. Important components of intimacy include the following:

- Caring—having an emotional investment in the well-being of another person.

- Sharing—giving or revealing a part of oneself to another.

- Liking and loving—having strong emotional attachments to others and desiring to be with them.

- Risk taking—being willing to risk disclosing part of oneself in order to be close to another.

- Self-disclosure—risking possible exposure by another person with whom we have been open; sharing of our secret parts.

As sexual human beings we can establish intimacy without engaging in sex. Young people, especially, need the opportunity to experience intimacy without having sex. The mature expression of sexuality includes intimacy that goes far beyond mere genital sex and is expressive of the totality of human relationships.

Sexual identity, often the most complicated aspect of sexuality, is the development of a sense of who one is sexually, including a sense of maleness or femaleness. Sexual identity develops gradually in three different areas. These include the following:

- Gender identity—a sense of maleness and femaleness that results from knowing whether one has a penis and scrotum or a vulva and breasts.
- Gender role identity—everything we do and feel that expresses our maleness or femaleness. Our development in this area often reflects society's messages about what it means to be male or female.
- Sexual orientation—whether our primary sexual attraction is to persons of the same or of the opposite gender, that is, homosexuality or heterosexuality.

All three aspects of sexual identity can have a profound effect on the well-being of a person: (1) Whether one is male or female largely determines how others perceive him or her. (2) Society's messages about gender roles, as well as how a person interprets these messages, can influence his or her feelings about self, interactions with others, and dreams for the future. (3) Sexual orientation can affect the entire quality of a person's life experience in our society.

Reproduction is the fourth and most familiar of the components of sexuality. Reproduction includes the attitudes and behaviors related to producing children and the consequences to society and individuals that result. Human reproduction includes many recognizable aspects of sexuality, which are as follows:

- The facts of life—information about reproduction, conception, contraception, and physical development.
- Feelings and attitudes—how we feel about pregnancy, birth control, abortion, and other issues related to human reproduction.
- Physiology and anatomy—what the male and female reproductive systems are and how they actually work.
- Sexual intercourse—the human behavior that can result in pregnancy and production of a new life.
- Teen pregnancy and sexually transmitted infections (STIs)—commonly occurring, unintended consequences of sexual activity that can have profound implications for young people.

Sexualism, represented in the fifth circle, is the final human element that constitutes sexuality. Sexualism is the use of sexuality to influence, control, or manipulate others. This last aspect of sexuality spans behaviors that range from harmless to sadistic and violent and includes such behaviors as flirting, seduction, withholding sexual intercourse, sexual harassment, sexual abuse, incest, and rape. In the area of sexualism we find the potentially dark and sinister side of our sexuality—therein lies the power to destroy another human being, just as in reproduction lies the ability to create life. We cannot understand ourselves as sexual beings until we acknowledge all aspects of our sexuality, including that of sexualism. In order to avoid being sexually manipulated, each of us needs to learn assertiveness skills that can protect us from sexualism.

God's Love

Having examined all five circles in Figure 1, we should have a complete definition of human sexuality. Yet something seems to be missing. Only if we draw a central circle—separate, yet connecting all the others—can we truly complete the picture. (See Figure 2.)

This center circle is God's love, which is essential for full realization of ourselves as sexual beings. God's love touches and influences all facets of our sexuality as represented by the five circles. God's love fashioned the bodies housing our sensuality; God's love is reflected in our loving, intimate relationships; God's love gave us our sexual identity; God's love forged our capacity to create new life in God's image; and God's love enables us to affirm our God-given sexuality and resist the urge to exploit our sexuality.

Our sexuality is a good gift to us from God, a gift that touches all parts of us as sexual beings. In order to cherish and use this gift wisely, we need to know as much about ourselves and our sexuality as we can. The framework of interlocking circles anchored in God's love that is provided in the older youth course can guide our thinking and studying about our sexual selves in relation to others and to God.

As you lead youth in thinking and studying, keep these two key points in mind:

1.   All aspects of our sexuality are related.
2.   Central to our sexuality is God's love for us.

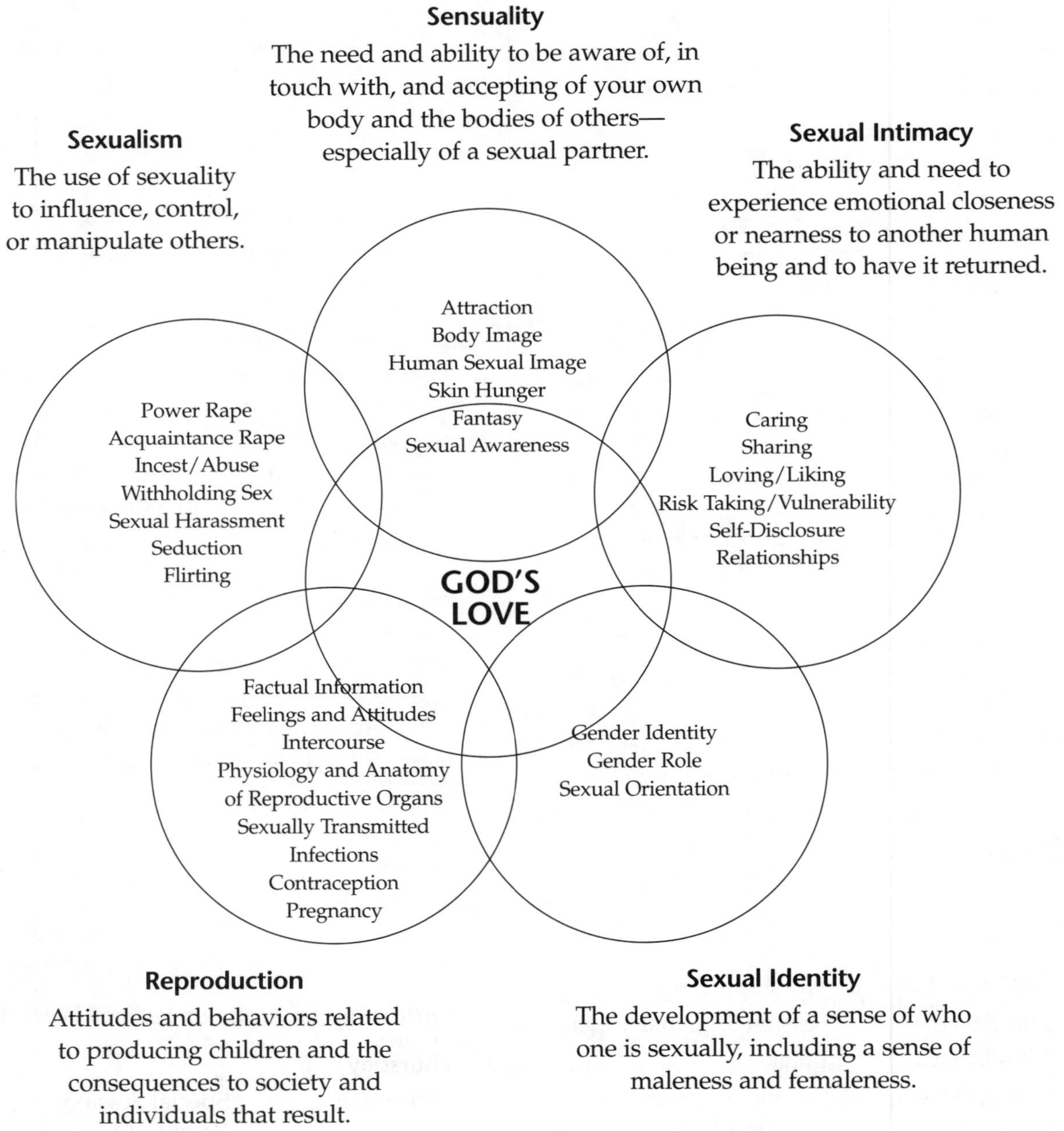

Sensuality
The need and ability to be aware of, in touch with, and accepting of your own body and the bodies of others—especially of a sexual partner.

Sexualism
The use of sexuality to influence, control, or manipulate others.

Sexual Intimacy
The ability and need to experience emotional closeness or nearness to another human being and to have it returned.

Attraction
Body Image
Human Sexual Image
Skin Hunger
Fantasy
Sexual Awareness

Power Rape
Acquaintance Rape
Incest/Abuse
Withholding Sex
Sexual Harassment
Seduction
Flirting

Caring
Sharing
Loving/Liking
Risk Taking/Vulnerability
Self-Disclosure
Relationships

GOD'S LOVE

Factual Information
Feelings and Attitudes
Intercourse
Physiology and Anatomy
of Reproductive Organs
Sexually Transmitted
Infections
Contraception
Pregnancy

Gender Identity
Gender Role
Sexual Orientation

Reproduction
Attitudes and behaviors related to producing children and the consequences to society and individuals that result.

Sexual Identity
The development of a sense of who one is sexually, including a sense of maleness and femaleness.

Figure 2

Sample Schedules for the Course

Younger Youth—One Weekend

Thursday

7:00–8:30 P.M.   Preparatory Session 1: Small-Group Leader Training

Friday

6:00–7:00 P.M.   Preparatory Session 2: Parent's Orientation

7:15–9:00 P.M.   Session 1: Anatomy and Physiology

Saturday

12:30–1:45 P.M.   Session 1: Anatomy and Physiology (*continued*)

1:45–2:00 P.M.   Break

2:00–5:00 P.M.   Session 2: Puberty

5:00–5:30 P.M.   Dinner

5:45–8:20 P.M.   Session 3: Relationships and Intimacy

8:20–8:30 P.M.   Break

8:30–9:30 P.M.   Session 4: The Consequences of Sex

Sunday

8:30–11:30 A.M.   Session 4: The Consequences of Sex (*continued*)

11:30 A.M.–1:00 P.M.   Worship/Lunch

1:00–3:00 P.M.   Session 5: Sexual Violence

3:00–3:10 P.M.   Break

3:10–5:45 P.M.   Session 6: Values and Decisions

6:00–7:00 P.M.   Dinner/Special Session: Parent's Overview

7:00–9:00 P.M.   Session 7: Parent/Youth Communication

Younger Youth—One Weekend with Follow-Up Sessions or Two Weekends

First Weekend

Thursday

7:00–8:00 P.M.   Preparatory Session 2: Parent's Orientation

8:00–9:30 P.M.   Preparatory Session 1: Small-Group Leader Training

Friday

7:00–10:00 P.M.   Session 1: Anatomy and Physiology

Saturday

9:00 A.M.–Noon   Session 2: Puberty

Sunday

3:00–9:00 P.M.   Sessions 3 and 4: Relationships and Intimacy; The Consequences of Sex

Follow-up Sessions or Second Weekend

Thursday

7:00–9:00 P.M.   Special Session: Parent's Overview

Sunday

2:00–6:30 P.M.	Sessions 5 and 6: Sexual Violence; Values and Decisions
6:30–7:15 P.M.	Dinner
7:15–9:15 P.M.	Session 7: Parent/Youth Communication

Older Youth—One Weekend

Thursday

6:00–7:30 P.M.	Preparatory Session 1: Small-Group Leader Training
7:30–8:30 P.M.	Preparatory Session 2: Parent's Orientation

Friday

5:30–7:30 P.M.	Session 1: Sexuality Redefined
7:30–9:40 P.M.	Session 2: Sensuality

Saturday

10:00 A.M.–Noon	Session 3: Intimacy
Noon–12:30 P.M.	Lunch
12:45–2:30 P.M.	Session 3: Intimacy (*continued*)
2:30–2:45 P.M.	Break/Snack
2:45–4:45 P.M.	Session 4: Sexual Identity
5:00–7:25 P.M.	Session 5: Good Health Habits
7:30–8:00 P.M.	Dinner
8:00–10:00 P.M.	Session 6: Contraception

Sunday

8:30–9:30 A.M.	Session 7: Sexually Transmitted Infections
9:45 A.M.–12:15 P.M.	Session 8: Parenthood
12:30–1:30 P.M.	Worship/Lunch
1:45–4:00 P.M.	Session 9: Sexual Violence
4:00–4:15 P.M.	Break
4:15–5:45 P.M.	Session 10: Decision Making
6:00–6:45 P.M.	Dinner
7:00–8:30 P.M.	Session 11: Building Blocks for Better Parent/Youth Communication

Older Youth—One Weekend with Follow-up Sessions or Two Weekends

First Weekend

Thursday

7:00–8:30 P.M.	Preparatory Session 1: Small-Group Leader Training

Friday

6:30–7:30 P.M.	Preparatory Session 2: Parent's Orientation
7:30–9:30 P.M.	Session 1: Sexuality Redefined

Saturday

10:00 A.M.–12:10 P.M.	Session 2: Sensuality
12:10–12:45 P.M.	Lunch
1:00–4:45 P.M.	Session 3: Intimacy

Sunday

9:00–11:00 A.M.	Session 4: Sexual Identity
11:00 A.M.–1:00 P.M.	Worship/Lunch
1:15–3:45 P.M.	Session 5: Good Health Habits

Second Weekend or Follow-Up Sessions

Friday

7:00–9:00 P.M.	Session 6: Contraception

Saturday

1:00–3:00 P.M.	Session 7: Sexually Transmitted Infections
3:00–3:15 P.M.	Break
3:15–5:45 P.M.	Session 8: Parenthood

Sunday

1:00–3:30 P.M.	Session 9: Sexual Violence
3:30–3:45 P.M.	Break
3:45–5:45 P.M.	Session 10: Decision Making
5:45–7:30 P.M.	Dinner/Session 11: Building Blocks for Better Parent/Youth Communication

Publicity Samples—Letters and Forms

Younger Youth
Human Sexuality Course*

For Grades 6–8

Dates: _____

Taught by: _____

God's Gift of Sexuality is a program for youth that picks up where the elementary-age sexuality curriculum, *God's Plan for Growing Up*, left off. Both of these courses were created in response to mandates of the General Assembly of the Presbyterian Church (U.S.A.).

God's Gift of Sexuality is based on the beliefs that:

God created us and gave us the gift of our sexuality.

God created us for life in the community.

Our church is a community of love.

Our church is a community of responsibility.

Our church is a varied community.

Our church is a community of forgiveness.

God gives us responsibility for our own decisions.

SCHEDULE

Program Content

The program is designed to examine all aspects of human sexuality and includes the following areas: sensuality, intimacy, sexual identity, reproduction, sexualism, and decision making. Presbyterian Church (U.S.A.) teachings and scriptural teachings will be an integral part of the entire program.

Youth *must* attend *all* youth sessions and parents are requested to attend all parent's meetings.

Deadline for registration is: _____

[ ] Yes, I give _____ permission to participate in this program.
                    (*youth's name*)

Phone No. _____

Parent's Signature _____

*Adapted from Robert Hay, First Presbyterian Church, Marietta, Georgia.

Older Youth
Human Sexuality Course*

For Grades 9–12

Dates: _____

Taught by: _____

     This is a program on human sexuality that continues the teachings in the younger youth portion of *God's Gift of Sexuality* and in the elementary-age sexuality curriculum, *God's Plan for Growing Up*. Both of these courses were created in response to mandates of the General Assembly of the Presbyterian Church (U.S.A.).

     God's Gift of Sexuality is based on the beliefs that:

God created us and gave us the gift of our sexuality.

God created us for life in the community.

Our church is a community of love.

Our church is a community of responsibility.

Our church is a varied community.

Our church is a community of forgiveness.

God gives us responsibility for our own decisions.

Youth *must* attend *all* youth sessions and parents are requested to attend all parent's meetings.

SCHEDULE

PROGRAM CONTENT

    Integral parts of the sessions will include teachings from Scripture and the Presbyterian Church (U.S.A.).

    The program is designed to examine all aspects of human sexuality. Sessions will include studies of self-esteem, relationships, and decision making.

Deadline for registration is:_____

[ ] Yes, I give _____ permission to participate in this program.
             (*youth's name*)

Phone No. _____

Parent's Signature _____

*Adapted from Robert Hay, First Presbyterian Church, Marietta, Georgia.

Memorandum*

TO: All Session Members
FROM: *[Coordinator of Youth Activities]*
DATE:
RE: Youth Sexuality Course

Education about sexuality for teenagers is a topic of great concern to all. The Presbyterian Church (U.S.A.), in response to mandates from its General Assembly, has developed programs about sexuality for junior high and senior high young people.

The intention of the developers was to write curriculum based on Presbyterian/Reformed biblical and theological understandings of human sexuality. The curriculum meets this objective.

I recommend that the church present an education course about sexuality for *[younger/older]* youth for the following reasons:

- There have been numerous requests from parents of *[younger/older]* youth for a sexuality education course.
- Research has shown that education helps demystify sex, helps put it into proper perspective, and helps reduce rather than intensify adolescent sexual activity.
- Sex education is available from many sources, but the church has a responsibility to emphasize the moral and social implications of sexuality.
- Sexuality education allows young people to discover and articulate their own beliefs and values before being faced with the challenge of making decisions about their own sexual conduct.

I recommend we use this particular curriculum, *God's Gift of Sexuality*, for the following reasons:

- It has a strong theological and biblical base.
- It presents sexuality as a positive aspect of personality, a gift from God of which we must be good stewards.
- There is a strong emphasis on parent-teen communication, and parents are included in the course.

The course would be conducted *[in a retreat/Sunday school/youth group]* on the following dates: _____

The cost will be _____ per person. Cost will include _____

The areas of sexuality to be covered will include _____

The expectations for parents, guardians, and participants are as follows: _____

_____

_____

_____

Thank you for considering this request.

*Adapted from Barbara Tucker, First Presbyterian Church, McAllen, Texas.

Letter to Parents/Guardians*

Dear _____,

On *[date]* the *[younger/older youth Sunday school class]* will begin a course on human sexuality that has been prepared by the Presbyterian Church (U.S.A.) in response to mandates from its General Assembly.

Young people in the middle and high school years need education about sexuality but often don't receive it. Parents may feel inadequate to provide it. They may be concerned that talking about sex will give their young person ideas or imply tacit permission to experiment sexually. To the contrary, knowledge helps people make informed decisions and act responsibly. Young people are having intercourse earlier than in previous eras. Often education about sexuality is postponed by parents and/or the schools until the young person has already begun to experiment sexually.

Because education about sexuality comes from many sources in a young person's life, accurate information and loving concern are needed to counterbalance the distorted images received from peers, as well as from advertisements, television programs, movies, music, and other media. This course on human sexuality, *God's Gift of Sexuality,* has been designed to help young people put their sexuality into perspective. It has been developed with several general principles in mind:

- Respect for young people is a primary theme. Leaders will respect their dignity and acknowledge the value of the opinions and beliefs they express.

- A good course about sexuality helps to reduce rather than increase adolescent sexual activity. When sex is talked about, put into perspective, and demythologized, young people begin to see it as a part of life as God has given it, not as a god in life that must be experienced.

- Sexuality is seen as a positive aspect of personality. Sex is seen as a gift of God over which we are to be good stewards.

- Most values are formed at an early age and are derived largely through observation rather than from verbal instruction. The young people will come to the course with their values already in place. There is no way this course can outweigh parental influence. What the course can do is to encourage young people to begin articulating the values they already hold. This will help them in situations that challenge and call into question those values.

- The teachings of the church and Scripture are used as valuable resources. This is an opportunity to strengthen the ties between faith and life.

We feel certain that your child will benefit from participating in this course. We hope, too, that you will join us during the last session, which will focus on parent/youth communication. The schedule for our meetings is as follows: [*Leader: Provide a schedule that includes dates, times, and meeting place.*]

The areas of sexuality to be covered include the following: _____

A parent's orientation before the program and a session on parent/youth communication at the end are important components.

The expectations for parent(s), guardians, and participants are as follows: _____

A fee of *[$]* per youth participant is to cover the costs of materials, videos, and food.

Young people are expected to attend all the meetings. (Exceptions may be negotiated with the leader if absolutely necessary.) Parent(s) and guardians are expected to participate in all parents' sessions and will be asked to help prepare or clean up for one meal.

This seems like an enormous amount of information to be sending you, but we want you to have a feel for what will take place during the next few weeks and to know the basic beliefs presented in the course. We want you to feel comfortable about what your child is learning. If you have questions, please call *[name]* at *[phone number]*. Please return the enclosed form to let us know if your child will be attending the course.

Sincerely,

---

*Adapted from Connie Stewart, First Presbyterian Church, Buffalo, New York, and Erik Spencer, First Presbyterian Church, West Seneca, New York.

Registration Form

The following young person(s) will be participating in the sexuality education program at _____

_____
(place)

on _____
(dates)

Name(s) of young person(s): _____

_____

_____

I will participate in the sessions for parent(s) and guardians and will help with one of the meals.

_____
(parent's signature)

Please detach on dotted line, sign, and return this registration form along with $ ____ by _____
(date)

to: _____
(name of coordinator)

_____
(address)

_____
(address)

Resources

Resources for the Leader

The following books are recommended for leaders of this course. They should be available in your local library or bookstore. They will help you prepare for teaching this course and will assist you in answering questions that may arise during the course.

Changing Bodies, Changing Lives, by Ruth Bell. New York: Vintage Books, 1988.

The Christian Response to the Sexual Revolution, by David R. Mace. Nashville: Abingdon Press, 1980.

Coming Out to God, by Chris Glaser. Louisville: Westminster/John Knox Press, 1991.

Confronting Domestic Violence: Not Just for Adults, by Sharon K. Youngs. Louisville: Curriculum Publishing, PC(USA), 1996.

Created by God, by Darlis Brown Glass. Nashville: Graded Press, 1989.

Dealing with Crisis, by Bob Tuttle. Louisville: Bridge Resources, 1997.

How to Raise Teenagers' Self-Esteem, by Harris Clemes, Bean Reynald, and Aminah Clark. Edited by Janet Gluckman. New York: Putnam Berkley Group, 1990.

It's Perfectly Normal, by Robie H. Harris. Cambridge, MA: Candlewick Press, 1994.

Let's Talk About . . . S-E-X, by Sam Gitchel and Lorri Foster. California: Planned Parenthood of Central California, 1989.

Meeting at the Crossroads: Women's Psychology and Girls' Development, by Lyn Mikel Brown and Carol Gilligan. New York: Ballantine Books, 1992.

The New Our Bodies, Ourselves, by Ruth Bell. New York: Simon & Schuster, 1992.

On Being Gay, by Brian McNaught. New York: St. Martin's Press, 1988.

People, Love, Sex and Families—Answers to Questions That Preteens Ask, by Eric W. Johnson. New York: Walker & Co., 1985.

Self-Esteem: A Family Affair, by Jean Illsley Clarke. San Francisco: HarperCollins, 1978.

Sex for Christians, by Louis B. Smedes. Grand Rapids: Wm. B. Eerdmans Publishing Co., 1989.

Striking Terror No More: The Church Responds to Domestic Violence, edited by Beth Basham and Sara Lisherness. Louisville: Bridge Resources, 1997.

Talking with Your Child About Sex, by Dr. Mary S. Calderone and Dr. James Ramey. New York: Ballantine Books, 1991.

To Love As We Are Loved, by Bruce C. Birch. Nashville: Abingdon Press, 1992.

What's a Virus Anyway? by Dr. David Fassler and Kelly McQueen. Vermont: Waterfront Books, 1990.

Who Am I? by Katherine Patterson. Grand Rapids: Wm. B. Eerdmans Publishing Co., 1994.

You Just Don't Understand: Men and Women in Conversation, by Deborah Tannen. New York: William Morrow & Co., 1990.

Resources for Youth and Their Parents

The following are resources that young people and their parents may find helpful. They should be available in local libraries or bookstores.

"Becoming an Askable Parent," a free brochure from the American Social Health Association, P.O. Box 13827, Research Triangle Park, N.C. 27709.

Building Community in Youth Groups, by Denny Rydberg. Loveland, CO: Group Publishing, 1990.

Coming Out as Parents: You and Your Homosexual Child, by David K. Switzer. Louisville: Westminster John Knox Press, 1996.

A Kid's First Book About Sex, by Joani Blank and Marcia Quackenbush. Santa Rosa, CA: Yes Press, 1989.

My Body, My Self: Workbook for Boys, by Linda Madaras. New York: Newmarket Press, 1995.

My Feelings, My Self. Workbook for Girls, by Linda Madaras. New York: Newmarket Press, 1993.

Our Sexuality: God's Gift, by Joan Miles. Nashville: Graded Press, 1989.

Raising Healthy Kids: Families Talk About Sexual Health. Contains two thirty-minute videos with accompanying study guides to help parents and their children communicate about issues of sexuality. Media Works, Inc., P.O. Box 15597, Kenmore Station, Boston, MA 02215; (978) 282-9970.

Red Light, Green Light: Preventing Teen Pregnancy, by Janet Ollila Colberg. Helena, MT: Summer Kitchen Press, 1997.

Speaking of Sex: Are You Ready to Answer Questions Your Kids Will Ask? by Meg Hickling. Kelowna, Canada: Northstone, 1996.

Talking About Sex. Contains a thirty-minute animated video with celebrity narration, a sixty-page resource guide for parents, and an activity workbook for children and youth ages 10–14. Contact your local Planned Parenthood clinic or call (800) 669-0156.

The What's Happening to My Body for Boys, by Linda Madaras. New York: Newmarket Press, 1995.

The What's Happening to My Body for Girls, by Linda Madaras. New York: Newmarket Press, 1995.

Sexuality Curriculum

God's Plan for Growing Up. A sexuality education curriculum for elementary-age children and their parents. Contains five pieces: *Wonderfully Made* (grades 2–3); *Amazing Stuff* (grades 4–5); *Parent's Guide; Leader's Guide; Listening In,* an audiocassette. Louisville: Curriculum Publishing, PC(USA), 1996.

In God's Image is a sexuality curriculum for young children and their parents. This curriculum is made up of three resources: *In God's Image,* a book for children; *In God's Image: Young Children and Sexuality, Parent's Guide;* and *In God's Image: Young Children and Sexuality, A Guide for Congregations.* Louisville: Bridge Resources; Witherspoon Press, 1998; (800) 524-2612.

Life Planning Education. Newly revised popular youth development resource that contains activities, leader's resources, handouts. Appropriate for pregnancy/AIDS prevention and sexuality/life skills education for youth ages 13–18. Washington, D.C.: Advocates for Youth, 1995.

Open and Affirming. A study packet to help churches as they study, pray, and act to be more inclusive of people of all sexual orientations. Prepared by the Massachusetts Conference of the United Church of Christ and the United Church Coalition for Lesbian/Gay Concerns. Contact UCCL/GC-ONA, P.O. Box 403, Holden, MA 01520; (508) 856-9316.

Sexual Abuse Prevention: A Course of Study for Teenagers, by Marie Fortune and Rebecca Voelkel-Haugen. Cleveland: United Church Press, 1996.

Videos

The following videos are available for rental at most state health centers, education service centers, and Planned Parenthood clinics, and for purchase from the addresses listed. As with any resource, preview these videos to be sure they are appropriate for your youth. Since many of these videos have been updated, be sure to get the most recent version.

Conception

The Miracle of Life (60 minutes)

> *Theme:* Human conception.
> *Focus:* Leadership training/resource.
> 1986. Crown Video Series. Produced by Swedish Television in association with WGBH-TV, Boston.

Contraception

Hope Is Not a Method IV (20 minutes)

> *Theme:* Birth control.
> *Focus:* Junior and senior highs.
> Perennial Education, The Altschul Group, 930 Pitner Ave., Evanston, IL 60203; (312) 328-6700.

General

Making Healthy Choices: A Key to Abundance (28 minutes)

> *Theme:* Making good decisions about health.
> *Focus:* Junior and senior highs.
> 1998. Bridge Resources, PC(USA), 100 Witherspoon St., Louisville, KY 40202; (800) 524-2612.

Sex, Lies, and the Truth (30 minutes)

> *Theme:* Sex in the '90s.
> *Focus:* Junior and senior highs/parents.
> 1993. Focus on the Family, Colorado Springs, CO 80995.

Youth, Sex, Sexuality (40 minutes)

> *Theme:* Youth and sex/sexuality.
> *Focus:* Training resource for adult leaders.
> YMTN Teleconference Special with Jim Burns and Robert Miniear; Mass Media Ministries, 2116 N. Charles St., Baltimore, MD 21218.

HIV/AIDS

AIDS: Everything You Should Know (28 minutes)

> *Theme:* AIDS awareness and prevention.
> *Focus:* Youth and adults.
> AIMS Media, 9710 DeSoto Ave., Chatsworth, CA 91311-4409; (800) 367-2467.

A Is for Aids (15 minutes)

> *Theme:* AIDS awareness and prevention.
> *Focus:* Younger youth.
> Perennial Education, The Altschul Group, 930 Pitner Ave., Evanston, IL 60203; (312) 328-6700.

Time Out: The Truth about HIV, AIDS, and You (42 minutes). Hosted by Magic Johnson and Arsenio Hall.

> *Theme:* HIV/AIDS.
> *Focus:* Junior and senior highs (preview before showing—needs some editing).
> 1992. Paramount Home Video.

Puberty/Sexual Development

Am I Normal? (23 minutes)

> *Theme:* Puberty from a boy's perspective.
> *Focus:* Junior highs.
> EcuFilm; (800) 251-4091.

Another Half (27 minutes)

> *Theme:* Struggling with the boundaries of masculinity.
> *Focus:* Junior and senior highs.
> Wadsworth Productions, 1413 W. 37th St., Austin, TX 70731; (512) 478-2971.

Boy to Man (19 minutes)

> *Theme:* Puberty from a boy's perspective.
> *Focus:* Junior highs.
> Churchill Media, 6901 Woodley Ave., Van Nuys, CA 91406; (800) 334-7830.

Dear Diary (24 minutes)

> *Theme:* Puberty from a girl's perspective.
> *Focus:* Junior highs.
> EcuFilm; (800) 251-4091.

Girl to Woman (22 minutes)

> *Theme:* Puberty from a girl's perspective.
> *Focus:* Junior highs.
> Churchill Media; (800) 334-7830.

Human Growth IV (23 minutes)

> *Theme:* Sexual development.
> *Focus:* Junior highs.
> Churchill Media; (800) 334-7830.

Then One Year (23 minutes)

> *Theme:* Physiological changes of adolescence.
> *Focus:* Junior highs.
> Churchill Media; (800) 334-7830.

What Kids Want to Know About Sex and Growing Up (60 minutes)

> *Theme:* Puberty, sex, sexuality.
> *Focus:* Junior highs/parents.
> 1992. Children's Television Workshop.

Self-Esteem

Building Self-Confidence (38 minutes; includes study guide)

> *Theme:* Self-esteem.
>
> *Focus:* Junior and senior highs.
>
> Sunburst Communications, 101 Castleton Street, P.O. Box 40, Pleasantville, NY 10570; (800) 431-1934.

I Like Being Me: Self-Esteem (30 minutes; includes study guide)

> *Theme:* Self-esteem.
>
> *Focus:* Junior highs.
>
> Sunburst Communication; (800) 431-1934.

Sexually Transmitted Infections

A Million Teenagers (23 minutes)

> *Theme:* Sexually transmitted infections.
>
> *Focus:* Youth.
>
> Churchill Media; (800) 334-7830.

Sexual Orientation

Can We Just Talk About It? The Church and Homosexuality (30 minutes)

> *Theme:* Homosexuality.
>
> *Focus:* Adults/Older youth.
>
> 1996. CTS Press, Decatur, GA.

On Being Gay: A Conversation with Brian McNaught (80 minutes)

> *Theme:* What is it like growing up gay?
>
> *Focus:* Students and leaders.
>
> EcuFilm; (800) 251-4091.

Project 10 (10 minutes)

> *Theme:* Homosexuality.
>
> *Focus:* Leadership training/older youth.
>
> Virginia Uribe, Fx HS, 7850 Melrose Ave., Los Angeles, CA 90046.

Sexual Violence

Play It Safe (8 minutes)

> *Theme:* Sexual abuse.
>
> *Focus:* Youth/adults. 1994.
>
> Interlink Video Productions, Inc., P.O. Box 1004, Merchantville, NJ 08109; (800) 662-1151.

When Dating Turns Dangerous (33 minutes; includes study guide)

> *Theme:* Dating violence and date rape.
>
> *Focus:* Senior highs.
>
> SunBurst Communications; (800) 431-1934.

Organizations

Advocates for Youth, Suite 200, 1025 Vermont Ave. N.W., Washington, D.C. 20005; (202) 347-5700.

Produces a variety of resources to increase the opportunities for and abilities of youth to make healthy decisions about sexuality. They provide information, advocacy, and training to youth-serving professionals, policy makers, youth, and the media.

AIDS National Interfaith Network, 1400 I St., Suite 1220, Washington, D.C. 20005; (202) 842-0010; www.thebody.com.

Links people of faith, mobilizes religious leadership, and fosters compassionate services to people with or affected by AIDS.

The Center for the Prevention of Sexual and Domestic Violence, 936 N. 34th St., Suite 200, Seattle, WA 98103; (206) 634-1903; www.cpsdv.org.

This interreligious ministry addresses issues of sexual and domestic violence and serves as a bridge between religious and secular communities.

Planned Parenthood Federation of America, 810 Seventh Ave., New York, NY 10019; (212) 261-4660; www.ppfa.org.

A national organization with more than nine hundred clinics in communities across the country providing reproductive health care and education. They are an excellent source for information, brochures, videos, and training about family planning, women's health care, sexuality education, sexually transmitted infections, and family communication.

SIECUS (Sexuality Information and Education Council of the United States), 130 W. 42nd St., Suite 350, New York, NY 10036; (212) 819-9770; www.siecus.org.

Develops, collects, and distributes information; promotes comprehensive education about sexuality; and advocates the right of individuals to make responsible sexual choices.

II. Younger Youth Course

Introduction

Middle school-age young people need education about sexuality but often don't receive it. Parents may feel inadequate to provide it. They may be concerned that talking about sex will give their young person ideas or imply tacit permission to experiment sexually. To the contrary, knowledge helps one make informed decisions and act in a responsible manner. Young people are having intercourse earlier than they did in previous eras. Often education about sexuality is postponed by parents and/or the schools until the young person has already begun to experiment sexually.

Because education about sexuality comes from many sources in a young person's life, accurate information and loving concern are needed to counterbalance the distorted images received from peers, movies, television shows, and advertisements.

Some young people in this course may have participated in *God's Plan for Growing Up*, the Presbyterian Church (U.S.A.) sexuality education curriculum for elementary-age children and their parents. But even if they have not, *God's Gift of Sexuality* is designed to help young people put their sexuality into perspective. To achieve this goal, the material has been developed with several general principles in mind:

1. Respect for young people is a primary theme throughout the course. Leaders will respect their dignity and acknowledge the value of opinions and beliefs they express. This course provides opportunities to discuss sexual issues with youth. Learning is enhanced when people share true feelings and experiences with one another rather than merely talking at or to one another.

2. A good course about sexuality helps reduce rather than increase the intensity of the adolescent sex drive. Often the power of our feelings can be reduced when these feelings are verbalized. When young people hear sex talked about, put into perspective, and its power explored, they begin to see it as a part of life as God has given it, not as a god in life that must be experienced. Rather than putting their sexuality into practice, they are shown how to put it into proper perspective, thus making such practice unnecessary.

3. Sexuality is seen as positive, not evil, wicked, nasty, or dirty. Rather than emphasizing the negative elements of sexual behavior, the material presents sex as a gift of God over which we are to be good stewards.

4. Beliefs and values are best taught by example. Many young people gain their values through a process of accepting and rejecting values held by significant adults in their lives. This course provides young people the opportunity to begin articulating the values they already hold, which will help them when their values are challenged and called into question. At the same time, good models are provided through a trained leader, small group leaders, and parents.

Teaching This Material in Your Church

This material can be taught in a variety of formats. (See "Sample Schedules" on pp. 27–28 in this guide.) It can be completed in one or two weekends. Activities for the first weekend are scheduled Friday evening through Sunday evening, with parent's orientation and small-group leader training taking place on Thursday evening. The second weekend has activities planned for all day Sunday.

The material can be taught in a retreat setting or in four blocks of five hours each. The course can also be conducted by teaching a small block once a week for several weeks, but the length of time between sessions makes it difficult to develop community and trust.

The complete course includes about twenty hours of coursework for the youth participants, plus additional time for meals and breaks. Select a time other than the youth fellowship hour. Not everyone in youth fellowship may want to participate, and the course works best when it is presented as an option. Night meetings seem to work better than after-school meetings. If the course is taught in a retreat setting, remember that parents must also participate at the end of the course. The group could come back to the church for this parent/youth session, or it could be held as a follow-up soon after the retreat. A third option is to hold the entire retreat at the church.

Keeping the students in small groups is the most important component of this course. The ideal small group is composed of six to eight young people of both sexes who are close in age. People teaching about sexuality sometimes separate males and females. This separation reinforces the attitude that males and females cannot discuss sexual matters together. One reason some young people become sexually active is that they are embarrassed to discuss their feelings. They may engage in unprotected intercourse for the same reason. The small-group time offers a rare opportunity for males and females to communicate with each other about beliefs, feelings, and concerns.

Each small group needs at least one leader, but ideally a team of one man and one woman should lead each small group. That is a good way to model that males and females can talk about sexuality together. Choose people who like young people and are good listeners to lead small groups. Because of the nature of the course, they do not need to have any special skills or knowledge. The course is designed to create opportunities for young people and adults to discuss, question, explore, and discover together. It is not dependent on adult lectures to young people. (See "Guidelines for Leaders" on pp. 3–7 in this guide for more suggestions about leaders.)

Parents are the primary source from which young people form values about sexuality. The purpose of the parent's sessions is to enhance their communication with their children about sexuality. Communication involves both talking and listening. The activities in this course encourage the sharing of information and views. For parents to attend the parent/youth session is important. There is no need for a young person to attend this particular session if his or her parent cannot attend, because the session is dependent on the families participating together. You may want to find a way to work with families who cannot attend this session so the value of this special interaction will not be lost.

One person from the church should serve as the coordinator to ensure that the course runs smoothly. This person publicizes the event, handles registration, recruits small-group leaders, assigns the young people to small groups, and secures needed equipment and supplies. He or she also helps set up activities and oversees the meals and/or refreshments.

Hold this course in a large room. The small groups can be arranged around the room, leaving space in the middle for the total group to gather for discussions, games, and videos.

This guide contains information about recruiting leaders, the values espoused in this course, publicity, various course formats, and videos and other resources. It also contains sections titled "A Reformed/Presbyterian Understanding of Sexuality" and "Guide for the Presbyterian Church (U.S.A.)," along with many other resources (see pp. 8–22 in this guide.)

Those of us who have worked on this resource have a particular bias. We believe young people who are not married should not engage in sexual intercourse. In plain terms, we believe having sex as an unmarried teenager is a mistake. We believe that in our society having sexual intercourse before marriage is hazardous to a teenager's health of body, mind, and spirit. Our intention is to respond to, communicate with, and be supportive of young people who are not having sex as well as those who decide to have sex anyway or who have already been sexually involved.

Preparatory Session 1

Small-Group Leader Training

Purpose: This session gives small-group leaders an orientation to the course and an opportunity to share their anxieties and expectations.

Time: One hour and thirty minutes

Materials Needed

- Course schedule
- "Tips for Working with Small Groups" (p. 45)
- Assignment of small groups
- *God's Gift of Sexuality, Leader's Guide*
- "Basic Principles for Education about Sexuality" (pp. 45–46)
- Copies of small-group activities

Activities

Expectations	15 minutes
Review of Principles	15 minutes
Review of Course Schedule	60 minutes

Background for the Leader

People are the most important variable in this course. Like any course that fosters growth, this one depends on sensitive, caring persons. You will need to enlist such people to serve as small-group leaders.

Small-group leaders should be chosen from the participating church if at all possible. It does not matter whether they have young people participating in the course as long as no two members of any one family are in the same small group. The persons selected must like young people and have the ability to listen actively to group members. Most important, they need to be themselves and accept others as they are. Small-group leaders do not have to be authorities on every topic; in fact, it is sometimes helpful to the group when the leaders admit they do not know an answer.

A good small-group leader keeps the overall goal of the course in mind and works toward that end. The small-group leader's task is to help young people express their feelings, ideas, and values. Leaders who can laugh, cry, and struggle to make sense out of what it means to be a sexual human being will have a profound opportunity to make a difference in the lives of the young people.

Procedures

Expectations (15 minutes)
Have small-group leaders share their anxieties about and expectations for the course.

Review of Principles (15 minutes)
Go over "Tips for Working with Small Groups" (p. 45) and "Basic Principles for Education about Sexuality" (pp. 45–46).

Review of Course Schedule (60 minutes)
Go over the schedule in detail and describe each activity. Decide who has responsibility for each item within each activity. Make small-group assignments. Close with prayer.

Homework: Read the "Guide for the Presbyterian Church (U.S.A.)" (pp. 14–22).

Tips for Working with Small Groups

1. Remember that the primary role of the small-group leader is to encourage and be supportive of the participation of the young people.

2. Silence doesn't mean nonparticipation. Sometimes, because of the subject, the only response young people will make is to listen. If they are listening actively, they will get great benefit from the course.

3. Communication will be encouraged by keeping the group in a circle facing each other and on the same level (either all on the floor or all in chairs).

4. Young people will rarely ask personal questions of the small-group leaders. If they do, an appropriate response is, "What happened with me may not be accurate for everyone. Let's see if we can find out what is true for most people." Their questions should then be dealt with in the large-group session.

5. Admitting that you don't know the answer to a question will encourage young people to relate to the leaders on the same level; that is, that the leaders, too, are learning about sexuality. The answers to specific questions should then be obtained from either an authority on the subject or an appropriate book or resource.

6. To create an atmosphere of trust, confidentiality is to be respected. Please do not share with anyone outside the group what is discussed or stated by any young person during the course. (An exception would be if a young person reports a case of rape or abuse to you. See "Recognizing and Reporting Abuse" on pages 6–7 for more information.)

Basic Principles for Education about Sexuality

1. A good course about sexuality respects young people. It respects their dignity and values their opinions and beliefs.

2. A good course about sexuality uses a banquet-table model of learning, providing information in a variety of ways. It does not make the assumption that young people are vessels waiting to have the right information poured into them; it allows students to choose and to wrestle with what is being taught.

3. A good course about sexuality sees sex as positive. Sex is not portrayed as evil, wicked, nasty, or dirty, but rather as a gift of God, which, if we are good stewards, must be used wisely and responsibly.

4. A good course about sexuality develops an atmosphere of trust. Sex is difficult to talk about under the best of circumstances; to talk about sex if trust does not exist is impossible. This course is designed with many activities that are not about sex but are used to build group trust and self-esteem.

5. A good course about sexuality teaches values. Most values are formed at an early age and largely through observation as opposed to verbal instruction. The young people will come into the course with their values already in place. They will have been with their parents for about as many years as the course has hours. The course cannot outweigh parental influence. However, what the course can do is to encourage young people to begin articulating the values they already hold. This will prove extremely helpful to them when their values are challenged and called into question.

6. A good course about sexuality uses the teachings of Scripture and the church as valuable resources. To do otherwise is to waste an opportunity to strengthen the ties between faith and life and to teach with incomplete information.

7. A good course about sexuality helps to reduce rather than increase the intensity of the adolescent sex drive. When sex is talked about and put into perspective, young people

begin to see it as a part of life created by God, not as a god in life that must be experienced. Rather than putting it into practice they have put it into proper perspective, making such practice unnecessary.

8.   A good course about sexuality teaches males and females together. To do otherwise is a wasted opportunity. Most of us will choose a member of the opposite sex as our sexual partner. Therefore, learning the similarities and the differences in the sexes and learning to communicate with people of the opposite sex about sex is important.

Preparatory Session 2

Parent's Orientation

Purpose: This session gives parents the opportunity to gain ownership in the course and to ask questions. The session also helps relieve their anxiety about the course. *Note:* Small-group leaders should attend this session.

Time: One hour

Materials Needed

- "Basic Principles for Education about Sexuality" (found on p. 26 in the *Parent's Guide*; pp. 45–46 in this guide)
- Course schedule

Activities

Group Building	20 minutes
Review of Principles	20 minutes
Review of Course Schedule	20 minutes

Procedures

Group Building (20 minutes)
Welcome the parents. Ask people to introduce themselves by telling something about the sexuality education they received as a child or something about the decision-making process in their household that prompted their young person to sign up to take this course.

Review of Principles (20 minutes)
Briefly cover the "Basic Principles for Education about Sexuality" that were used to create this course (see pp. 45–46 in this guide).

Review of Course Schedule (20 minutes)
Introduce the small-group leaders and others involved in leading the course. Review the course schedule and details with the parents. Invite their questions about the various activities. Remind parents of the closing parent's overview session and ask whether they will be participating with their children in the parent/youth communication session. This session depends on parents and young people participating in family groups. Tell parents that if they cannot be present for the parent/youth communication session, there is no need for their young person to attend. If you, as the leader, can make other arrangements or can find a time to work with families individually, feel free to do so.

If time permits, select an activity from one of the sessions in the course and let the parents participate in it. Close with prayer.

Session 1

Anatomy and Physiology

Purpose: Session 1 begins with exercises to form a group, reduce anxiety, and build trust. This process is essential if young people are going to share their feelings about something as personal as sexuality.

A set of agreements is provided to help the group function smoothly and establish a spirit of working together. The physiology sheets provide a working vocabulary for the rest of the course and serve as a yardstick for measuring the participant's knowledge. The theological study is used to emphasize the positive aspects of sexuality as a gift of God.

Language often serves as a barrier in teaching young people about sexuality. This course uses the proper names of sexual organs and activities. These may be new to some young people. The slang word exercise is used to alleviate the tension between the two vocabularies and to set the framework for open discussion. In addition, it helps the young people relax with the topic of sexuality.

Time: Three hours

Materials Needed

- *Younger Youth Guide* (Session 1)
- Pencils
- Videocassette recorder (VCR) and television monitor
- Video: "Then One Year"
- 8 1/2" x 11" white paper (one sheet for each small group)
- 3" x 5" index cards (two colors)
- Name tags

Activities

Registration	15 minutes prior to starting
Group Building	40 minutes
Introductions and Community Agreement	10 minutes
Anatomy and Physiology Sheets	15 minutes
Video: "Then One Year"	20 minutes
Break	15 minutes
Review Anatomy/Physiology Sheets	20 minutes
Slang Word Exercise	15 minutes
Question Cards	5 minutes
God Created Us and Gave Us the Gift of Our Sexuality	40 minutes

Procedures

Registration (15 minutes prior to starting)

Group Building (40 minutes)

Find Someone Who . . .

Have students turn to "Find Someone Who . . . " in Session 1 of the Younger Youth Guide (p. 16). At the given signal people mill about trying to complete their sheet as quickly as possible. Give them about ten minutes. You can make up your own "Find Someone Who . . ." sheet if you prefer.

Continuums

Divide into groups of ten or twelve and have people line up in order for certain categories. Use any or all of the following suggestions:

1. The day of your birth (for example: Jan. 1–Dec. 31)
2. Alphabetical order according to first name (Amy–Zeb)
3. Alphabetical order according to the kind of toothpaste used
4. Alphabetical order according to the kind of deodorant used
5. Alphabetical order according to favorite foods
6. Fewest to most pets
7. Birthplace from nearest to farthest from the city where you are

Three Truths and a Lie

Announce the small group assignments at this time and divide into groups. To help group members get to know one another, have each person tell four things about himself or herself, three of them true and one of them a lie. The group tries to guess which statement is not true. Example: Tell your favorite food, movie, pet peeve, and way to spend time. Fib about one of these.

Introductions and Community Agreements (10 minutes)

Have the group gather in a large circle. If the room is carpeted, chairs won't be necessary. Begin with prayer. Next, introduce the leader and cover the agreements necessary for the group to function smoothly. You may want to write the following on newsprint, on a chalkboard, or use as a handout:

Attendance—Tonight can be a trial session to see if you are interested in this course. If you like it and come back next time, can we agree that this is an indication of your commitment to attend all the sessions and to be on time? If, after tonight's session, you decide not to come back, please tell your small-group leader.

Confidentiality—We will be talking about some things that people may consider personal. It is important for each of you to feel free to say what is on your mind. In order to do this, we will need to agree not to talk outside the group about what happens or is said during the group meetings. If you want to discuss things with your parents, this is an exception. Can we agree to this?

Comfort—We are going to be doing activities in these sessions. Can we agree that no one has to do any activity with which they are not comfortable?

Boredom—Your time and mine are too valuable to waste. If you are bored, tell me, and we can do something else. Will you agree to tell me if this happens?

Housekeeping—Have the coordinator give instructions about boundaries within the facility, where bathrooms are, where meals will be served, who else is using the facility, and so forth.

Anatomy and Physiology Sheets (15 minutes)

Divide into small groups and ask the students to complete the anatomy and physiology sheets found in Session 1 of the *Younger Youth Guide* (pp. 17–23). Young people should be assured that no one will see their answers. They may work in pairs.

Video (20 minutes)

After the sheets are completed, gather the group to view "Then One Year" or a similar video on anatomy, physiology, and human development.

Break (15 minutes)

Review Anatomy and Physiology Sheets (20 minutes)

Call the participants back together and review the anatomy and physiology sheets. This may develop into a question-and-answer session.

Slang Word Exercise (15 minutes)

Give each small group a sheet of paper with the following words written across the top: penis, vagina, intercourse. Each group is to brainstorm and write down as many synonyms as possible in three to four minutes. Baby words, street language, slang, or formal language are all acceptable. Share the list in the large group. Have the leader read them aloud. The leader then says the following:

> Language has a great deal of power. Often people use words to exclude others or to make them feel they are ignorant. For our purposes in this course, we will be using the scientific terms simply because they are more accurate terms. If you want to ask a question and can't think of the scientific word, use the word with which you are most comfortable. In this course there aren't any good or bad words. You know these words, and we adults know them. You know that we know, and we know that you know. We've all heard the slang terms before, and we don't need to let them get in the way of talking with each other.

Question Cards (5 minutes)

Distribute blank 3" x 5" index cards. Give girls one color and boys another. Tell the participants to write down any question they want answered but don't want to ask aloud. Explain that they may ask a question a friend has asked them to which they did not know the answer. Each person should write something on the card. If they don't have a question, they should write "no comment." Do not put a name on the card. Pass around a container for them to put the cards in. Tell them that all these questions will be answered at the next session.

God Created Us and Gave Us the Gift of Our Sexuality (40 minutes)

Theological concepts to understand:

- God created us as sexual beings.
- Our sexuality affects all of who we are.
- Our sexuality is good.

Read the theological section "God Created Us and Gave Us the Gift of Our Sexuality" (p. 23 in the *Younger Youth Guide*; p. 58 in this guide).

In the small groups, have the students individually write the answers to the questions given at the end of this session (p. 24 in the *Younger Youth Guide*; p. 59 in this guide). Discuss the answers.

After completing the discussion in small groups, come back together as a total group and compile the one-word answers from question 10. Record the answers on newsprint and post in the room. Ask someone to read again the Scripture lesson from Genesis and Ephesians. Ask for any other questions or thoughts about this part of the session. Join in a prayer of thanksgiving for the gift of our sexuality.

Gather the group in a circle. Thank the group for their participation and express appreciation for their willingness to deal with a topic that requires risk. Close with prayer or use the litany for Session 1 (p. 25 in the *Younger Youth Guide*; p. 60 in this guide).

Find Someone Who . . .

Directions: Find different people in your group who match these statements and ask them to sign their names beside that statement. Do not sign your own name.

Find someone who . . .

1. has not been to a movie in the last month. _____

2. walks to school. _____

3. has three sisters. _____

4. is going to high school next year. _____

5. is allergic to chocolate. _____

6. dislikes pizza. _____

7. is over 5' 6" tall. _____

8. you have never met before. _____

9. you have met before. _____

10. cannot rollerblade. _____

11. gets Bs or better in math. _____

12. is left handed. _____

13. has never been on water skis. _____

14. prefers yellow as a favorite color. _____

15. knows how to play hockey. _____

16. is an only child. _____

17. has a part-time job. _____

18. prefers hamburgers to pizza. _____

Anatomy Drawing (Male)

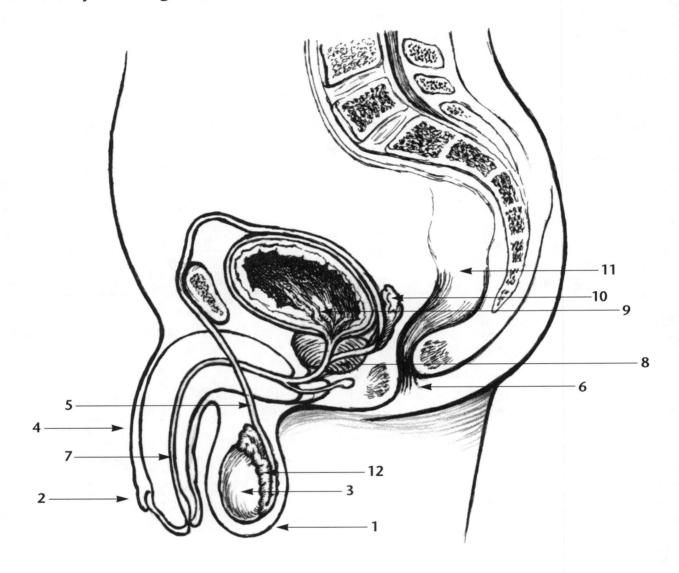

Scrotum   Penis   Anus
Vas deferens   Prostate gland   Glans penis
Testis   Urethra   Epididymis
Bladder   Rectum   Seminal vesicle

1. _____   7. _____
2. _____   8. _____
3. _____   9. _____
4. _____   10. _____
5. _____   11. _____
6. _____   12. _____

Anatomy Drawing (Female—Internal)

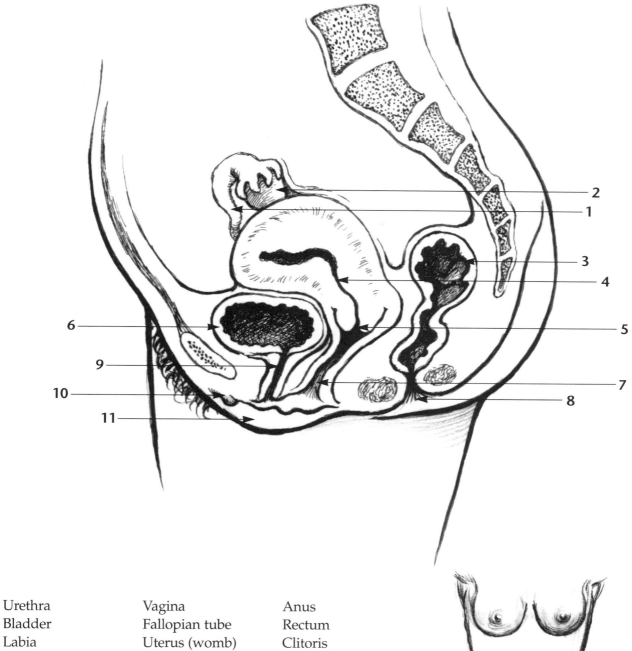

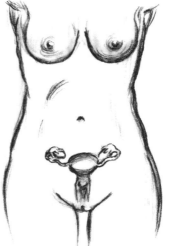

Urethra	Vagina	Anus
Bladder	Fallopian tube	Rectum
Labia	Uterus (womb)	Clitoris
Cervix	Ovary	

1. _____   7. _____
2. _____   8. _____
3. _____   9. _____
4. _____   10. _____
5. _____   11. _____
6. _____

Anatomy Drawing (Female—External)

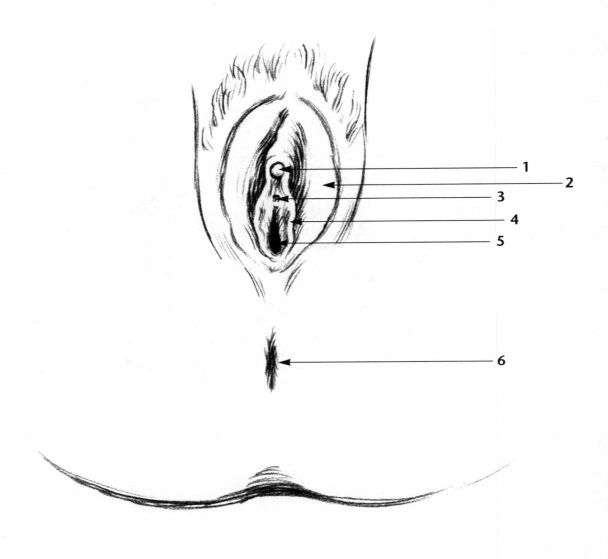

Labia minora (inner lips)   Anus (opening)   Labia majora (outer lips)
Urethra (opening)   Clitoris   Vagina (opening)

1. _____   4. _____
2. _____   5. _____
3. _____   6. _____

Anatomy Drawings—Answer Key

Male

1. Scrotum
2. Glans penis
3. Testis
4. Penis
5. Vas deferens
6. Anus
7. Urethra
8. Prostate gland
9. Bladder
10. Seminal vesicle
11. Rectum
12. Epididymis

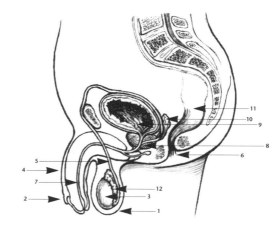

Female (Internal)

1. Fallopian tube
2. Ovary
3. Rectum
4. Uterus (womb)
5. Cervix
6. Bladder
7. Vagina
8. Anus
9. Urethra
10. Clitoris
11. Labia

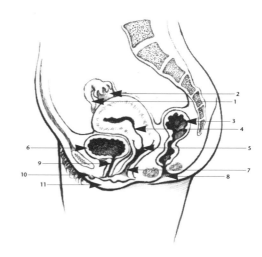

Female (External)

1. Clitoris
2. Labia majora (outer lips)
3. Urethra (opening)
4. Labia minora (inner lips)
5. Vagina (opening)
6. Anus (opening)

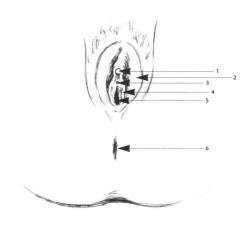

Male Physiology Sheet

A. Semen
B. Circumcision
C. Glans
D. Erection
E. Epididymis

F. Impotence
G. Penis
H. Ejaculation
I. Scrotum
J. Foreskin

K. Vas deferens
L. Testes
M. Sperm
N. Premature ejaculation
O. Seminal vesicles

1. _____ The stiffening of the penis because of an increased flow of blood.

2. _____ Male sex cells that fertilize the ovum or egg.

3. _____ The sack of skin that forms a pouch containing the testicles.

4. _____ Tube through which the sperm travel from testicles to the seminal vesicles and urethra.

5. _____ Male sex organ used in urination and intercourse.

6. _____ Whitish fluid in which sperm is transported and ejaculated.

7. _____ The inability to achieve an erection.

8. _____ Covering of the tip of the penis that is often removed.

9. _____ A vast group of microscopic tubes where sperm are stored.

10. _____ Orgasm and discharge of semen before the penis has completely entered the vagina or just after entry.

11. _____ The tip of the penis.

12. _____ Surgical removal of the foreskin of the penis, which covers the glans.

13. _____ Male sex glands.

14. _____ Pouches that open out into the sperm ducts.

15. _____ The rapid discharge or expulsion of sperm and semen during orgasm.

Female Physiology Sheet

A. Abortion
B. Fallopian tube
C. Ovary
D. Vulva
E. Cervix

F. Hymen
G. Ovulation
H. Vagina
I. Clitoris
J. Labia

K. Placenta
L. Ovum
M. Douche
N. Menarche
O. Uterus

1. _____ The name of the female sex cell, derived from the Latin word for egg.

2. _____ A process used mistakenly as a contraceptive and sometimes to cleanse the vagina.

3. _____ The place where the egg is fertilized.

4. _____ A center of sexual response for women.

5. _____ The start of menstruation.

6. _____ The approximate monthly release of an ovum.

7. _____ The removal of a fetus from the uterus prior to birth, sometimes occurring spontaneously.

8. _____ The lips or folds of skin covering the vaginal opening. There are two sets: majora and minora.

9. _____ The term that applies to both sets of the structures referred to in number 8.

10. _____ The twin storage places for ova (eggs) in the female.

11. _____ A thin membrane across the opening of the vagina.

12. _____ A pear-shaped organ where the fertilized ovum develops into a fetus.

13. _____ The opening, sometimes called the birth canal, where the penis enters during intercourse.

14. _____ The neck of the uterus where the vagina and uterus are joined.

15. _____ The lining of the uterus through which the baby is fed during pregnancy.

Male and Female Physiology Sheets—Answer Key

Male Physiology

1. D
2. M
3. I
4. K
5. G
6. A
7. F
8. J
9. E
10. N
11. C
12. B
13. L
14. O
15. H

Female Physiology

1. L
2. M
3. B
4. I
5. N
6. G
7. A
8. J
9. D
10. C
11. F
12. O
13. H
14. E
15. K

God Created Us and Gave Us the Gift of Our Sexuality

> Then God said, "Let us make humankind in our image, according to our likeness; and let them have dominion over . . . the earth." So God created humankind in [God's] image, in the image of God [God] created them; male and female [God] created them . . . God saw everything that God had made, and indeed, it was very good.
>
> (Gen. 1:26, 27, 31a)

> For we are what [God] has made us, created in Christ Jesus for good works.
>
> (Eph. 2:10)

God created us and called us very good. God did not create us only as spirits, nor only as bodies. God created us as total persons—body and spirit. And God called this entire creation very good.

Not only did God create us, but God created us to be God's very own image in the world. All that we are—including our bodies, including our sexuality—is God's gift to us.

Our sexuality is our way of being male or female in the world. Our sexuality is very basic; it affects our thoughts, feelings, and actions. Because our sexuality is called good by God and because it is God's gift to us, we can feel good about our sexuality.

Questions

1. The first point in understanding our sexuality is to understand that it is God's good gift to us. What is good for you about being male or female?

_____

_____

_____

_____

2. Do you think most people your age believe sexuality is a positive part of their lives? If not, how do they feel about their sexuality?

_____

_____

_____

_____

3. What is difficult about being female or male?

_____

_____

_____

4. What do you not understand about being a male?

_____

_____

_____

5. What do you not understand about being a female?

_____

_____

_____

6. Do you think it is easier for males or for females to feel good about their sexuality? Why?

_____

_____

_____

7. Do you think your parents feel good about your sexual development? Do they talk to you about your sexual development?

_____

_____

_____

8. Your body may be going through many changes. What changes would you describe as embarrassing, as difficult, or as very good?

_____

_____

_____

9. Your body is still in the process of changing. What changes do you still want to see happen?

_____

_____

_____

10. In one word, God described your sexuality as "good." What one word would you use?

_____

_____

_____

_____

Litany

Leader: In the book of Genesis, God said: "Let's make humankind in our own image . . . " So God created humankind in God's own image, in the image of God was the human being created; male and female God created them.

All: God created us together—to be together. That is what Scripture says. God made us male and female, boys and girls, men and women. That is all part of God's plan for the enjoyment and fulfillment of human life.

Girls: To be a growing female is hard. I like being a girl, but it is hard to understand and to know what life holds for me. I feel so mixed up at times. I want to laugh and cry at the same time. I want to feel like a woman. I am glad God created me female. Thank you, God!

Boys: To be a growing male is hard. I like being a boy, but it is hard to understand and to know what life holds for me. At times I feel all mixed up inside, like I should hide. I want to feel like a man. I am glad God created me male. Thank you, God!

All: Creator of us all, we need you as our friend and guide as we grow to be men and women. Teach us the way of love as we spend time together, as we talk, play, and live together. Teach us the meaning of love as we learn and grow, as we date and form relationships with one another.

Teach us the depths of love as we learn to give of ourselves to others.

Creator of goodness and beauty, you tell us that love is beautiful and good. Let our activities together express your love. Let us treat our bodies as holy temples. Let us care for each other as you care for us. Amen.

Session 2

Puberty

Purpose: This session focuses on the participant's sexual development. The presentations in this session cover the changes that are taking place within each young person. The normality of these changes will be stressed. The Sex Charades activity is a fun way to reinforce proper terminology and help young people further relax with the topic of sex. The "I'm Glad I Am . . . / If I Were . . . " exercise helps young people become aware of their feelings about their gender. Answering the question cards from the previous session shows the participants that this course respects and takes seriously the issues that concern young people.

Time: Three hours (You may choose to omit some of the group-building activities if you have less than three hours.)

Materials Needed

- Pencils
- VCR and television monitor
- Videos: "Am I Normal?" and "Dear Diary"
- 3" x 5" index cards with Sex Charade terms
- 3" x 5" index cards with questions from previous session
- 3" x 5" index cards for new questions
- Felt-tipped markers and newsprint
- 8½" x 11" white paper

Activities

Group Building	30 minutes
Question Cards	30 minutes
Video: "Dear Diary"	30 minutes
Break	10 minutes
Video: "Am I Normal?"	25 minutes
Sex Charades	20 minutes
"I'm Glad I Am . . . / If I Were . . . " (optional)	35 minutes

Procedures

Group Building (30 minutes)

People to People

Ask the entire group to stand in one area of the room and pair off, with pairs facing each other. Assure participants that it doesn't matter who their partners are because they will be changing frequently. Explain that this game is about human touch. Give these instructions: "Listen as the leader calls out a position, then assume that position with your partner. Change partners when the leader calls 'People to people,' but assume the same position."

When you are sure everyone understands, call out the first position. Once all pairs have assumed a position, call out a new one and allow time for partners to assume the new position. Start with simple, less-threatening positions and go on to those that are more complicated. Begin with nose to elbow; finger to forehead; elbow to knee; toe to toe; knee to knee; elbow to hand. Then move to neck to neck; forehead to forehead; nose to nose.

After several positions have been called, call "People to people" and have pairs change partners, then reassume the previous position. Go on to call several new positions.

Care Coil

Have the group form a circle while holding hands. One person lets go of one hand and stands still while the rest of the circle begins to spiral around them. Slowly the circle will begin to tighten into a clumped group. Have a group hug. Next have the stationary person duck and crawl under the still-linked hands. With no one letting go, let the others follow until the group unwinds itself back into the original circle.

The Lap Game

Everyone in the group stands shoulder to shoulder in a circle. Next the group, as a body, turns 90 degrees to the right, maintaining the circle and standing as close to one another as possible. Next, very gently, everybody sits down on the lap of the person who is behind. Those who succeed should then try to stand up again.

Knots

Have individuals stand shoulder to shoulder in a circle and place their hands in the center. When the signal is given, members join hands with others in the group. No one should grab both hands of the same person or take the hand of the person immediately on the right or left. The object is to untie the knot that has formed without letting go of the hands.

Question Cards (30 minutes)

Read aloud the questions written on cards in the previous session. Give the answer. Be concise. It is best to have read the cards ahead of time, in case you need to research any of the answers. Often someone will ask for additional explanations and answers during this time. Tell the youth they may fill out more question cards and leave them with you to answer next week.

Video (30 minutes)

Introduce and show "Dear Diary," the video on female puberty. Then divide into small groups for discussion or, if the group members are feeling comfortable with each other, the discussion can be done in the large group. The following are some questions for discussion:

- Do you think "Dear Diary" presents a realistic picture of girls? Why or why not? (Explain that although the video is dated, the issues remain much the same.)
- Did you think the main character's friends were mean to her? Why do you think we tease each other about sexual things and love?
- Why do you think some people become "girl crazy" or "boy crazy"?
- What's the hardest thing for you about growing up?

Break (10 minutes)

Video (25 minutes)

Introduce and show "Am I Normal?" the video on male puberty. Then break into small groups for discussion, or discuss the film in the large group. Discussion questions should include the following:

- In what ways was "Am I Normal?" true or not true to life? (Again, if necessary explain that even though the video is dated, the issues remain the same.)
- Are most adults as understanding about sexual questions as the movie portrayed them?
- What could Jimmy or his father have done to make their talk more helpful?
- Are friends good sources of information concerning sexuality? Why or why not?
- Why do you think people have such a hard time talking about sex?
- Having seen "Dear Diary" and "Am I Normal?" what do you think the advantages are for males and for females as you grow up?

Sex Charades (20 minutes)

Have each small group sit in a circle on the floor. Give each group a stack of white paper and one felt-tipped marker. The leader is positioned in the middle of the room, holding a stack of 3" x 5" index cards. Each card has one sex-related term on it.

One member from each group comes to the leader. When all are ready, the leader shows the term to them. They run back to their small groups and draw something on the paper to illustrate the term. The person who is drawing the term cannot say anything or use words or letters to depict the term. The other group members try to guess what the term is. When the term has been correctly identified, the group members yell the term aloud so the leader can hear. The first group to yell the correct term wins that round. A second person then goes to the leader to get the term for round two. Continue until every person in the group, including the small-group leader, has had a chance to draw. Give the winning group a cheer.

Note: Prepare the charade cards ahead of time. Suggested terms include the following: breast, fallopian tube, circumcision, sperm, erection, urethra, navel, hymen, foreskin, puberty, virgin, pubic hair, pregnant, seminal vesicle, penis, scrotum, epididymis, cervix, clitoris, placenta, testicles, fetus, vas deferens, vagina, ova, labia, ejaculation, scrotum, menarche.

"I'm Glad I Am . . . / If I Were . . . " (optional) (35 minutes)*

This activity can help young people become more aware of their feelings about their gender. Divide the group into several small groups of the same sex. Ask each group to come up with as many endings as they can for the following sentences:

Boys' group(s): "I'm glad I'm a man because . . ."
Girls' group(s): "I'm glad I'm a woman because . . ."

Give an example to help the groups get started. Have each group record the endings on a sheet of newsprint. Allow about ten minutes and then give the groups another piece of newsprint. Ask the groups to think of as many endings as they can for another sentence:

Boys' group(s): "If I were a woman, I could . . ."
Girls' group(s): "If I were a man, I could . . ."

Have the groups record endings to the second sentence on the other sheet of newsprint in the same way as before. Allow ten minutes. Hang the sheets on the wall and use the following questions for discussion:

- Were any of the responses the same for both genders?
- Was it any harder for the boys or the girls to come up with reasons why they are glad of their gender?
- Was it harder for the boys or for the girls to state the advantages of being the opposite gender?
- Which of the advantages of being a man are real reasons and which are stereotyped reasons?
- Which of the advantages of being a woman are real reasons and which are stereotyped reasons?
- Is it possible to be a "man" and still have or do some of the things listed under "woman"?
- Can you think of a woman you know who has some of the traits listed under "man"?

*Used by permission from *Life Planning Education* (Washington, D.C.: Advocates for Youth, 1985).

Session 3

Relationships and Intimacy

Purpose: This session helps young people to understand how we live together in relationships and to identify the characteristics of healthy relationships. The "Defining Love" exercise provides an opportunity for seeing friendship as the basis of love. As young people share their definitions and ideas about friendship and love, they will begin to see the two as related.

Included in this session is a study of homosexuality. Young people are sometimes fearful and confused about homosexuality. Often they are misinformed about it. This session gives accurate information about homosexuality and discusses it in the context of the teachings and values of the Presbyterian Church (U.S.A.).

Time: Two hours and thirty-five minutes (three hours and fifty minutes with the optional activities)

Materials Needed

- *Younger Youth Guide* (Session 3)
- Newsprint
- Felt-tipped markers
- Pencils
- 8 ½" x 11" sheets of white paper (one for each participant)
- 3" x 5" index cards
- 3" x 5" index question cards from last week

Activities

Group Building	15 minutes
Question Cards	15 minutes
God Created Us for Life in Community	20 minutes
Defining Love	25 minutes
Break	10 minutes
Likes/Dislikes (optional)	40 minutes
Video: "Another Half" (optional)	35 minutes
Understanding Homosexuality	35 minutes
Our Church Is a Varied Community	35 minutes

Procedures

Group Building (15 minutes)

How Do You Like Your Neighbor?

Have the participants sit in chairs in a circle. Have them count off one, two, three, four; one, two, three, four; until they each have a number. Have one person stand in the middle of the circle without a chair and take away any extra chairs from the circle. The person in the middle then moves to someone who is sitting and asks, "How do you like your neighbor?" The person sitting can say one of two statements. He or she can say "I like my neighbor just fine," which is a signal to the group that everyone must change their chairs as quickly as possible, or the person can say, "I don't like him (or her)." If this is the response, the person in the middle must then ask, "Well, who do you like?" The person sitting responds by saying, "I like ones and twos," or "threes, fours, and ones," or "threes," using any combination of the numbers one, two, three, and four. The people whose numbers are called must change chairs as quickly as possible. The original person in the middle tries to get a chair when everyone moves, leaving a new person in the middle, and the game begins all over.

Question Cards (15 minutes)

Answer the questions written on the cards in the previous session. Allow time for follow-up questions and for the young people to ask questions for clarity. Tell them they may use the cards to write more questions for the next session.

God Created Us for Life in Community (20 minutes)

Theological concepts to understand:

- God created us to be together.
- We are together in relationships and in communities.
- In God's community, we can best learn who God created us to be.

Ask participants to read "God Created Us for Life in Community" (see p. 3 in the *Younger Youth Guide*; p. 72 in this guide).

Break into small groups. Because the idea of "relationship" or "community" can best be understood by looking at friendship, have the young people describe someone who they think is a good friend to someone else. On a sheet of newsprint labeled "Friendships," write down the words or phrases the young people use to describe a good friend. Hang the sheet on the wall.

Using the list of characteristics of a good friend, discuss the following:

- Which of the characteristics listed would you most like to develop?
- What experiences help make people friends?
- Do you find it easier to be friends with boys or girls?
- What makes it difficult to be friends with girls?
- What makes it difficult to be friends with boys?
- How important is friendship in your life right now?

Refer to the theological statement "God Created Us for Life in Community" on p. 72 in this guide. Conclude this section with a prayer, thanking God for friends and asking for help in becoming better friends to others.

Defining Love (25 minutes)

This activity is designed to help young people discern the different kinds of love found in human relationships. For the purpose of this discussion, the kinds of love have been simplified into three categories: friendship, infatuation, and love. Ask the group to read "Love, Infatuation, and Friendship Definitions" (see p. 26 in the *Younger Youth Guide*; p. 68 of this guide). Working in small groups, ask the young people to use the definitions to describe the situations given in "Love, Infatuation, and Friendship Situations" on page 68 of this guide. (Some of the situations may include more than one kind of love.) In the large group, discuss why people described the situations as they did.

Break (10 minutes)

Gather in a large circle and give back rubs or do the Lap Game activity described in Session 2 (p. 62).

Likes/Dislikes* (optional) (40 minutes)

This activity helps young people identify qualities in the opposite sex that they like and don't like. Explain to the group that you want them to think about the things they like—as well as the things that they don't like about members of the opposite sex.

Have the males form one group, the females another. Give each group a felt-tipped marker and two sheets of newsprint. Each group is to brainstorm and make two lists: things they like about members of the opposite sex and things they don't like. For the "Dislikes" list, they should think about the following questions: What would keep them from wanting to meet or get to know a person? What kinds of approaches bother them? For the "Likes" list, they should think about members of the opposite sex they like and why. What made them want to get to know the person? How does she or he behave?

After about fifteen minutes, have the two small groups come together to share their lists.

Establish these rules for reporting:

1.   When the girls report, the boys must keep quiet and listen.

2.   The boys can say nothing unless they are seeking clarification.

3.   After the girls have reported, the boys must tell the girls what they heard and understood.

4.   After they have demonstrated that they understand, the boys can comment on what the girls have said.

The same rules apply for the boys' report.

After both groups have reported, discuss the following:

- What have you learned about the opposite sex?
- Is everyone attracted to the same characteristics in the opposite sex?
- If you had a magic wand, what is one characteristic you would change about the opposite sex?

*Adapted by permission from *Life Skills and Opportunities* (Philadelphia: Public/Private Ventures, 1986).

Video (optional) (35 minutes)

The video "Another Half" should increase the young people's awareness of male gender (sex) roles and stereotypes, how these develop, and how they affect male attitudes about responsibility in sexual relationships. Introduce it with the following explanation:

> This is a story about two teenage boys, Scott and Rob, who are good friends and have grown up together. Rob's nickname is "Fluteman" because he likes to play music. In the beginning of the film Rob has been badly hurt, and Scott is waiting in the hospital to find out if he is okay. While he waits, Scott remembers different things from their childhood. He also thinks about a girl named Connie who may be pregnant with his baby.

Show the video, and discuss the following questions:

1.   How did you feel about this film? Is it realistic?

2.   Who did you like best, Scott or Rob? Why?

3.   What are some of the stereotyped sexual attitudes and behaviors that Scott developed as he grew up? (Boys don't cry; boys are always interested in sports and athletics; boys should not back down from a fight; playing a musical instrument or being in the band is "sissy"; girls are supposed to take care of birth control if they have sex; girls who have sex are promiscuous [they will have sex with anybody and everybody]; pregnancy is a girl's problem.)

Suggest that "being a man" in a relationship used to mean being a stud (a guy who had sex with a lot of women, taking advantage of girls sexually and not caring about their feelings or what might happen to them). It doesn't have to be that way. A man can be caring, sensitive, and take responsibility for birth control if he and his partner decide to have intercourse. A boy doesn't prove that he's a real man by getting his girlfriend pregnant.

Understanding Homosexuality (35 minutes)

Ask each person to take the homosexuality quiz. (See p. 27 in the *Younger Youth Guide*; p. 69 in this guide.) Allow only a few minutes for completing the quiz so that the young people will give their initial, spontaneous responses.

Next, ask each young person to turn to the section on homosexuality in the "Guide for the Presbyterian Church (U.S.A.)" on pages 13–15 in the *Younger Youth Guide*. Ask someone to read aloud from the section on homosexuality in the guide, one question at a time. The leader then reads the answer to the question.

Then have participants fill in their "Beliefs about Homosexuality" sheets (p. 71), using the "Guide for the Presbyterian Church (U.S.A.)" as a reference. Be clear that you are reading statements from the Presbyterian Church (U.S.A.).

The purpose of this activity is to have the young people translate the church's understanding of homosexuality into their own words. This is not a test. The last two questions are discussion questions.

If questions are raised that you cannot answer, tell the young people that you do not know the answers but will search for the correct answers and share them the next time you meet. It would be especially helpful to discuss the last question. There is no right answer.

Then ask everyone to look again at the homosexuality quiz. Ask if anyone wants to change his or her answers in light of the previous discussion. Give the correct answers found on page 70 of this guide and discuss the answers as needed.

Our Church Is a Varied Community (35 minutes)

Theological concept to understand:

- There are a variety of ways in which people choose to live out their relationships.

Ask the group to read the theological section "Our Church Is a Varied Community" (see p. 5 in the *Younger Youth Guide*; p. 73 in this guide).

Since the Bible verses for this section talk about the body of Christ as being one with many different parts, ask the group to describe the different kinds of family groups in their congregation. Are there people who have always been single? Are there some who are married, divorced, or widowed? Are there some with children, some without? Are there single-parent families?

Ask each person to write on the paper in her or his own words what the Bible verses mean. Share these in small groups.

Use the remaining time to answer any questions about this session.

Close with prayer, and sing "They Will Know We Are Christians by Our Love."

Love, Infatuation, and Friendship Definitions

Love . . .

is a slowly developing and exciting experience.

is energizing.

lets people enjoy everything in life.

occurs between two people who feel good about themselves.

rarely involves jealousy or possessiveness.

comes from two people honestly sharing their feelings.

involves a commitment over time and through difficulty.

Love . . .

is patient and kind.

is not jealous or conceited or proud.

is not ill-mannered or selfish or irritable.

does not keep a record of wrongs.

is not happy with evil.

is happy with the truth.

never gives up.

is faith, hope, and patience that never fails.

is eternal.

(paraphrased from 1 Cor. 13)

Infatuation . . .

is a quickly developing experience.

is exhausting—people can think of nothing else.

keeps people from focusing on other parts of life.

is sometimes motivated by a desire to be taken care of.

occurs when someone feels that he or she is a nobody who can become somebody with the other person.

is often jealous and possessive.

comes from two people denying their conflicting feelings.

does not last over time or through difficulty.

Friendship . . .

occurs with communication.

occurs among people who share common interests.

involves listening.

may turn into love.

occurs with acceptance and trust.

occurs between two people who enjoy each other.

can last over time and through difficulty.

Love, Infatuation, and Friendship Situations

Jill and Eric both play the clarinet in band. They have known each other for three years and often practice together. Wednesday, Eric asked Jill to go to the basketball game.

Martin met Shawna while on vacation at the beach last year. They spent lots of time together during the week and had a great time. Martin knew Shawna was special. He knew he was in love. This fall they have written each other several times, but now the letters are coming less frequently.

Sam and Soon Lee have been looking at (but pretending not to notice) each other for several weeks now. Finally, Sam called Soon Lee and asked her to go steady. She said yes. After hanging up, she called her friend Julie and told her she was in love.

Rose and Jim have lived down the street from each other for years. About twice a month they go for a bicycle ride. Lately when they reach the park, they stop and talk about school, parents, and friends.

Marcus and Cindy have been going steady for one year. They occasionally have "real" dates, but often they spend time together doing things with their families. What Cindy and Marcus like most about their relationship is the way they can talk to each other. Once in a while they have an argument, but they keep talking until things are worked out.

Juan and Jeff are inseparable. They go to the movies together, are on the same football team, spend the night at each other's houses, and often study with each other.

Ann and Joon have been going together for fourteen weeks. Lately Ann has become angry at Joon when he talks to other girls.

Homosexuality Quiz

Directions: Answer each statement True (T), False (F), or do not know (DK).

1. _____ Homosexuality is feeling attracted to or turned on mostly by members of one's own sex.

2. _____ We know homosexuality is caused by an imbalance of hormones.

3. _____ Homosexuals are born that way.

4. _____ More males than females are homosexual.

5. _____ You can easily tell homosexuals by the way they dress or act.

6. _____ Most homosexuals are child molesters.

7. _____ Once a person has a homosexual experience, then he or she is a homosexual.

8. _____ Most churches see homosexual behavior as sinful.

9. _____ About one-third of all males engage in homosexual behavior at some point in their lives.

10. _____ Almost all people have homosexual feelings at one time or another, but they usually won't admit it.

11. _____ Women who are successful in their careers are often lesbians (a term for female homosexuals).

12. _____ Homosexuals are more creative than heterosexuals.

13. _____ A male can do things traditionally considered feminine and not be a homosexual.

14. _____ A female can do things traditionally considered masculine and not be a homosexual.

Homosexuality Quiz—Answer Key

1. Homosexuality is feeling attracted to or turned on mostly by members of one's own sex. **True.**

2. We know homosexuality is caused by an imbalance of hormones. **False.**

3. Homosexuals are born that way. **Do not know.**

4. More males than females are homosexual. **True.**

5. You can easily tell homosexuals by the way they dress or act. **False.**

6. Most homosexuals are child molesters. **False.**

7. Once a person has a homosexual experience, then he or she is a homosexual. **False.**

8. Most churches see homosexual behavior as sinful. **True.**

9. About one-third of all males engage in homosexual behavior at some point in their lives. **True.**

10. Almost all people have homosexual feelings at one time or another, but they usually won't admit it. **True.**

11. Women who are successful in their careers are often lesbians (a term for female homosexuals). **False.**

12. Homosexuals are more creative than heterosexuals. **False.**

13. A male can do things traditionally considered feminine and not be a homosexual. **True.**

14. A female can do things traditionally considered masculine and not be a homosexual. **True.**

Beliefs about Homosexuality

1.   What is homosexuality?

2.   What do people believe the causes of homosexuality may be?

3.   What does our church say about the relationship between membership in the church and being homosexual?

4.   What is homophobia?

5.   What additional information would help you better understand homosexuality?

6.   How would you express your feelings about those who are homosexual?

Definitions

Usually, people are attracted to someone of the opposite gender—males to females, and females to males. We don't know why. It's the way God created them. It's just a part of who they are deep inside. A word used to describe people who are sexually attracted to people of the opposite gender is *heterosexual*.

Some people are sexually attracted to people of the same gender—males to males, and females to females. We don't know why. Most of the people who are this way think it's because God created them this way. A word used to describe people who are sexually attracted to people of the same gender is *homosexual*.

God Created Us for
Life in Community

> Owe no one anything, except to love one another; for the one who loves another has fulfilled the law. The commandments, "You shall not commit adultery; You shall not murder; You shall not steal; You shall not covet"; and any other commandment, are summed up in this word, "Love your neighbor as yourself." Love does no wrong to a neighbor; therefore, love is the fulfilling of the law.
>
> (Rom. 13:8–10)

God created us to be together. From the very beginning, God's purpose was for us to be together—with God and with one another.

One word to define this togetherness is "relationship." A *relationship* is the connection between two people. The connection might be the result of birth or adoption, as with our parents and brothers and sisters. Or the connection might be the result of feelings and commitments, as with acquaintances, friends, and partners. God creates us with a basic need to form and be in relationships with others. Our relationships are answers to the loneliness we feel. They give our lives meaning.

Another word to define this togetherness is "community." A *community* is a group of people who join with one another. You are a part of many communities: your neighborhood, your town or city, your own particular group of friends, your church. God created us to be together in communities to give meaning and identity to our lives.

The very heart of what it means to be in the image of God is to be in community—joined with God and with other people. When we gather in God's name, we are the church in the world. In this community, the church, we can best learn to be who God created us to be.

Our Church Is a Varied Community

For just as the body is one and has many members, and all the members of the body, though many, are one body, so it is with Christ. For in the one Spirit we were all baptized into one body—Jews or Greeks, slaves or free—and we were all made to drink of one Spirit. . . . Now you are the body of Christ and individually members of it.

(1 Cor. 12:12–13, 27)

There is no longer Jew or Greek, there is no longer slave or free, there is no longer male and female; for all of you are one in Christ Jesus.

(Gal. 3:28)

The young need to see in the church role models of both sexes who communicate by life, even more than by words, the goodness of our femaleness and maleness and the equal opportunity of both for service, responsibility, and authority in the life of the church. They need to see the varied responsible ways in which one can live out one's maleness and femaleness and be helped to affirm the goodness of their own sexuality.

("The Nature and Purpose of Human Sexuality," lines 469–475)

The many ways in which people choose to live out their relationships include casual acquaintanceship, friendship, and marriage. In all our relationships we must relate to one another lovingly and responsibly.

Some people remain single all their lives. They have friendships and close, loving relationships without having sexual intercourse. Sometimes people become widowed or divorced; they must then renew friendships and other relationships as single people.

Marriage is a covenant of love and responsibility in which a couple makes a commitment of faithfulness. Sexual intercourse is the ultimate expression of this mutual and lasting covenant. Some people choose to become parents, making a commitment to love, protect, and support their children.

The ways we live out our relationships are influenced by many factors: our families, our friends, our early sexual experiences, and the sex education we receive all have an effect. We are also affected by the particular economic, racial, and/or ethnic group to which we belong, by our community, and by the neighborhood in which we live. Sometimes we live out our relationships in sexist ways—stereotyping one another in particular ways and assigning one another superior or inferior status merely because we are male or female. Sometimes we live out our relationships in racist ways and stereotype particular groups of people merely because of their race. In our own church, we have held, and sometimes still hold, sexist and racist views. To avoid these views we must embrace the diversity within our community and strive toward a good, positive, and healthy view of our sexuality, as God intends.

Whether we are children, youth, or adults; single, divorced, married, or widowed; male or female; heterosexual or homosexual; and whatever our economic status or racial/ethnic heritage, we are all loved by a God who is faithful and just.

Session 4
The Consequences of Sex

Purpose: When people choose to become sexually active, there are consequences to those actions. In the context of a committed relationship, those consequences can be quite wonderful indeed, with the possibility for intense feelings of connection and intimacy and love. There can be a sharing of body and soul in a union that is like no other. One of the positive choices that can come from that union is the birth of a child, who can bring a powerful sense of love and life to a family.

Every act of sexual intercourse has the potential to result in a pregnancy. It is essential for our young people to have information about how pregnancy occurs and about birth control options that can minimize the possibility of conception. In the context of this discussion, young people will have questions about abortion, and therefore it is important to make sure they have the information they need.

Another possible consequence we face when becoming sexually active is exposure to a sexually transmitted infection (STI). Education about STI prevention and detection can give young people information they need in order to make the healthiest choices for themselves, choices that might even include saving their lives.

The challenge in talking with young people about the consequences of becoming sexually active is that our fears for their safety cause us to want to warn them of the dangers of casual sex, of unplanned pregnancies, of STIs, and even of death from AIDS. There is the possibility they will see sexuality as something to be feared and dreaded. On the other hand, between two people in a committed relationship, the consequences can be among the most life affirming and life giving of God's gifts to us. The real goal is to affirm God's gift of sexuality while realistically presenting the possible consequences when our sexuality is misused.

Time: Four hours (May be divided into two sessions)

Materials Needed

- Pencils
- 3" x 5" cards
- Three sheets prepared for "Talking about Consequences" (p. 75)
- Index card prepared for "STI Handshake" (pp. 75–76)
- VCR and television monitor
- Videos: "A Million Teenagers" and "Hope Is Not a Method IV"
- "Sexually Transmitted Infections" chart (pp. 79–80)
- "Ten Most Commonly Asked Questions about STIs" (p. 81)
- "Birth Control Chart" (p. 82)
- "Beliefs about Abortion" questions (p. 83)

- Candy and bowls for pregnancy game
- Birth control kit

Activities

Group Building	15 minutes
Question Cards	15 minutes
Talking about Consequences	20 minutes
STI Handshake	15 minutes
STI Video	30 minutes
STI Discussion	25 minutes
Suggestions for Further Study	(optional)
Break	15 minutes
Pregnancy Game	15 minutes
Birth Control Video	20 minutes
Birth Control Discussion	20 minutes
Break	15 minutes
Beliefs About Abortion	25 minutes
Closing	10 minutes

Procedures

Group Building (15 minutes)

Say, "Give a hug to someone wearing blue." The participants are then to find someone wearing blue and give that person a hug. Continue, using the following categories:

someone in the band

someone not from your school

someone wearing tennis shoes

someone taller than you

someone wearing glasses

someone wearing a watch

someone with a pierced ear

someone with brown eyes

someone wearing socks

Vary the game by having the participants suggest their own categories (someone of the same sex, someone of the opposite sex, etc.).

Vary the game by changing the activity from a hug to a back rub, a handshake, or a pat on the back.

Question Cards (15 minutes)

Answer the questions from the previous session. Give the opportunity for the participants to write new questions.

Talking about Consequences (20 minutes)

Using the information from the "Purpose" section, talk to the young people about the possible consequences of sexual intercourse: an intimate relationship, a pregnancy, a sexually transmitted infection. Divide the participants into three groups, each with the assignment to take the questions provided for them, to decide together how to answer the questions, and to be ready to report back to the group in seven minutes with their answers.

Sheet #1: An Intimate Relationship

- What circumstances are necessary for sexual intimacy to be a good and loving experience for both people?
- What things might make it a bad experience?

Sheet #2: A Pregnancy

- Under what circumstances would a pregnancy be a good thing to happen as a result of sexual intercourse?
- Under what circumstances would a pregnancy be a bad result?

Sheet #3: Sexually Transmitted Infections

- What ways might you ensure that you would not get a sexually transmitted infection?
- What would be bad about having a sexually transmitted infection?

If you have a large group, you might want to assign the questions to more than one small group and compare their answers. Have each group share their responses with the total group.

STI Handshake (15 minutes)

In advance: Count out enough 3" x 5" index cards and pencils so that each member of the group gets just one. Mark the back of one of the cards with a very small x.

Gather the group in the middle of your room and have the participants pass around the cards and pencils, one for each participant. (One person will receive the card with the x on the back, but should not notice it since everything is being passed out and you are giving directions.) Instruct the group to shake hands with three different members of the group. After each handshake, the two people shall sign each other's cards. Tell the participants to sit down as soon as they have three signatures on their card.

When the participants have finished shaking hands, announce that one card has an *x* on the back, representing a sexually transmitted infection. Ask the person with the *x* to stand up and read the three names on the card, disclosing those who have contracted the infection.

Instruct these three to stand as their names are read. Then have them read the names of those with whom they shook hands after shaking person *x*'s hand, with each of those people standing. Continue until all infected people are identified. If someone's name reappears, that person raises a hand to demonstrate reinfections. For a large group, you might have everyone get five signatures instead of three.

Be sure to emphasize that you do not get STIs by shaking hands. The purpose of the game is to demonstrate graphically and personally how quickly and widely STIs can spread. Ask the person with the *x* how he or she felt about having the *x* and about spreading it to so many in the group. Ask all group members to discuss the following questions:

- How did you feel about having been given an infection without any intention on your part?
- Was the infection more widespread than you would have expected?
- If you'd known it was possible to get an infection in this way, how might you have protected yourself from the infection?
- What might you have done if you had known in advance that someone was carrying the infection?

STI Video (30 minutes)
Introduce and show the video "A Million Teenagers." This video has been updated several times to give the most accurate information for young people. Be sure to get the latest version. The video explains the physiology, transmission, symptoms, and dangers of sexually transmitted infections, including AIDS. It is a good, basic presentation. The video stresses responsible behavior. There are questions at the end of the video for discussion, which you might want to use. The video is available in English and Spanish.

STI Discussion (25 minutes)
Have youth look at the STI chart (pp. 30–31 in the *Younger Youth Guide*; pp. 79–80 in this guide), which gives information on the nine most common STIs. Spend a few minutes introducing the chart.

Have youth look at the "Ten Most Commonly Asked Questions about STIs" (p. 32 in the *Younger Youth Guide*; p. 81 in this guide). Go around the room and answer the questions together, having each participant read a question and attempt an answer. By having the young people answer, you can get a good idea of how much knowledge they have, and you can help answer their misconceptions in discussion about each question. Make sure the young people get all the correct information.

Suggestions for Further Study (optional)
If you have more time, or feel a need to explore further, you might consider one of the following videos, and use the discussion questions provided:

- *A Is for AIDS* (15 minutes)—The animated character Dr. Andy explains the basic facts about HIV and AIDS. This would be a good introduction, especially for younger groups.
- *AIDS: Everything You Should Know* (28 minutes)—This is a video produced for young people, with Whoopi Goldberg presenting the facts about HIV and AIDS, explaining how HIV destroys the immune system, how HIV is passed, and how to avoid getting it. Young people are encouraged to postpone sexual involvement until a faithful, monogamous relationship develops during adult life.

Break (15 minutes)

Pregnancy Game (15 minutes)
The purpose is to help the young people experience the possibility of getting pregnant if they are having sexual intercourse.

Tell the young people that these are the statistics for sexually active people:

- If no birth control is used for a period of one year, there is an 85 percent chance of becoming pregnant.
- If birth control is used, there is a 15 percent chance of becoming pregnant. (Some methods are more effective than others, but overall, an average of 15 percent become pregnant, even using birth control.)

Tell the young people that in order to dramatize the likelihood of becoming pregnant, you have a game for them to play. Provide a kind of candy that comes in red and blue (or two other distinctive colors). One bowl is marked "No Birth Control. Red = pregnant. Blue = not pregnant." Have the young people put in enough pieces of candy for each person in the group to have one. Make approximately 85 percent of them red and 15 percent of them blue. Tell the young people to close their eyes and pick a candy from the bowl. Then tell them, "If you draw a red candy, it means you (or your partner) would be pregnant in one year of unprotected sex. If you draw a blue candy, it means you (or your partner) would not be pregnant." Discuss how they feel being "pregnant" or "not pregnant." Do the statistics become more real when they see they are the ones who are pregnant?

Now move to the other bowl, marked "Birth Control. Red = pregnant Blue = not pregnant." Have the young people put in enough pieces of candy for each person in the group to have one. Make 15 percent of them red and 85 percent of them blue. Tell the young people to close their eyes and pick a candy from the bowl. Then tell them, "If you draw a red candy, it means you (or your partner) would be pregnant. If you draw a blue candy, it means you (or your partner) would not be pregnant." Discuss how they feel being "pregnant" or "not pregnant" and how this game shows the possibility of their being pregnant, even when using birth control.

Birth Control Video (20 minutes)

Introduce the video by reminding the young people that the primary purpose of sexual intercourse is to express love and intimate commitment. A secondary purpose is the creation of a new life. Therefore the decision to have a child is one that a couple should make intentionally. Knowledge of birth control allows a couple to make informed decisions. The video "Hope Is Not a Method IV" covers all methods of birth control. It includes information about side effects and how each method works. It is a straightforward presentation of methods, with an emphasis on responsibility. It continues to be updated, so be sure to get the most recent version.

Birth Control Discussion (20 minutes)

Provide birth control products that the young people can see and examine. Many schools and agencies will provide you a sample kit that will include samples of pills, an implant, an IUD, a diaphragm, and a male and female condom. Pass them around so all the young people can see and touch them.

Refer to the "Birth Control Chart" (p. 33 in the *Younger Youth Guide*; p. 82 in this guide), which shows a picture of each method and has information on how to use it and the effectiveness rate. In advance of the class, copy and cut out the pictures of the method. Divide your young people into three groups and give each group a complete set of pictures. On a poster board, have each group arrange in order their pictures according to one of the following criteria:

Group One: The rate of effectiveness, with the most reliable at the top and the least reliable at the bottom (the correct order is as follows: abstinence, implant, sterilization, injection, pill, IUD, condom, diaphragm, natural family planning).

Group Two: The cost, with the least expensive at the top and the most expensive at the bottom. (The list is debatable, but should be close to this: abstinence, natural family planning, diaphragm, condom, IUD, implant, injection, pill, sterilization.)

Group Three: Ease of use, with the easiest at the top and the most difficult at the bottom. (This list is debatable, but will show you how the young people perceive the use of each of the methods.)

When the three groups have finished, compare the lists, and discuss the following questions:

- What are the similarities and differences in the lists?
- What is your overall impression of the reliability of birth control?
- Which choices seem unwise and which ones seem most reasonable?

At this point, it is important to refer to our basic beliefs, which state that abstinence is the method appropriate for unmarried teenagers.

Break (15 minutes)
This break is important, so that the discussion of abortion is not considered a part of the presentation about birth control. Abortion is not a form of birth control and should not be chosen as a convenience or to ease embarrassment. It is a very serious and far-reaching decision, and it should be presented to the young people in this manner.

Beliefs about Abortion (25 minutes)
Young people have heard about abortions in various settings, and particularly through the media. The activity that follows gives them the opportunity to talk about what they have heard in the context of what our church's understanding of abortion is. "Beliefs about Abortion" (p. 34 in the *Younger Youth Guide*; p. 83 in this guide) should be worked through a question at a time, allowing time for discussion and giving clear answers. All the information in this section is taken from official church documents as stated in the "Guide for the Presbyterian Church (U.S.A.)" on pages 14–22 in this guide.

Closing (10 minutes)
Tell the participants: One of the affirmations of our study is that "our church is a community of responsibility." We can be sure we are acting responsibly when we keep God's Spirit as the guide of our lives. We will know God's Spirit is guiding us when we see the result of God's Spirit in our lives. For "the fruit of the Spirit is love, joy, peace, patience, kindness, generosity, faithfulness, gentleness, and self-control" (Gal. 5:22–23a).

Close with a circle prayer, with participants naming one fruit of the Spirit they see in their lives and giving thanks to God. For example: Thank you, God, for love, which allows me to love my family; thank you, God, for patience, which allows me to get along with my younger brother; thank you, God, for gentleness, which allows me to forgive myself.

Sexually Transmitted Infections (STIs)

Acquired Immune Deficiency Syndrome (AIDS)

What is it?
AIDS, caused by HIV, a virus that destroys the body's immune system allowing life-threatening illnesses to attack the body.

How do I get it?
By the transfer of infected body fluids through sex, sharing dirty needles, or from contaminated blood.

Is it common?
It continues to spread.

How do I get rid of it?
There is no cure, but new medications are being developed to help control it.

Chlamydia

What is it?
Bacterial infection in the urinary and reproductive organs.

How do I get it?
Close sexual contact with someone infected, even without intercourse.

Is it common?
It is the most common STI in the United States, with four million new cases each year.

How do I get rid of it?
The right antibiotic.

Gonorrhea

What is it?
Bacterial infection inside the body.

How do I get it?
Close sexual contact with someone infected, even without intercourse.

Is it common?
There are one million new cases each year.

How do I get rid of it?
The right antibiotic.

Hepatitis B

What is it?
Viral infection causing inflammation of the liver.

How do I get it?
Exposure to infected blood or body fluids or dirty needles.

Is it common?
Very common.

How do I get rid of it?
Bed rest for several weeks, maybe months.

Herpes

What is it?
Painful blisters on the penis, vagina, or anus.

How do I get it?
The virus enters the body through cuts or sexual contact.

Is it common?
There are five hundred thousand to one million new cases each year.

How do I get rid of it?
No cure, only medical relief of pain.

Human Papilloma Virus (HPV)

What is it?
HPV, also known as genital warts, a viral infection that causes warts.

How do I get it?
The virus enters the body through sexual contact or use of damp linens or bathing suits that have been used by someone infected.

Is it common?
It is spreading rapidly among teenagers.

How do I get rid of it?
The warts are treated with ointment, frozen, or burned off with a laser or electric needle.

Scabies, Lice

What is it?

Lice are tiny crabs that live in the hair around the penis or vagina; scabies are tiny bugs that burrow under the skin.

How do I get it?

Sexual contact with someone infected, or by using a towel, toilet seat, bedding, or clothing used by someone infected.

Is it common?

Fairly common.

How do I get rid of it?

Creams, lotions, shampoos that clean the body.

Syphilis

What is it?

Bacterial infection.

How do I get it?

Sexual contact with sores from infected person to an open cut on another.

Is it common?

It is increasing among teenagers.

How do I get rid of it?

Penicillin or other antibiotic.

Trichomoniasis

What is it?

Infection of vagina in women, urethra in men, caused by tiny protozoa.

How do I get it?

Sexual contact with someone infected, or by using a towel, toilet seat, bedding, or clothing used by someone infected.

Is it common?

Very common.

How do I get rid of it?

A specific antibiotic.

Ten Most Commonly Asked Questions about STIs

1. Can I get AIDS if I'm not gay?

Yes. AIDS is a disease caused by a virus (HIV), so anyone exposed to the virus can get AIDS. AIDS is decreasing among gay people (education is encouraging them to employ healthy behaviors to avoid HIV), but it is increasing among the heterosexual population, especially young women.

2. Are STIs, other than AIDS, really a serious threat?

Yes. Many of them are life-threatening if not treated. Some are not life-threatening, but cannot be cured and can cause pain for a lifetime. Some can lead to the development of other illnesses, including cancer, and can cause pregnancy complications.

3. Are women at a greater risk for STIs?

Yes. It is often easier for a woman's body to catch and hold diseases, and often those infections are difficult to detect. Annual exams help women protect themselves.

4. Could I have an STI and not even know it?

Yes. Many people with STIs experience no noticeable symptoms. Regular check-ups help people discover disease.

5. Can condoms prevent STIs?

Maybe. Latex condoms, when used correctly, are effective in *reducing* the transmission of most infections. But condoms often are used incorrectly or only occasionally. No method except abstinence is 100 percent effective.

6. Can STIs be cured?

Some can, some can't. Bacterial STIs (including gonorrhea, chlamydia, and syphilis) can be cured with antibiotics. Viral STIs (including AIDS and herpes) cannot.

7. Can I test myself for STIs?

You can start the process. You might be able to recognize what could be symptoms of an STI. Or you could use a home HIV test. But laboratory tests are necessary to confirm an STI and to prescribe proper treatment.

8. Can I get AIDS from shaking hands with someone who has AIDS?

No. You cannot get AIDS from shaking hands, drinking from a water fountain, touching, hugging, or kissing. You also cannot get AIDS from toilet seats, swimming pools, public showers, sneezes, coughs, donating blood, or being around someone who has AIDS.

9. Can I get an STI from a towel or a toilet seat?

Yes. Lice, scabies, and trichomoniasis can be caught from infected towels, clothes, or sheets (and maybe in a rare instance from a toilet seat), but most STIs are spread only through direct sexual contact.

10. Is there such a thing as safer sex?

Yes. Safer sex means using a condom and being sure your partner has no STI. Safe sex happens if a couple has no STIs and is in a committed relationship where they have no other sexual partners.

Birth Control Chart

Method	How to Use It/Cost	Actual Rate of Effectiveness
Pill	Woman takes one pill a day, which prevents release of egg. ($25 to $45 for a month's supply)	97%
Implant	Woman has six small tubes implanted in her upper arm, which prevent release of egg. ($450 to $900 for implanting; lasts five years)	99.91%
Injection	Woman receives an injection, which prevents release of egg. ($30 to $65 for the injection, which lasts three months)	99.7%
IUD	A doctor places the IUD in the woman's uterus, which keeps eggs from implanting. ($250 to $750 for the device, which can last ten years)	99.2%
Diaphragm	A soft, rubber dome is placed far inside the vagina, over the cervix, which prevents sperm from entering the uterus. ($20 to $50 for the diaphragm)	82%
Condom	For a male, a latex sheath is placed over the penis, which prevents sperm from entering the woman. (Each condom costs 50 cents to $3.50 and can be used only once.) For a female, a latex sheath is placed to line the vagina and cover the cervix so sperm cannot enter the uterus. (Each condom costs $1.50 to $3.50 and can be used only once.)	Male condom, 88% Female condom, 79%
Abstinence	No sexual intercourse (no cost)	100%
Sterilization	For a female, the tubes are cut, which keeps the egg from entering the uterus. For a male, the tube carrying the sperm from the testes to the penis is cut so that the sperm cannot be ejaculated. (Costs vary greatly for the surgery, which is permanent.)	Male, 99.85% Female, 99.6%
Natural Family Planning	Woman does not have sexual intercourse during the times in her cycle when she is most likely to get pregnant. (Cost is for a thermometer and chart to keep track of the monthly cycle).	65% to 80%

Beliefs about Abortion

Listed below are some conflicting viewpoints about abortion. Pick the one that represents our church's belief. Tell why it is our belief. Tell whether you agree or disagree with it.

1. A. Choosing to have an abortion might be the right choice for a Christian to make.

    B. Choosing to have an abortion would never be the right choice for a Christian to make.

    C. Choosing to have an abortion is always the right choice for a Christian to make.

Answer: A. Abortion might be the right choice in situations such as when serious genetic problems arise or when the resources are not adequate to care for a child.

2. A. We can trust in God's Spirit, God's Word, and God's people to help us make the right decision about an abortion.

    B. God's Word tells us that abortion is always wrong.

    C. The church teaches us that humans do not have the ability to make life-and-death choices; only God does.

Answer: A. We can trust in God's Spirit to guide us in all our decisions; the gospel reminds us again and again of God's grace; we are part of the community of faith and we can be sure that the community will be there to help and sustain us in our decisions.

3. A. The ultimate decision about an abortion is the responsibility of the doctor of the woman who is pregnant.

    B. The ultimate decision about an abortion is the responsibility of the woman who is pregnant.

    C. The ultimate decision about an abortion is the responsibility of the church.

Answer: B. Biblical faith emphasizes the need for personal moral choice, with each individual ultimately accountable to God. The choice for an abortion is to be made by the woman who is in the position to make the decision, and it is, above all, her responsibility.

4. A. Abortion should be available to anyone who can pay for it.

    B. Abortion should be available for anyone who can show a reasonable reason for choosing it.

    C. Abortion should be available to anyone who chooses it.

Answer: C. We have responsibility to guarantee every woman the freedom to choose for herself.

5. A. It is wrong for a woman to think about an abortion.

    B. It is wrong for a woman to think about an abortion, and then decide not to have one.

    C. It is okay for a woman to think about an abortion.

Answer: C. It is better to give birth intentionally than to feel that the diagnosis of pregnancy constitutes an absolute obligation to bear a child. A woman who considers abortion should never be made to feel guilty that she has thought about it.

6. A. Abortion is often an easy and convenient choice for a woman who does not want to be pregnant.

    B. Abortion is a good way to ease the embarrassment some women might feel if they are pregnant.

    C. Abortion is not a form of birth control.

Answer: C. Abortion is a very serious and far-reaching decision, so it should not be considered as a form of birth control or chosen as a convenience or to ease embarrassment.

7. A. Most people in our church believe abortion is morally wrong.

    B. Most people in our church believe abortion is morally acceptable.

    C. There are varieties of beliefs about abortion within our church.

Answer: C. There are many beliefs and a great variety of words that people in our church would use to describe their beliefs concerning abortion. Many of the varying beliefs are held very strongly by individuals. It is for this reason that the church has been led to the conviction that the decision regarding abortion must remain with the individual, to be made on the basis of conscience and personal religious principles.

Session 5

Sexual Violence

Purpose[1]

In this session, participants will

- understand that sexuality and violence are two different things.
- understand that sexual violence is a misuse of power.
- understand that power comes from resources.
- increase their understanding of rape and sexual harassment.
- recognize their own power and vulnerability and how they might use them responsibly.

Time: About three hours

Materials Needed

- Newsprint and markers, chalkboard and chalk, or overhead projector, transparencies, and markers
- Two newspaper articles describing an assault (cross out the names of any of the parties involved)
- VCR, TV, and video "Out of Bounds" (order in advance and preview)
- Contact person at a local sexual assault center or battered women's shelter

Activities

Group Building (optional)	15 minutes
Introduce the Session	15 minutes
Discuss Sexuality	20 minutes
Discuss Violence	20 minutes
When Violence and Sexuality Are Mixed	20 minutes
Power and Resources	15 minutes
Sexual Harassment	30 minutes
Rape	30 minutes
What We Need to Know	10 minutes

Background for the Leader[2]

This session has as its core understanding the belief that sexuality is a gift from God. It relies on the rest of the course to help participants come to a greater understanding of what that means. In particular, we will look at sexual violence. There are three concepts we want to convey:

1. Sexuality and violence are two very different things.

2. When talking about sexuality and violence, it is important to understand power and resources.

---

1. In preparation, it is recommended that you contact the Center for the Prevention of Sexual and Domestic Violence, which is an interreligious organization working on issues of sexual and domestic violence prevention. In order to obtain a list of their resources, please write to the following address: CPSDV, 936 North 34th Street, Suite 200, Seattle, WA 98103, (206) 634-1903.

2. Much of this information is taken from *Sexual Abuse Prevention: A Course of Study for Teenagers*, by Rebecca Voelkel-Haugen and Marie Fortune (Cleveland: United Church Press, 1996), pp. 1–8.

3. Sexual violence is an example of the misuse of power.

1. Sexuality and violence are two very different things.

God blessed us with the gifts of bodiliness and sexuality. God created us with longings for intimacy and connectedness with one another. A sexual relationship can be one expression of deep intimacy and love. But our sexuality is more than what we do genitally. Our sexuality is "the divine invitation to find our destinies, not in loneliness but in deep connection."[3]

Contrasted to our sexuality is violence. Violence is the antithesis of connection and intimacy; for it not only destroys trust, but it also violates and degrades another's humanity.

Although sexuality and violence have often been viewed as opposites, they were still seen as related. Rape/sexual violence was at one end of the spectrum; "normal" sexual activity was at the other. In other words, rape was seen as sex that just "got out of hand."

Although it may seem obvious to *us* that sex and violence are completely different, our society constantly confuses the two. In music videos, advertising, movies, magazines, the Internet, and much of the culture that young people have contact with, we are taught that "good" sex is violent and violence is sexy. We are taught that our sexuality is about dominance and sub-mission. For men this means that, to be a man, we need to be in control and get what we want, no matter what. For women, this means that, to be feminine, we need to give up choices and let others take control; whatever someone does to us is okay.

This session takes as its first premise the belief that this intermingling of sex and violence is wrong. It is harmful and it leads to sexual harassment and sexual violence that deeply hurts and can destroy its victims.

2. When talking about sexuality and violence, it is important to understand power and resources.[4]

In order to understand sexual violence, it is necessary to understand power and the way in which we choose to use the power we have. However, it is important to define what we mean by power because it may differ from the common understanding.

Power, as used here, has two very important components: relational and contextual.

- Power as Relational—Power is not an absolute trait, like skin color or height; it is relative. Person A may have power in relation to Person B but not in relation to Person C. That is why it is inaccurate to simply say that someone "has power" or "is powerful." For example, a business executive may have power in relation to those she manages, but in relation to her doctor who is older and male, she has less power.

- Power as Contextual—A person's power or lack of it is not a constant but varies with the context. A twenty-year-old walking down the street may be more powerful than a thirteen-year-old he meets, but when the twenty-year-old is in class, his professor is more powerful.

Both of these concepts rest on the idea that power is a measure of one person's (or group's) resources as compared to another person's (or group's) resources. Those who have greater resources than others have power relative to them; those who command fewer resources are vulnerable relative to them.

It is important to note that resources can be anything that can be a source of strength, anything that can be drawn on to take care of a need or be used to one's advantage. Resources can include money, knowledge, job skills, gender, race, or physical strength, among other things. (The older youth session on Sexual Violence will

---

3. *Sexuality and the Sacred: Sources for Theological Reflection,* edited by James B. Nelson and Sandra P. Longfellow (Louisville: Westminster/John Knox Press, 1994), xiv.

4. Much of the information on power and resources in this session is taken from *Clergy Misconduct: Sexual Abuse in the Ministerial Relationship—Trainer's Manual* (Seattle: Center for the Prevention of Sexual and Domestic Violence, 1992), IV-62 to IV-66.

go into more specifics about this. For now, it is sufficient to discuss this concept in general terms.)

The other important distinction about power is how we use it. Power can be used to control or manipulate. We define this as "Power Over." Power is also defined as the capacity to do things or make things happen, to act, including on behalf of others. This is "power to do/make" or "Power With." Examples of this distinction are as follows:

Power Over	Power With
To control others (e.g., a coach who uses his/her role to coerce his/her player into a sexual relationship)	To provide leadership (a coach who uses his/her role to guide the team with genuine care for the players)
To preserve privilege and power of gender, race, body size, etc. (e.g., a teenaged boy harassing a classmate who is a girl)	To respect and protect the vulnerable, i.e., those who have less power

3. Sexual violence is an example of the misuse of power.

As seen in the two examples of "Power Over," sexual violence is an example of one person using his or her power to hurt another. In this session we will look at two examples of sexual violence—harassment and rape.

For our purposes, we use the U.S. Federal Equal Employment Opportunity Commission's definition of sexual harassment:

> The use of one's authority or power, either explicitly or implicitly, to coerce another into unwanted sexual relations or to punish another for his or her refusal; or the creation of an intimidating, hostile or offensive . . . environment through verbal or physical conduct of a sexual nature.

The definition we use for rape in this session is as follows:

> . . . [T]he most comprehensive definition [of rape] refers to forced penetration by the penis or any object of the vagina, mouth, or anus against the will of the victim.[5]

In this above-mentioned definition, we see that rape is usually perpetrated by a man against a woman. However, about 10 percent of rape victims are men. In these cases, nearly all the perpetrators are also men. But women can rape, too, and it is important to share this fact. Regardless of the circumstances, rape is a crime.

In this session, we will look at date/acquaintance rape, which we will define as follows:

> In acquaintance rape, the rapist and the victim may know each other casually—having met through a common activity, mutual friend, at a party, as neighbors, as students in the same class, at work, on a blind date, or while traveling. Or they may have a closer relationship—as steady dates or former sexual partners. Although largely a hidden phenomenon because it is the least reported type of rape (and rape, in general, is the most underreported crime against a person), many organizations, counselors, and social researchers agree that acquaintance rape is the most prevalent crime today.[6]

In both acquaintance/date rape and sexual harassment, the perpetrator uses his or her power over another. Therefore, it is important to recognize that in any case of harassment or rape, it is the perpetrator's responsibility. It is never the victim's fault. The particularities of what the victim was wearing, what she or he had done in the past, whether or not she or he had been drinking, and so forth, do not matter. Abuse of power through sexual harassment or date/acquaintance rape is the perpetrator's choice. It is his or her responsibility.

5. *Sexual Violence: The Unmentionable Sin*, by Marie M. Fortune (New York: The Pilgrim Press, 1983), 7.
6. *Never Called It Rape: The Ms. Report on Recognizing, Fighting, and Surviving Date and Acquaintance Rape*, by Robin Warshaw (New York: Harper & Row, 1988), 12.

Procedures

Group Building (optional) (15 minutes)

It is hoped that by this point in the course, there will be a level of trust and community among participants. If this is not the case, do some community-building exercises. An example of this might be breaking into pairs and having each person talk about their favorite movie, favorite type of music, and their favorite actor. Then bring the group back together and have each person introduce her or his partner to the group using this information. Another example might be asking participants to review some of what they've learned from the previous sessions.

Introduce the Session (15 minutes)

Begin by asking participants what they've heard about this session and this topic. What are their expectations? As individuals respond, be aware of their answers. For males, note if they discount the importance of this information, or if they say they don't need to know about harassment and rape. Be prepared to share examples that will help focus their awareness on the fact that males can also be victims. (One such example is that one in seven boys are sexually abused before they reach age 18 and that 10 percent of reported rapes are of boys and men.)[7]

In addition to noting resistance, be aware that there is a high likelihood that at least one of your students will be a survivor. Tell the group that you will be available to talk if anyone needs to. Be prepared with names and phone numbers of local resources, such as the sexual assault clinic, the battered women's hotline, the YWCA, or the local women's center.

Go over the session plans briefly. Identify which expectations they have raised that you plan to cover. Be clear with the students that the subject matter is very important and can be painful and difficult. Lay out some ground rules. Because this is painful and difficult material, it is very important that everyone respect one another. This means listening to others, not making fun of what another person has said, paying attention to whoever is speaking, and keeping confidential things that are said in the group. Ask participants if they have other ground rules that they would like to set.

Discuss Sexuality (20 minutes)

Ask participants to go over with you what they've learned from the first few sessions in this course. Ask participants to define what sexuality is. On a sheet of newsprint, on an overhead transparency, or on the chalkboard, make a list of their definitions.

Using these words and the definition provided in the "Background for the Leader" (pp. 84–86 in this guide), identify sexuality as being essentially about connection, with God and with one another. Note where this may be different from what they have listed and clarify what the difference is.

Discuss Violence (20 minutes)

Ask participants to define violence. List the words and phrases they provide on newsprint, an overhead, or on the chalkboard.

Bring some articles from newspapers or magazines that describe an assault or other form of physical violence. Have several members of the group, males and females, read the articles aloud. Ask the group to discuss the articles. (You may want to acknowledge that it's hard to do this because it's hard to talk about people getting hurt.) Using the words the group listed above and the discussion about the articles, discuss what violence is.

Put the list of words that define sexuality next to the list of words that define violence. Ask the participants to compare them. What do they notice? What is the difference between sexuality and violence? Highlight that one of the main things that you hope they will remember from this session is that sexuality and violence are two very different things.

(*Note:* The most important difference to note is the element of choice and consent. Violence is the use of power over someone else. It is against her or his will. It is against her or his choice or consent. It harms because it inflicts physical pain, but it also harms because it degrades and violates

7. Cited in *The Courage to Heal*, by Ellen Bass and Laura Davis (New York: Harper & Row, 1994).

another's humanity. Sexuality is a gift from God that is based on respect for the other, mutuality, equality, and honesty. It is based on the ability to choose.)

When Violence and Sexuality Are Mixed (20 minutes)

Read the stories "Julie" and "André" on page 90 in this guide. Acknowledge that it is difficult to hear stories like this, and remind youth that you are available if they want to talk privately afterward.

Ask participants if they know people like Julie and Matt or like André and Brad. Ask them how they think Julie and André felt. Then ask the participants, if they had experienced something like this, what could they do in response? Who could they tell? Do they think that Julie or André had a choice? Why or why not?

(*Note:* Be aware that any story about a male either sexually abusing or harassing another male usually brings up reactions from participants about the offender or the victim being gay. [In fact, this is one of the biggest barriers for boys who have been victimized by other boys or by men in reporting the incident. They are afraid that people will think they are gay.] It is important to remind participants that most men who molest children, either boys or girls, are heterosexual. And just because a boy experiences harassment or assault by another male, does not make him gay. Being gay is a sexual preference, and it is not related to violence. Being molested or harassed by someone does not necessarily influence your sexual orientation. If someone molests or harasses you, they perpetrate violence against you.)

Power and Resources (15 minutes)

Ask participants to define both power and vulnerability, and list their responses on newsprint, the chalkboard, or an overhead. Using the information provided in the "Background for the Leader" on pages 85–86 in this guide, talk in general terms about resources, emphasizing with the participants the importance of context and relationship. Introduce the concepts of "power over" and "power with."

On a piece of newsprint, a chalkboard, or on an overhead, ask them to list examples of people using their power "over" another person and

people using their power "with" someone. Role-play some of these examples, or use the following:

- A male teacher giving an assignment to a female student
- A high school coach telling a player that he's not following the play correctly
- A popular senior asking a sophomore out on a date

Act out the role plays in two ways. First, as an example of "power over"; second, as an example of "power with."

Sexual Harassment (30 minutes)

Introduce the concept of sexual harassment. Ask participants what they think it means. Share the definition given in the "Background for the Leader" on page 86 in this guide. Point out the fact that harassment is an example of someone using his or her power over another in order to control, manipulate, or humiliate them.

Show the video "Out of Bounds." (Be sure to preview it to make sure that it is appropriate for your group.) Then divide the group in two, with males in one group and females in another. Try to have a discussion leader who is the same gender as the group she or he is working with. Have the groups discuss the following questions:

- Was the situation real to you? Does this ever happen in your school?
- What things did Gus and Juan, and later Gus, Juan, and Kyle, do? Do you ever do things like this?
- Why did the narrator say it was about "power" and "attitude"?
- How is the situation in the video the same or different from André's experience?
- How did Freddie respond to Gus, Juan, and Kyle? How might André respond? How might you respond if someone sexually harasses you?
- Does your school have a sexual harassment policy?

Rape (30 minutes)

Begin by asking participants how they would define rape. Add any information from the "Background for the Leader" on page 86 in this guide. Point out that rape is another example of someone using their power over another. It is about force and takes place against the will of the victim. Remind participants again that anyone can be a victim, including boys and men.

Ask the group to define date/acquaintance rape. Write the definition on a piece of newsprint, an overhead, or the chalkboard. Clarify the definition using the information provided in the "Background for the Leader" on page 86 in this guide.

(*Note:* Be sure to highlight that the relationship between the rapist and the victim is irrelevant. Regardless of whether the couple has had sex before, just met, or has been dating for a while, if one person forces another to have sex against her or his will, it's rape.)

Re-read Julie's story on page 90 in this guide. Ask participants to discuss how date rape is similar to or different from sexual harassment. Examples of similarities might be: both involve the use of power over another person, both are a misuse of sexuality, both make the victim feel bad about themselves. Examples of a difference might be the degree of physical contact.

What We Need to Know (10 minutes)

Recap the session and ask if anyone has any questions or comments.

Ask participants what they think they need to know in order to help them and others avoid being a perpetrator or victim of sexual harassment or rape. See the list on page 91 for some examples.

End with a prayer of your own, or use the following:

> Gracious and Loving God, You have created each of us in Your image and we give You thanks. For our sexuality that is a gift, we rejoice. But sometimes we get confused. And sometimes your gift of sexuality gets mixed up with violence. Sometimes we hurt someone else or we get hurt. So we ask for your guidance and your healing. Help us to use our power responsibly. Help us to respect and love each other. Help us to follow Your way. Amen.

Sexuality and Violence

Julie

When Julie was thirteen, she had her first date. Matt was also thirteen and one of the cutest guys in the eighth grade. Julie was really excited to go out with him. All of her friends had been talking about their boyfriends and now she had a date. On Friday night, he told her he was babysitting for his younger brother and asked her to come over to watch a movie. When she got there, Matt's younger brother was just going to bed. She and Matt hung out for a while and then they started the movie. During the movie, Matt sat really close to Julie, which felt good to her. But then he started kissing her too hard. When she said "no," Matt held her down and forced her to have sex with him.

André

When André was twelve, he was still pretty short and slim for his age. He went out for the football team, but he didn't ever start. He mostly warmed the bench. He also played in the orchestra and was really good. One day he bumped into Brad by mistake. Brad was really popular and was a starter on the football team. Brad got really mad and pushed him. From that day on, whenever Brad saw André, he would push him and tell him he was gay because he played the violin. In the locker room during gym class, Brad and his friends would make fun of André's body as he changed clothes.

What We Need to Know*

Males

Regarding Rape

- Understand that "no" means "no."
- Know it is never okay to force yourself on a girl, even if you think she's been teasing you and leading you on.
- Know that it is never okay to force yourself on a girl, even if you've heard that women say "no" when they really mean "yes."
- Know that it is not "manly" to use force to get your way.
- Know that it is never okay to force yourself on a girl, even if you feel physically that you've got to have sex.
- Know that it is never okay to force yourself on a girl, even if she is drunk.
- Know that whenever you use force to have sex you are committing a crime called *rape*, even if you know her or have had sex with her before.
- Be aware of peer pressure to "score," and work against it by listening to what your date is saying.
- Be aware of what society may tell you it means to be a "real" man, and work against it by forming your own values based on respect, honesty, good listening, and so forth.
- Recognize that you can be raped too.

Regarding Harassment

- Be aware of what your peers may be telling you about being "cool"; avoid putting other boys down who may not act like you.
- Work on your own self-image, which is based on respect for other people rather than being better than someone else.

Females

Regarding Rape

- Say "no" when you mean "no"; say "yes" when you mean "yes"; stay in touch with your feelings so you know the difference.
- Believe in your right to express your feelings and learn how to do so assertively.
- Be aware of stereotypes that prevent you from expressing yourself, such as "anger is unfeminine," "being polite, pleasant, and quiet is feminine."
- Be aware of specific situations in which you do not feel relaxed and "in charge."
- Be aware of situations in which you are vulnerable and have fewer resources.
- Be aware that if you are raped, it is not your fault, you didn't deserve it, and you can get help.

Regarding Harassment

- Remember that you have the right to your feelings and your space.
- If you have experienced harassment, remember you are not alone, you can report it and get help.

*From *Sexual Abuse Prevention: A Course of Study for Teenagers*, by Rebecca Voelkel-Haugen and Marie Fortune (Cleveland: United Church Press, 1996), p. 22. Used by permission.

Session 6

Values and Decisions

Purpose: In this session, participants will hear attitudes, beliefs, and values expressed in a Christian context and will learn to examine their own beliefs and values. Young people need the opportunity to explore, to share, and to express their opinions, thoughts, and ideas on sexual matters. They need to be listened to and to learn to listen to others as they clarify their beliefs and values. Decision making is discussed in the context of sexuality that is expressed both as an act of love and responsibility. The young people will learn a method of responsible decision making that can become a model for their lives.

Time: Two hours and forty minutes (two hours and fifty-five minutes with the optional activity)

Materials Needed

- *Younger Youth Guide*
- One roll of toilet paper for each small group
- The Appropriate Game board and cards, one set for each small group (see directions in the activity description)
- Pencils
- 3" x 5" index cards
- Five sheets of paper, each labeled with one of the following terms: "Strongly Agree," "Agree," "No Opinion," "Disagree," and "Strongly Disagree"

- Newsprint
- Felt-tipped markers

Activities

Group Building	30 minutes
Question Cards (optional)	15 minutes
Our Church Is a Community of Forgiveness; God Gives Us Responsibility for Our Own Decisions	30 minutes
Statements on Relationships and Intimacy	20 minutes
The Appropriate Game	20 minutes
Our Church Is a Community of Love and Responsibility	20 minutes
Break	10 minutes
Decision-Making Guide	25 minutes
Litany	5 minutes

Procedures

Group Building (30 minutes)

Move __ Seats to the _____

Have the participants sit in chairs in a circle. The leader stands in the middle and asks the group members to move a certain number of seats in a given direction if they are in a certain category. Examples:

1. Move three seats to the right if you are wearing high-top sneakers.

2. Move two seats to the left if you are taking Spanish.

3. Move five seats to the right if you like pizza.

4. Move six seats to the left if you are wearing something blue.

5. Move four seats to the right if you are fourteen years old.

Take as Little or as Much as You Need

Give each small group a roll of toilet paper. Pass the roll around to each person in the small group, saying, "Take as little or as much as you need." Give no other instructions until everyone has torn off a length of toilet paper. When group members have their paper, they take turns telling the group one thing about themselves for each segment of paper they took.

Question Cards (optional) (15 minutes)

Answer any question cards that were filled out in the previous session.

Our Church Is a Community of Forgiveness; God Gives Us Responsibility for Our Own Decisions (30 minutes)

Theological concepts to understand:

- We are God's good creation.
- We have all misused our sexuality and are called to confession and forgiveness within the bounds of the community.
- Our decisions, based on love, responsibility, and forgiveness, are discovered in relationship with God, with one another, and with ourselves.

In the small groups, read Gen. 1:26–27, 31a. Give each person enough index cards so that he or she has one for every other member of the small group. Using a different card for each member, have each person complete the following statement about the other small group members: "I like your . . . " or "I admire you for . . . "

Remind the group that God's creation is good, and stress that the statements are to be affirmations only; no negative comments should be made. Suggest that they focus on qualities such as warmth, caring, friendliness, or honesty, as opposed to achievements or activities such as playing baseball or making good grades. Once the cards are completed, pass each card to the intended person. Everyone in the group should have an affirmation from every other member. Have each person read aloud what was written about him or her. The small group leader then leads a discussion using the following questions:

- How did it feel to see the comments? to read them aloud?
- Did the comments make you feel better or worse about yourself?
- Did they make you feel stronger or weaker?

The preceding exercise helps the young people feel a sense of self-esteem. On a sheet of newsprint, write "Self-esteem is . . . " Have the group complete the sentence by reflecting on the feelings they had in the previous exercise. List their answers on the sheet of newsprint. Possible answers would be: "when we feel good about ourselves," "when we like ourselves," "when we trust ourselves," "when we stand up for what we believe when it is questioned by someone else," or "when we feel loved."

Have the young people work through the activity sheets "Self-Esteem Exercise" and "Amy and Joe." (See pp. 36–37 in the *Younger Youth Guide*; pp. 97–98 in this guide.)

Discuss the two activity sheets, using statements such as the following:

- The hardest question for me to answer was . . .
- The easiest question for me to answer was . . .
- The part of this exercise that impressed me the most was . . .
- Self-esteem is . . .
- If Amy had more self-esteem, she would have . . .
- If Joe had more self-esteem, he would have . . .
- My own feelings of self-esteem are . . .
- The person I know who has a good sense of self-esteem is . . .
- I believe I could develop better self-esteem by . . .

Discuss how, in the following examples, self-esteem might determine how we act out our sexuality:

1. If we feel good about ourselves, we are not as likely to need attention from other people or try to find our worth in the way they treat us.

2. If we feel good about ourselves, we have less need to please others in an unhealthy way, especially if they want us to do something we may not want to do.

3. If we feel good about ourselves, we see things in a larger perspective and are less likely to get caught up in the moment.

Read "Our Church Is a Community of Forgiveness" and "God Gives Us Responsibility for Our Own Decisions" (see p. 5 in the *Younger Youth Guide*; p. 99 in this guide). This will begin to set the stage for the activities that follow.

Statements on Relationships and Intimacy (20 minutes)

This is a feelings/values exercise that gives young people an opportunity to share with each other and to learn from each other by looking at the choices they make. Only when young people begin to make their own choices and evaluate the actual consequences do they develop their own values. The process of evaluating their own choices will come in the exercises on decision making.

Put the sheets of paper that say "Strongly Agree," "Agree," "No Opinion," "Disagree," and "Strongly Disagree" up along the wall. Divide the large group in half. Half the group will participate and the other half will observe. Alternate groups after discussing a few statements. Read a statement from the list that follows. Tell the members of the participating group to stand beside the sheet of paper that represents their response to the statement. A young person may choose not to respond to a statement. Have the members of the group discuss why they chose their particular positions. Do not be judgmental about the positions taken. Have the group return to the middle of the room before reading the next statement in order to avoid someone standing in the same spot throughout the exercise. Change groups and continue the process until the statements are completed.

1. Love is the only important consideration in choosing whom to marry.

2. Marriage is a lifetime commitment.

3. If two high school students are in love and have been going steady for six months, it is okay for them to make love.

4. Males and females should share equally in housework and child care.

5. Looks and bodies are the main ingredients in two people being sexually attractive to each other.

6. Only boys should plan and pay for dates.

7. Having sexual intercourse will make a good relationship better.

8. To keep from having sexual intercourse when you're making out and get carried away is impossible.

9. Being a virgin until you get married is old-fashioned.

10. Teenage girls prefer a close, kissing relationship with their boyfriends without sexual involvement.

11. Most women do not want to be independent; they want a man to take care of them.

12. It is all right for thirteen-year-olds to date.

13. Teenage boys prefer a sexual relationship with their girlfriends.

14. If a boy and girl are going together, the girlfriend should do what her boyfriend tells her.

The Appropriate Game (20 minutes)

Write each of the following behaviors on a different 3" x 5" index card. Make one set of cards for each small group.

In the middle of each group, place a poster board with the following categories: "Child," "Teen," "Teen Sometimes," "Adult," and "Never." Give each group member a few of the index cards. Have the group members quickly place their cards on the poster board under the category they think is most appropriate. For example, holding hands may be appropriate for the "Child" category, marriage for "Teen Sometimes," and seeing an X-rated movie for "Never." Members of the group can place their cards at the same time to avoid embarrassment. The small-group leader then picks the cards from one category and reads them. Have the group discuss if they agree or disagree and why. Continue through each category.

Go parking

French kiss

Marry

Get pregnant

Get a divorce

Have a baby

Pet

Cuss

Flirt

Get engaged

Read *Playboy* or *Playgirl*

Have sexual intercourse

Pick your nose in public

See an X-rated movie

Tell a dirty joke

Gossip about a friend

Fondle each other above the waist

Have a sexual encounter with someone of the same sex

Masturbate

See an R-rated movie

Chew gum during the worship service

Fondle with clothes off

Buy birth control pills

Talk to your parents about sex

Go nude in the presence of the opposite sex

Our Church Is a Community of Love and Responsibility (20 minutes)

Theological concept to understand:

- Our sexuality is to be expressed lovingly and responsibly.

Ask everyone to read the theological statements in "Our Church is a Community of Love and Responsibility" (p. 38 in the *Younger Youth Guide*; p. 100 in this guide). Then say something like:

> In the decision-making activity that we will do in a moment, one of the central questions is "What values have I learned from my family, church, and friends that I need to consider in making my decisions?" The values defined by our community are love and responsibility. What does our church say about love and responsibility?

Then ask the group members to write the phrases that they believe are important in helping them define "love" and "responsibility." Use their phrases to compile a list on newsprint. The statements your group develops should be similar to the following: An act can be described

as "loving" if it is mindful of love for God, is loving of the other person, and is respectful of self. An act can be described as "responsible" if it is motivated by love and is within the boundaries understood by our church.

Read the examples that follow. Using the definitions of "loving" and "responsible" developed in the previous activity, decide as a group if these situations follow the values of our church. Allow the young people to think up situations and use the same method to evaluate them.

Example 1: Bob and Virginia are high school juniors. They have been dating for six months and are very much in love. They feel strongly that they will someday get married. They want to make love with one another. Is it okay? (To apply our values to this situation, you would need to go step by step through the definitions of "loving" and "responsible." To help understand the boundaries of the church, see the "Guide for the Presbyterian Church (U.S.A.)," particularly the section on premarital sex (pp. 10–11 in the *Younger Youth Guide*; pp. 17–18 in this guide).

Example 2: One of your friends comes to you for help because her sister is pregnant. She wants to know which choice would be the best to discuss with her sister: marrying her boyfriend, keeping the baby, having an abortion, or placing the baby for adoption. Help her think through her values on each of these alternatives.

(Follow the steps as above. Check the "Guide for the Presbyterian Church (U.S.A.)," particularly the sections on premarital sex and abortion.)

Break (10 minutes)

Decision-Making Guide (25 minutes)

Divide the group in half. Ask the young people to turn to the "Decision-Making Guide Dilemmas" (p. 40 in the *Younger Youth Guide*; p. 102 in this guide). Ask them to pick two of the dilemmas as practice situations. For each dilemma the group should follow the steps that are outlined. Give each group newsprint and markers. Have one person in each group act as a recorder. When each group has done at least two of the dilemmas (or after ten minutes), bring the two groups back together to report on how they dealt with each dilemma. Work through the first dilemma as a whole group.

Use the questions that follow for discussion:

- How difficult was it to use the decision-making process to solve this problem?
- Would you use the process in real life situations? Why or why not?

Litany (5 minutes)

Read together the "Litany for Decision Makers" (p. 41 in the *Younger Youth Guide*; p. 103 in this guide).

Self-Esteem Exercise

1. The good feelings of esteem come from a variety of places—from other people, from things you do, from special times and places. From what other sources might people receive reinforcement of their self-esteem? Add them to the list.

- your mother
- your father
- a grandparent
- a brother or a sister
- a teacher
- an adult at church
- God
- an accomplishment at school
- some special words of praise
- a good friend
- a celebration, such as a birthday or Christmas
- something you did for someone else
- a special skill you have
- a certain thing about your personality
- something brave you did
- a special place you like to be
- your own feelings about yourself
- _____
- _____
- _____

2. Circle the things above that are sources of esteem for you. Then beside each one you have circled, explain exactly how it is a source of esteem.

3. Self-esteem happens when we realize:

   We were created by God.
   God believes we are one of God's good creations.
   Others love and affirm us.
   All of us make mistakes but when we recognize and admit our mistakes, God is with us, forgiving us, no matter what we have done.

Amy and Joe*

Amy and Joe have been going together for three months. Joe leaves town with his parents for a long summer vacation. Amy and Joe have agreed not to date anyone else in the meantime.

David, a friend of Joe's, knows that Joe and Amy are going together, but he asks Amy out anyway. She doesn't know whether to accept or say no, so she asks the advice of her friend Jane. Jane says, "Just do what you think is best."

Amy decides to go out with David. They have several dates while Joe is on vacation. They stop dating when Joe returns.

Joe confesses to Amy that he dated a girl while he was on his vacation. Amy gets very angry with Joe and feels hurt. She tells him she never wants to see him again and that she no longer trusts him.

1. Who did you like best in the "Amy and Joe" story? Why?

2. Who did you like least in this story? Why?

3. Which of the three characters acted most responsibly? Why?

4. Which one acted most irresponsibly? Why?

5. Which of the following dating patterns do you think is best?

a.   To go out with one person exclusively.

b.   To go out with a lot of different people and be honest about it.

c.   To go out with whomever you want but not mention to any of your dates that you are also dating others.

6. Which of the following do you think is the worst thing to hear about a friend?

a.   The friend has an STI.

b.   The friend is "sleeping around" with a lot of people.

c.   The friend is telling lies about the people he or she is dating.

*Adapted from "My Feelings Are Me," in *Growing Up to Love*. Youth Elect Series (St. Louis: Christian Board of Publication), p. 31. Used with permission.

Our Church Is a Community of Forgiveness

> Do not judge, and you will not be judged; do not condemn, and you will not be condemned. Forgive, and you will be forgiven; give, and it will be given to you. A good measure, pressed down, shaken together, running over, will be put into your lap; for the measure you give will be the measure you get back.
>
> (Luke 6:37–38)

Sometimes we do not use our sexuality responsibly. Sometimes we are not grateful for the gift of our sexuality. We all fall short at times of the high calling God has for us, including the use of our sexuality. Even though we do fall short, we are still a part of the church and called to confession and forgiveness within the bounds of the church.

We can be grateful that the church is a community of forgiven people and not people who never do wrong or sin. In our church, we can honestly acknowledge our mistakes. God's forgiveness makes such honesty possible and helps us to change our lives to reflect God's love; the Holy Spirit enables us to change and guides us. In the church we can experience forgiveness and receive help in living out our sexuality.

We are then all the more willing to forgive the failings of others because we have experienced God's love in such abundance.

God Gives Us Responsibility for Our Own Decisions

> I appeal to you therefore, brothers and sisters, by the mercies of God, to present your bodies as a living sacrifice, holy and acceptable to God, which is your spiritual worship. Do not be conformed to this world, but be transformed by the renewing of your minds, so that you may discern what is the will of God—what is good and acceptable and perfect.
>
> (Rom. 12:1–2)

In our decision making we should be instructed by God's Word to us. We are to be influenced by our Christian beliefs. We should be aware of other influences—what our friends believe, how we feel, and what we have learned about our sexuality. We need to learn to sort out those different factors because some may be sexist, racist, or the result of pressures from others.

The guiding principles that define our church are love, responsibility, obedience, and forgiveness. Keeping these principles in mind and exploring their meaning within our community will lead us to make responsible decisions for our own lives.

Talking about how we make decisions for ourselves and how we communicate those decisions to others is important. Our decisions (based on love, responsibility, and forgiveness) are discovered in relationship with God, with one another, and with ourselves.

Our Church Is a Community of Love and Responsibility

> By contrast, the fruit of the Spirit is love, joy, peace, patience, kindness, generosity, faithfulness, gentleness, and self-control.
>
> (Gal. 5: 22–23a)

> God has told you . . . what is good; and what does the Lord require of you but to do justice, and to love kindness, and to walk humbly with your God?
>
> (Micah 6:8)

We are created to be in community, in relationship with God and with one another. God has loved us, does love us, and will love us faithfully. In the same way, we should love God and one another.

Jesus said to love God and love your neighbor as yourself. We should be concerned about others' needs and feelings without discounting our own. Physical intimacy can be as simple as a handshake or a hug, or as total as the intimacy of marriage. Sometimes we ask, What is the right kind of intimacy? We must remember that sexual intercourse should be reserved for marriage.

Some people say responsible sexual behavior is simply a matter of following rules for right and wrong. Other people say it is an individual matter of deciding for yourself what is right and wrong. Our understanding of responsible sexuality is not found at either of these two extremes. We are part of the community of faith. Joined together, we read and study God's Word, pray and listen for God's guidance for us, study the beliefs of our church in the past, and then—being guided by all this—we make statements together that express our beliefs. We take definite stands on issues. At the same time, we uphold the right of each person to maintain the dignity of his or her conscience in the light of the Scriptures.

We know that God's Spirit is present when there is love, joy, peace, patience, kindness, goodness, fidelity, gentleness, and self-control. We can be sure that we are acting responsibly when we keep God's Spirit as the guide of our lives.

Decision-Making Guide*

Step 1: What is the decision to be made?

Step 2: What are three possible solutions?

1.

2.

3.

Step 3: What have my family, church, and friends said about the choices that I need to consider?

Step 4: What would be the positive and the negative results of each solution?

    Solution 1 (from above)
      Positive Results   *Negative Results*

    Solution 2 (from above)
      Positive Results   *Negative Results*

    Solution 3 (from above)
      Positive Results   *Negative Results*

Step 5: Compare all the alternatives, make a choice, and write down your choice here.

Step 6: What steps need to be taken to carry out this choice?

*Used with permission from *Life Skills and Opportunities* (Philadelphia: Public/Private Ventures, 1987).

Decision-Making Guide Dilemmas

Dilemma 1: Tony and Sara are growing in their relationship. They are very attracted to each other, and when they are alone they get so sexually excited that they both feel out of control. What should they do?

Dilemma 2: Robert feels bad about himself because he wants to wait until marriage to have sex. According to his friends, the movies, and television, he is the only person in the world who feels this way. He is rethinking his beliefs and wonders whether he perhaps would have sex before marriage if the right girl were to come along. What should he do?

Dilemma 3: Jamaal's parents are not sure that a thirteen-year-old should be dating. Jamaal wants to go out on a double date with his brother, who can drive. What should his parents do?

Dilemma 4: Maria's boyfriend wants her to look at sex magazines with him. She feels uncomfortable and embarrassed; he keeps insisting. What should she do?

Dilemma 5: Kumiko is interested in going with Mark, but he has not paid much attention to her. Her friends say she has to wait until he calls her. Can she make the first move? What should she do?

Litany for Decision Makers

Leader: O God, you have made us responsible.

Group: Responsible to you.

Leader: We are responsible to you, God, for the decisions we make.

Group: But decision making is hard.

Leader: We want to do what is right, what you want us to do, God.

Group: But we hear other voices.

Girls: Friends.

Boys: Television.

Girls: Magazines.

Boys: Music.

Group: And the voices are so loud!

Leader: Help us, God, to stand for what is right. Help us to make good decisions.

Group: And forgive us when we mess up.

Leader: You have given us choices, O God.

Group: Help us be responsible decision makers. Amen.

Special Session

Parent's Overview

Purpose: Parents are the primary educators of their children about sexuality. As life becomes more complicated and sexual decisions more confusing, parents are seeking help to provide support and guidance for their teens. This session gives parents an overview of the information given to their children in this course. In doing this, a natural basis for communication is also provided. The video "Raising Healthy Kids: Families Talk About Sexual Health" portrays real people who reflect a wide range of values sharing their experiences and thoughts about communicating with their children about sexuality. The video models ways that parents can be understanding and "askable" in relation to sexuality.

Time: One hour and thirty-five minutes (two hours and five minutes if you do the optional activity)

Materials Needed

- *Parent's Guide*
- Video: "Raising Healthy Kids: Families Talk About Sexual Health"
- VCR and television monitor

Activities

Introduction	10 minutes
Video: "Raising Healthy Kids: Families Talk about Sexual Health" (optional)	30 minutes
Review Large-Group Activities	40 minutes
Review Small-Group Activities	40 minutes
Litany	5 minutes

Procedures

Introduction (10 minutes)
Ask parents if there has been any response at home from their child about this course. This is a good time to talk about further help for parents in discussing sex with their children. Refer to the "Resources" section on pages 34–37 of this guide and pages 21–24 of the *Parent's Guide*.

Video (optional) (30 minutes)
Introduce the video "Raising Healthy Kids: Families Talk About Sexual Health" by saying that it discusses a variety of real-life situations in which parents have found ways to talk about sex with their children. After showing the video discuss such questions as the following:

- Why is it important for a child to learn about sexuality from a parent?
- What are some barriers to talking about sex in your family?

Review Large-Group Activities (40 minutes)
Tell parents to fill out the Anatomy/Physiology sheets at home (see pp. 31–32 in the *Parent's*

Guide.) They can ask their young persons to help them.

Explain the value of the Slang Word Exercise included in Session 1 (see pp. 49–50 in this guide.)

Read the statement "God Created Us for Life in Community" on page 72 in this guide.

Discuss how you encouraged the youth to make decisions with an understanding of love and responsibility. Point out the "Love, Infatuation, and Friendship Definitions" and the "Situations" (p. 68).

Explain how you talked to youth about consequences related to sex. Refer to the sections on sexually transmitted infections (STIs), HIV/AIDS, pregnancy, abortion, rape, and sexual harassment. Stress the parent's role of being an "askable" parent in times of crisis.

Go over a sampling of question cards and report how they were answered.

Review Small-Group Activities (40 minutes)
Parents should gather in small groups with the small-group leaders of their child. Stress that leaders will not discuss an individual nor break confidentiality.

Review "God Created Us and Gave Us the Gift of Sexuality" (p. 33 in the *Parent's Guide*; p. 58 in this guide). Then look at the questions that follow. Parents may be interested in discussing some of the questions from their own perspective and from their child's.

Ask the parents to do the homosexuality exercises on pages 36–38 in the *Parent's Guide*. Go over the answers with the parents.

Have the parents read and discuss the "Decision-Making Guide" and the "Decision-Making Guide Dilemmas" (pp. 45–46 in the *Parent's Guide*).

Ask the parents to do the "Self-Esteem Exercise" on page 44 in the *Parent's Guide*. Discuss how their children's self-esteem, or lack of it, will affect how they handle different situations.

Litany (5 minutes)
Close with one of the litanies used in the course (see pp. 60 and 103).

Session 7

Parent/Youth Communication

Purpose: This session will help parents give guidance to their children by increasing the ability of families to communicate about sexuality. Communication is talking and listening. The activities in this session encourage family members to exchange views and share information.

Time: Two hours

Materials Needed

- Make sure each participant and parent has a guide or copies of exercises used in this session.
- Pencils
- Clusters of two to four chairs set up in the room. Have each family sit in a chair cluster.

Activities

Group Building	5 minutes
Introduction	5 minutes
"So You Think You Know . . . "	30 minutes
Word Choice	30 minutes
Care Coil, Back Rubs	10 minutes
Messages About Sex	20 minutes
Evaluation of the Course	10 minutes
Closing	10 minutes

Procedures

Group Building (5 minutes)
Start the session by playing "People to People," the group-building activity found on pages 61–62 in this guide.

Introduction (5 minutes)
Thank people for coming, and explain that most of the activities this afternoon will be done in family groups.

"So You Think You Know . . . " (30 minutes)
Have the parents fill out the "So You Think You Know Your Teen?" worksheet on page 47 in the *Parent's Guide* (p. 108 in this guide), and have the young people fill out the "So You Think You Know Your Parent(s)?" worksheet on page 42 in the *Younger Youth Guide* (p. 109 in this guide). When they are finished filling out the sheets, have the parents and children exchange sheets and discuss each other's answers.

Word Choice (30 minutes)
This activity is designed for a parent and child to do together. Have each family group turn to the worksheet "Better Communication—Word Choice" in their guides and complete the exercise, following the instructions on the sheet.

Care Coil, Back Rubs (10 minutes)
Divide the total group in half. Ask them to start in a circle and do the "Care Coil" activity from page 62 in this guide. End with circle back rubs and then have them return to their family groups.

Messages about Sex (20 minutes)

This activity is also designed for a parent and child to do together. Have group members turn to the "Messages about Sex" worksheets on page 49 in the *Parent's Guide* (p. 44 in the *Younger Youth Guide*; pp. 111–112 in this guide) and follow the instructions on the sheet.

Evaluation of the Course (10 minutes)

Ask both parents and young people to evaluate the course by completing the evaluation sheets (see p. 85 in *Parent's Guide;* p. 46 in *Younger Youth Guide*).

Closing (10 minutes)

When the parents and young people are finished with the evaluation sheets, gather them in a circle and close with the litany on page 115 in this guide.

So You Think You Know Your Teen?

Parent Worksheet

As parents, we are often so caught up in the hustle and bustle of daily life that we forget some of the details of our children's lives. This activity will help you realize how much—or how little—you know about your son or daughter.

   Directions: Answer the following questions about your child. Ask your son or daughter to fill out the worksheet "So You Think You Know Your Parent(s)?" at the same time. When you are finished, exchange and correct each other's worksheets.

1. What color are your child's eyes?

2. What is your child's favorite food?

3. What is your child most proud of about himself/herself?

4. Which type of video would your child rather see: action, comedy, or romance?

5. If your child could visit any country in the world, which one would it be?

6. What is your child's favorite after-school activity?

7. Name three of your child's closest friends.

8. What was the last book your child read?

9. Which room in the house does your child prefer to spend time in?

10. What is your child's favorite musical group/singer?

11. What is your child's favorite subject in school?

12. What does your child like to eat for breakfast?

   Note: You and your child might enjoy making up your own questions for this activity. You also may want to take the test every few months, so you don't lose track of the details of your child's life.

So You Think You Know Your Parent(s)?

Teen Worksheet

You probably think you know your parent(s) pretty well. After all, you probably see him or her almost every day. But there may be a lot you don't know. This activity will help you realize how much—or how little—you know your parent(s).

   Directions: Answer these questions. At the same time, your mother or father (stepmother or stepfather) will answer the questions on "So You Think You Know Your Teen?" When you are finished, exchange and correct each other's worksheets.

1. What color are your mom's/dad's eyes?

2. What is your mom's/dad's favorite restaurant?

3. How would your mom/dad describe their work?

4. What kind of music did your mom/dad listen to when they were your age?

5. When visiting a big city, would your mom/dad rather visit a museum, attend a sporting event, go shopping, or dine in a fancy restaurant?

6. Which room of the house does your mom/dad prefer to spend time in?

7. Would your mom/dad rather drive a truck, a sports car, a station wagon, or a luxury car?

8. What type of movie does your mom/dad like best: action, comedy, or romance?

9. Who is your mom's/dad's closest friend?

10. Did your mom/dad have a favorite childhood pet?

11. What does your mom/dad like to eat for breakfast?

12. If your mom/dad could visit any country in the world, which one would it be?

   Note: In the future, you and your parent(s) might enjoy making up your own questions for this activity. You also might want to take this test every few months so you don't lose track of the details of your parent's life. *Remember:* Knowing or wanting to find out about someone shows that you truly care. What's more, it can be fun.

Better Communication—Word Choice

When we communicate with others, the words we use can mean the difference between getting our point across clearly and making someone feel hurt, angry, or rejected. This activity is designed to help you find better ways to communicate with your child or parent.

Directions: The sentences that follow are examples of poor word choice. Parents and children should take turns reading these sentences and discussing your reactions to them.

Parent: I just can't trust you.
Youth: You never let me do anything.
Parent: You never do what I say.
Youth: You're so old-fashioned. Everyone is doing it.
Parent: I can't believe you did that.
Youth: You never trust me.

Parents

Write down something your son or daughter says that gets a negative reaction from you.

My son/daughter says: _____
_____
_____
_____
_____ .

Discuss this statement with him/her, and then reword it to make it more effective communication.

I'd rather hear my son/daughter say: _____
_____
_____
_____
_____ .

Youth

Write down something your parent says that gets a negative reaction from you.

My mom/dad says: _____
_____
_____
_____
_____ .

Discuss this statement with your mom or dad and then reword it to make it more effective communication.

I'd rather hear my mom/dad say: _____
_____
_____
_____
_____ .

Messages about Sex

Parent Worksheet

Parents are the most important educators of their children about human sexuality. Often, though—despite your best intentions—the messages you intend to give about sexuality are not the same as the ones they receive. This activity will help you be sure that the messages you are sending your son or daughter are the ones you intend to give.

Directions: Ask your child to fill out his/her worksheet while you do yours. Write three messages about sex you think you've given him or her, either verbally or by example through the way you live your life and express your sexuality.

1.

2.

3.

After you have both written three messages on your worksheets, get together and read the messages you have written. Ask your child whether these messages have been clearly and completely understood. If not, explain further.

Messages about Sex

Teen Worksheet

Your parents are the most important educators and role models for human sexuality that you will have. However—despite their best intentions—the messages they send are often not the same as the ones you receive. This activity will help you be sure the messages you get from your parent or parents about sexuality are the messages they intend to give.

Directions: Complete this worksheet while your parent or parents do theirs. Write three messages your parent(s) have given you about sex. These messages may be actual statements they have made, such as "Sex should be a private act." They may be messages about sex that you haven't actually heard your parent(s) say, but think they believe. Or they may be messages you've received from observing your parent's lives and relationships.

1.

2.

3.

After you and your parent(s) have written three messages on your worksheets, get together and read the messages you have written. Ask your parent(s) whether these are the messages he or she intended to give. If so, discuss whether you have clearly and completely understood the messages. If they are not messages your parent(s) meant to give, discuss why you perceived them in this way and find out how the misunderstood message differs from your parent's actual beliefs.

Sexuality Course Evaluation

Youth

I would rate the sexuality education course as:

UNINTERESTING	SLIGHTLY INTERESTING	OK	GOOD	GREAT
☐	☐	☐	☐	☐

The most interesting part of the course was:

The thing I enjoyed most about the course was:

The thing I enjoyed least about the course was:

The part of the course most important to me was:

I wish there had been more:

Other comments:

Sexuality Course Evaluation

Parent

I would rate the sexuality education course as:

UNINTERESTING	SLIGHTLY INTERESTING	OK	GOOD	GREAT
❐	❐	❐	❐	❐

My perception of my teen's impression of the course is:

The aspect of the course most important to me was:

Because of this course, the lines of communication between me and my child about sexuality will:

IMPROVE	STAY THE SAME	BE DAMAGED
❐	❐	❐

I wish there had been more:

Other comments:

Litany

People: God did a curious thing when we were created. Sometimes it is hard to understand that God made us so different. Girls' behavior is different from boys' behavior and boys' behavior is different from girls' behavior, and all this is part of sexuality. From the beginning, sexuality has been a part of God's creation. God created us as sexual beings—to be boys and girls, men and women.

Leader: So this curious thing that God has done becomes a tremendous experience—our experience! Scripture says that when God made male and female, man and woman, God said, "It is good."

People: It *is* good—it is great! Our sexuality, our femaleness and maleness, is who we are. It is what we will be. We are turned loose to think, talk, and decide.

Leader: It makes us feel strange to be so free. There is so much we want to know. Thinking of God and sex at the same time and saying both in the same breath reminds us of how all love comes from one source.

People: It makes us feel good. We want to think, talk, know, and be the best girl or boy, man or woman, we can be. We want to use the gift of our sexuality to its fullest.

Leader: Praise God that we are sexual beings. Right?

People: Right!

Leader: Thank God that we are free to discover, examine, and decide.

People: Right!

Leader: Amen.

People: And Amen.

III. Older Youth Course

Introduction

Young people are trying to understand their sexuality in relationship to their faith and future. Young people turn to the church when trying to understand how their faith relates to their sexuality and how to make decisions about their sexuality based on their faith.

This course is designed to help young people understand those natural questions, feelings, and experiences that are related to sexuality from the perspective of their faith. There are facts about young people that suggest a tremendous need for education about sexuality grounded in religious faith and teaching:

- More than one million teenaged women in the United States become pregnant each year.[1]
- Fifty-six percent of young women and 73 percent of young men today have had sexual intercourse by age eighteen.[2]
- Only one-third of the teenagers in an extensive survey conducted by Louis Harris had discussed sex as well as contraceptives with their parents. Another third had never discussed sex with their parents.[3]
- An estimated one out of four girls and one out of five boys are sexually assaulted before their eighteenth birthdays.[4]
- Rape is the most frequently committed violent crime in the United States, and 85 percent of rapes occur between people who know each other (friend, neighbor, family member, etc.). Approximately 30 percent of all women under the age of twenty have experienced some kind of dating violence.[5]
- In 1993 AIDS became the leading killer of Americans between the ages of twenty-five and forty-four. With the long and variable lag time between HIV infection and death, many of these people were probably infected as teenagers.[6]

These statistics call us to give young people an opportunity to deal seriously with their sexuality. However, more important than the statistics and the tragedies they represent are the young people themselves and their need, as well as their right, to have accurate information and sensitive guidance regarding their sexuality. The activities in this course were designed specifically for young people in grades nine through twelve (older youth). They may be appropriate for college students as well. Some principles that undergird this course and these activities are the following:

1. "Pregnancy and Childbearing Among U.S. Teens" (New York: Planned Parenthood Federation of America, 1997).
2. *Sex and America's Teenagers* (New York: Alan Guttmacher Institute, 1994), p. 20.
3. Cited in *The Insiders* (New York: Planned Parenthood Federation of America, 1987).
4. *Striking Terror No More: The Church Responds to Domestic Violence*, edited by Beth Basham and Sara Lisherness (Louisville: Bridge Resources, 1997), p. 41.
5. Ibid., p. 49.
6. "HIV and AIDS: Trends in the Epidemic" (Washington, D.C.: Centers for Disease Control and Prevention, 1995).

- Parents are the primary educators of their children about sexuality. Churches, schools, and other community agencies serve to supplement what families are already doing.
- Young people need to have accurate information about the physical, emotional, and social aspects of their sexuality.
- The worth and dignity of all people should be treated with respect regardless of a person's gender, race, religion, culture, or sexual orientation.
- Individuals are responsible for their own sexual behavior and its consequences.
- Before making important decisions regarding sexual behavior, each person should weigh the current and future consequences for self, significant others, family, and society, and each should do this within the framework of his or her faith.
- Open communication is an important part of healthy relationships with others.
- Sexual intercourse should be reserved for marriage.

Teaching This Material in Your Church

This material can be taught in a variety of formats. (See "Sample Schedules, Older Youth" on p. 28 in this guide.) It can be completed in two weekends. Activities for the first weekend are scheduled Friday evening through Sunday evening, with parent's orientation and small-group leader training taking place on the previous Thursday evening. The second weekend calls for activities all day Sunday.

The material can also be taught in a retreat setting or in four blocks of five hours each. The course can also be conducted by teaching a small block once a week for several weeks, but the length of time between sessions makes it difficult to develop community and trust.

The complete course includes about twenty-five hours of coursework for the youth participants, plus additional time for meals and breaks. Select a time other than the youth fellowship hour. Not everyone in youth fellowship may want to participate, and the course works best when it is presented as an option. Night meetings seem to work better than after-school meetings. If the course is taught in a retreat setting, remember that parents must also participate at the end of the course. The group could come back to the church for this parent/youth session, or it could be held as a follow-up soon after the retreat. A third option is to hold the entire retreat at the church.

Keeping the students in small groups is the most important component of this course. The ideal small group is composed of six to eight young people of both sexes who are close in age. People teaching about sexuality sometimes separate males and females. This separation reinforces the attitude that males and females cannot discuss sexual matters together. One reason some young people become sexually active is that they are embarrassed to discuss their feelings. They may engage in unprotected intercourse for the same reason. The small-group time offers a rare opportunity for males and females to communicate with each other about beliefs, feelings, and concerns.

Each small group needs at least one leader, but ideally a team of one man and one woman should lead each small group. That is a good way to model that males and females can talk about sexuality together. Choose people who like young people and are good listeners to lead small groups. Because of the nature of the course, they do not need to have any special skills or knowledge. The course is designed to create opportunities for young people and adults to discuss, question, explore, and discover together. It is not dependent on adult lectures to young people. (See "Guidelines for Leaders," pp. 3–7 in this guide for more suggestions about leaders.)

Parents are the primary source from which young people form values about sexuality. The purpose of the parent's sessions is to enhance their communication with their children about sexuality. Communication involves both talking and listening. The activities in this course encourage the sharing of information and views. For parents to attend the parent/youth session is important. There is no need for a young person to attend this particular session if his or her parent cannot attend, because the session is dependent on the families participating together. You may want to find a way to work with families who cannot attend this session so the value of this special interaction will not be lost.

One person from the church should serve as the coordinator to ensure that the course runs smoothly. This person publicizes the event, handles registration, recruits small-group leaders, assigns the young people to small groups, and secures needed equipment and supplies. He or she also helps set up activities and oversees the meals and/or refreshments.

Hold this course in a large room. The small groups can be arranged around the room, leaving space in the middle for the total group to gather for discussions, games, and watching videos.

This guide contains information about recruiting leaders, the values espoused in this course, publicity, various course formats, and videos and other resources. It also contains sections titled "A Reformed/Presbyterian Understanding of Sexuality" and "Guide for the Presbyterian Church (U.S.A.)," along with many other resources (see pp. 8–22 in this guide.)

Those of us who have worked on this resource have a particular bias. We believe young people who are not married should not engage in sexual intercourse. In plain terms, we believe having sex as an unmarried teenager is a mistake. We believe that in our society having sexual intercourse before marriage is hazardous to a teenager's health of body, mind, and spirit. Our intention is to respond to, communicate with, and be supportive of young people who are not having sex as well as those who decide to have sex anyway or who have already been sexually involved.

Preparatory Session 1

Small-Group Leader Training

Purpose: This session gives small-group leaders an orientation to the course and an opportunity to share their anxieties and expectations.

Time: One hour and thirty minutes

Materials Needed

- Course schedule
- "Tips for Working with Small Groups" (p. 123)
- Assignment of small groups
- *God's Gift of Sexuality, Leader's Guide*
- "Basic Principles for Education about Sexuality" (pp. 123–124)
- Copies of small-group activities

Activities

Expectations	15 minutes
Review of Principle	15 minutes
Review of Course Schedule	60 minutes

Background for the Leader

People are the most important variable in this course. Like any course that fosters growth, this one depends on sensitive, caring persons. You will need to enlist such people to serve as small-group leaders.

Small-group leaders should be chosen from the participating church if at all possible. It does not matter whether they have young people participating in the course as long as no two members of any one family are in the same small group. The persons selected must like young people and have the ability to listen actively to group members. Most important, they need to be themselves and accept others as they are. Small-group leaders do not have to be authorities on every topic; in fact, it is sometimes helpful to the group when the leaders admit they do not know an answer.

A good small-group leader keeps the overall goal of the course in mind and works toward that end. The small-group leader's task is to help young people express their feelings, ideas, and values. Leaders who can laugh, cry, and struggle to make sense out of what it means to be a sexual human being will have a profound opportunity to make a difference in the lives of the young people.

Procedures

Expectations (15 minutes)
Have small-group leaders share their anxieties about and expectations for the course.

Review of Principles (15 minutes)
Go over "Tips for Working with Small Groups" (p. 123) and "Basic Principles for Education about Sexuality" (pp. 123–124).

Review of Schedule (60 minutes)

Go over the schedule in detail and describe each activity. Decide who has responsibility for each item within each activity. Make small-group assignments. Close with prayer.

Homework: Read the "Guide for the Presbyterian Church (U.S.A.)" found on pages 14–22.

Tips for Working with Small Groups

1. Remember that the primary role of the small-group leader is to encourage and be supportive of the participation of the young people.

2. Silence doesn't mean nonparticipation. Sometimes, because of the subject, the only response young people will make is to listen. If they are listening actively, they will get great benefit from the course.

3. Communication will be encouraged by keeping the group in a circle facing each other and on the same level (either all on the floor or all in chairs).

4. Young people will rarely ask personal questions of the small-group leaders. If they do, an appropriate response is, "What happened with me may not be accurate for everyone. Let's see if we can find out what is true for most people." Their questions should then be dealt with in the large-group session.

5. Admitting that you don't know the answer to a question will encourage young people to relate to the leaders on the same level; that is, that the leaders, too, are learning about sexuality. The answers to specific questions should then be obtained from either an authority on the subject or an appropriate book or resource.

6. To create an atmosphere of trust, confidentiality is to be respected. Please do not share with anyone outside the group what is discussed or stated by any young person during the course. (An exception would be if a young person reports a case of rape or abuse to you. See "Recognizing and Reporting Abuse" on pp. 6–7 for more information.)

Basic Principles for Education about Sexuality

1. A good course about sexuality respects young people. It respects their dignity and values their opinions and beliefs.

2. A good course about sexuality uses a banquet-table model of learning, providing information in a variety of ways. It does not make the assumption that young people are vessels waiting to have the right information poured into them; it allows students to choose and to wrestle with what is being taught.

3. A good course about sexuality sees sex as positive. Sex is not portrayed as evil, wicked, nasty, or dirty, but rather as a gift of God that must be used wisely and responsibly.

4. A good course about sexuality develops an atmosphere of trust. Sex is difficult to talk about under the best of circumstances; to talk about sex if trust does not exist is impossible. This course is designed with many activities that are not about sex but are used to build group trust and self-esteem.

5. A good course about sexuality teaches values. Most values are formed at an early age and largely through observation as opposed to verbal instruction. The young people will come into the course with their values already in place. They will have been with their parents for about as many years as the course has hours. The course cannot outweigh parental influence. However, what the course can do is to encourage young people to begin articulating the values they already hold. This will prove extremely helpful to them when their values are challenged and called into question.

6. A good course about sexuality uses the teachings of Scripture and the church as valuable resources. To do otherwise is to waste an opportunity to strengthen the ties between faith and life and to teach with incomplete information.

7. A good course about sexuality helps to reduce rather than increase the intensity of the adolescent sex drive. When sex is talked about and put into perspective, young people begin to see it as a part of life created by God,

not as a god in life that must be experienced. Rather than putting it into practice they have put it into proper perspective, making such practice unnecessary.

8.   A good course about sexuality teaches young males and young females together. To do otherwise is a wasted opportunity. Most of us will choose a member of the opposite sex as our sexual partner. Therefore, learning the similarities and differences in the sexes and learning to communicate with people of the opposite sex about sex is important.

Preparatory Session 2

Parent's Orientation

Purpose: This session gives parents the opportunity to gain ownership in the course and to ask questions. The session also helps relieve their anxiety about the course.

Note: Small-group leaders need to attend this session.

Time: One hour

Materials Needed

- "Basic Principles for Education about Sexuality" (p. 26 in the *Parent's Guide*, pp. 123–124 in this guide)
- "Basic Principles for Learning about Sexuality" (p. 52 in the *Parent's Guide*, p. 126 in this guide)
- Course schedule

Activities:

Group Building	20 minutes
Review of Principles	20 minutes
Review of Course Schedule	20 minutes

Procedures

Group Building (20 minutes)
Welcome the parents. Ask people to introduce themselves by telling something about the sexuality education they received as a child or something about the decision-making process in their household that prompted their young person to sign up to take this course.

Review of Principles (20 minutes)
Briefly cover the "Basic Principles for Education about Sexuality" that were used to create this course (see pp. 123–124 in this guide). Also review "Basic Principles for Learning about Sexuality" (p. 126 in this guide).

Review of Course Schedule (20 minutes)
Introduce the small-group leaders and others involved in leading the course. Review the course schedule and details with the parents. Point out to parents that sample pages from the *Older Youth Guide* have been included in the *Parent's Guide*. Invite their questions about the various activities. If time permits, select an activity and let the parents participate in it. Close with prayer.

Note: Show parents the "Family History" (p. 172) and "Personal History" (pp. 173–174) sheets found in Session 5 in this guide. Explain that the students will need the parent's help to fill in the information requested. Tell parents you will be sending these sheets home after Session 5. Or, if you are teaching this material in a retreat setting, give the sheets to the parents and ask them to help the students complete them. Have the students bring the forms to the retreat.

Basic Principles for Learning about Sexuality

- Parents are the primary educators of their children about sexuality. Churches, schools, and other community agencies serve to supplement what families are already doing.

- Young people need to have accurate information about the physical, emotional, and social aspects of their sexuality.

- The worth and dignity of all people must be respected, regardless of a person's gender, race, religion, culture, or sexual orientation.

- Each person is responsible for her or his own sexual behavior and its consequences.

- Before making important decisions regarding sexual behavior, people need to weigh the current and future consequences for themselves, significant others, their families, and society.

- Open communication is an important part of healthy relationships with others.

- Sexual intercourse is to be reserved for marriage.

Session 1

Sexuality Redefined

Purpose: This session includes welcoming participants, explaining what the program will be like, introducing ground rules for participation, and exploring a new definition of sexuality. The activities in this session include group building, an explanation of how the course will be handled, and a brief look at the content of the course through the use of circles that describe us as sexual beings.

Time: Two hours (two hours and thirty minutes if both group-building activities are used)

Materials Needed

- Newsprint and felt-tipped markers
- 3" x 5" index cards
- Pens and pencils
- Shoe box or container marked "Questions"
- *Older Youth Guide*

Activities:

Introduction to the Program	30 minutes
Group Building	30 minutes
Find Someone Who OR Name Tags	30 minutes
Program Principles and Group Expectations	25 minutes
Sexuality Redefined	30 minutes
Question Box	5 minutes

Procedures

Introduction to the Program (30 minutes)

Welcome participants in your own words, introduce yourself to the group, and then ask participants to introduce themselves by giving their name and mentioning something special about one member of their family.

Explain the content of the program in your own words, being sure to include the following points:

- The program is designed to examine all aspects of human sexuality.
- The program includes the following content areas: sensuality, intimacy, sexual identity, reproduction, and sexualism (using sex to control others). Integral to the entire program are Scripture and the teachings of the Presbyterian Church (U.S.A.).
- The program also addresses decision making and self-esteem as they relate to all aspects of sexuality.
- The program is experiential. (That means everyone will learn by participating in the activities.)

Go over your timetable for the program and tell the group how many sessions there will be as well as what will be covered in those sessions. Also point out when and where subsequent sessions will be held. Encourage young people to plan to attend all sessions. Finally, examine the following ground rules for group participation, explaining that these are important since the program will cover sensitive subjects about which people may have strong feelings. (The ground rules are also printed on page 20 in the *Older Youth Guide*.)

Ground Rules

Establish ground rules for group behavior so that young people know their limits as members of the group. Examples of appropriate rules include the following:

- *Full participation:* Group members are expected to actively participate in activities and discussions. Participation may sometimes mean just listening, but everyone is encouraged to share his or her thoughts and feelings.

- *Right to "pass":* Everyone is encouraged to participate in each session, but if a question or activity makes a person feel too uncomfortable, he or she always has the right to say "I pass."

- *Nonjudgmental approach:* Members are expected to respect each other; put-downs and teasing are not allowed. It is okay to disagree with others, but not to make judgmental or negative remarks, call people names, or make fun of someone.

- *Confidentiality:* Confidentiality is required. Participants may not quote one another outside of this program. They should talk over sessions with family and friends but not identify specific individuals.

- *Appropriate sharing:* Members are not to bring in personal business of friends or family members and share it with the group. They may share stories or experiences but should be careful not to use anyone's real name. Also, they are never to talk specifically in the group about their own sexual behavior.

- *Openness:* To be open and honest is important, but this does not mean sharing your own or other people's (family, neighbors, friends) personal or private lives. To discuss general situations is okay, but using names is not.

- *I-statements:* To preface personal feelings or values with "I," such as "I believe . . . " or "I feel . . . ," is best.

- *There are no "dumb" questions:* All questions will be answered so it is all right to ask any question, no matter how silly it seems. A question box will be provided so questions can be asked anonymously.

- *Acceptance:* To feel embarrassed or uncomfortable when talking about sensitive topics like values or sexuality is all right.

You may choose to add more ground rules of your own.

Group Building (30 minutes)

Find Someone Who . . .

Distribute pencils or pens and ask participants to turn to the "Find Someone Who . . . " sheet in their guides. Explain that the goal of this activity is to get as many autographs as possible. Any person can autograph an item if he/she can answer "yes" to that item. If the item asks for factual information, the person autographing must give the answer. Ask participants to get up, move around the group, and find someone to autograph each item on their sheet. They should continue circulating until they obtain many different signatures, particularly from people they do not already know. Tell them to resist the temptation to get several autographs from a friend.

After five to ten minutes, bring the group together and pose a few questions for a group response, such as: "How many of you have an older brother? Raise your hand." This identifies similarities among group members.

Admit that asking questions about personal topics can be awkward, especially with people you don't know well.

Questions for discussion include the following:

- How many different autographs did you obtain?

- Were there any questions that were hard to ask?

- Were you unable to obtain autographs for any items?

- Did you approach females for autographs on certain questions, males for autographs on others? Which ones? Why?
- Was it easier to approach members of the same sex or the opposite sex? Why?

Name Tags

Distribute 3" x 5" index cards. Instruct participants to make name tags that answer each of the following questions (the questions can be altered depending on the group):

Center of the card: Name you want to be called in this group

Top left corner: Favorite TV personality and why

Top right corner: Something you do really well

Lower left corner: A job you would like to have

Lower right corner: Age you think people should be to have a baby and why

After all participants have completed their name tags, ask them to form pairs or groups of three people and spend a few minutes sharing what they wrote on their name tags. Reconvene the large group after five to ten minutes and discuss the following:

- How did it feel to talk about yourself, especially regarding something you do well?
- Did anyone choose a job that is nontraditional for your gender?
- How old should people be before having children? What reasons did you give? Why do you think so many teenagers have babies?

Program Principles and Group Expectations (25 minutes)

Divide the whole group into two groups and give each group one of the following tasks:

1. Identify the questions and concerns that teenagers often have about sexuality.
2. Identify the basic beliefs or principles that teenagers generally have regarding information about sexuality, communication, responsibility, rights, and behavior.

Give examples of questions and concerns (e.g., "When does a person know if he or she is ready for sex?") as well as principles (e.g., "Young people have the right to be accurately informed about the physical, emotional, and social aspects of their sexuality.") to get the groups started.

Ask each group to make a list of their answers on newsprint. Allow about ten minutes, then ask each group to post their list and go over it with the whole group. Using another piece of newsprint, add other concerns and/or principles to the lists as necessary. Ask people to turn to "Basic Principles for Learning about Sexuality" on page 20 in the *Older Youth Guide* (p. 126 in this guide). Read and then discuss these principles, asking questions such as:

- Are there any questions some adults might not want teenagers to have answered? Why?
- Are there any principles some people might not agree with?

Conclude by reassuring the group that in this program their questions will be answered and their concerns will be addressed, and the principles will be used to guide discussion and learning.

Sexuality Redefined (30 minutes)

Note: Before this part begins, draw a large-scale diagram of Figures 1 and 2 on newsprint.

Many people find it difficult, at the outset of a discussion, to talk about sex and sexuality. As the leader, you will want to acknowledge that some people in the group may be feeling embarrassed or uncomfortable. That is okay. You may want to tell the group that you sometimes get embarrassed, too, but that we can all learn to be more comfortable talking about sexuality. Practice will help. Point out that our feelings of comfort or discomfort with the topic of sexuality come from our family, friends, religion, and culture.

Ask the group to think about something related to sex or sexuality they have seen on television, heard in music, or read about in the last week. Record the incidents or scenes they relate on newsprint. Review the list and comment on the nature of the items included. If they represent a narrow definition of sexuality (e.g., sexual intercourse, seduction, sensuous scenes), point out that most groups usually come up with similar examples, equating sexuality with intercourse and related activities, and suggest that a broader definition exists. If the list represents a broader definition (e.g., sex roles, reproduction, body image, affection, parenting), tell the group they did an excellent job of defining sexuality more broadly than many people do.

Explain that you are going to redefine sexuality in a broader way using a model that was developed by a social scientist at the University of Kansas.* Display the drawing of interconnecting circles (Figure 1) and point out that it depicts a new and broader definition of sexuality that is called "sexual beingness." Explain that each circle represents one aspect of our sexuality. In order to fully understand the term *sexuality* as it is used in this program, everyone will need to understand the concepts in each individual circle and what they include. Use the section "Sexuality Redefined" (pp. 131–133 in this guide) to discuss definitions of each circle. (Be sure to have read the fuller explanation in the chapter titled "Sexuality Redefined" on pages 23–26 in this guide.)

Once you have examined all five circles of the diagram, tell the group that our definition of human sexuality should be complete. Yet something seems to be missing. Only if we draw a central circle—separate, yet connecting all the others—can we truly complete the picture (Figure 2). This center circle is God's love, which is essential for full realization of ourselves as sexual beings. God's love touches and influences all facets of our sexuality as represented by the five circles. God's love fashioned the bodies housing our sensuality; God's love is reflected in our loving, intimate relationships; God's love gave us our sexual identity; God's love forged our capacity to create new life in God's image; God's love enables us to affirm our God-given sexuality; and God's love can heal us when our sexuality is exploited.

Our sexuality is a good gift to us from God, a gift that touches all parts of us as sexual beings. In order to cherish and use this gift wisely, we need to know as much about ourselves and our sexuality as we can. The framework of interlocking circles anchored in God's love that is provided in this course should be of help in guiding our thinking and studying about our sexual selves in relation to others and to God.

Explain that the sessions that follow will focus on the many aspects of our sexuality. Piece by piece we will be challenged to explore, examine, rethink, and redefine our own sexuality. Everyone should keep two key points in mind during all the sessions:

1. All aspects of our sexuality are related.
2. Central to our sexuality is God's love for us.

Some questions for discussion include:

- Is there an aspect of sexuality as we have defined it that you never considered to be "sexual" before?
- Is there any aspect of sexuality you feel is missing from our model?
- Who will you share this model with? Why?

*Dennis M. Daily, "Sexual Expression and Aging," in *The Dynamics of Aging: Original Essays on the Processes and Experiences of Growing Old*. Edited by Forrest J. Berghorn, Donna E. Schaefer, et al. (Boulder, CO: Westview Press, 1981), pp. 311–330.

Question Box (5 minutes)

The question box is a way for young people to ask questions that they don't feel comfortable asking aloud. Tell them that they can put any question in at any time during the program. Distribute index cards and ask each person to write a question about any aspect of sexuality. Everyone is to write down something. If they don't have a question themselves, they may write down a question that they think other young people or parents might want answered or write "No comment." Remind the group that no questions will be considered "dumb." Also encourage them to use whatever language they know to communicate their question. Collect cards in the box.

If time allows, begin to answer the anonymous questions by drawing several out of the box and choosing one or two to answer. Selecting a question you feel you can answer right on the spot is advisable; save the others until a future session after you have had time to think about your answer or to research the answer, or answer the question when it fits in with the material under discussion. Close with prayer.

Sexuality Redefined

Sensuality is the need and ability to be aware of others, especially a sexual partner. Sensuality is that sexual part of ourselves that lets us feel good about our bodies—how they look and what they can do—and that allows us to enjoy the pleasure our bodies can give to us as well as to others. Sensuality includes several different aspects of our sexuality:

- Awareness of our physiology—understanding and appreciation of how and why our bodies function as they do.
- Body image—includes our feelings about how our bodies look and work; whether we feel satisfied or dissatisfied with our bodies.
- Attraction—an aspect of our sexuality (determined by the brain, our most powerful sex organ) that enables us to feel attracted to some people, but not to others.
- Satisfaction of skin hunger—our need to touch, to be held by, and to make contact with another person.
- Release of sexual tension—the unique human sexual response cycle that enables human beings to experience arousal, followed by a release of sexual tension through orgasm. Males and females experience this process differently.
- Importance of sensory expression—our ability to experience sensuality through our many senses, as well as through fantasy and memory. It has been demonstrated that sexual fantasies are normal and are generally unrelated to sexual behavior.

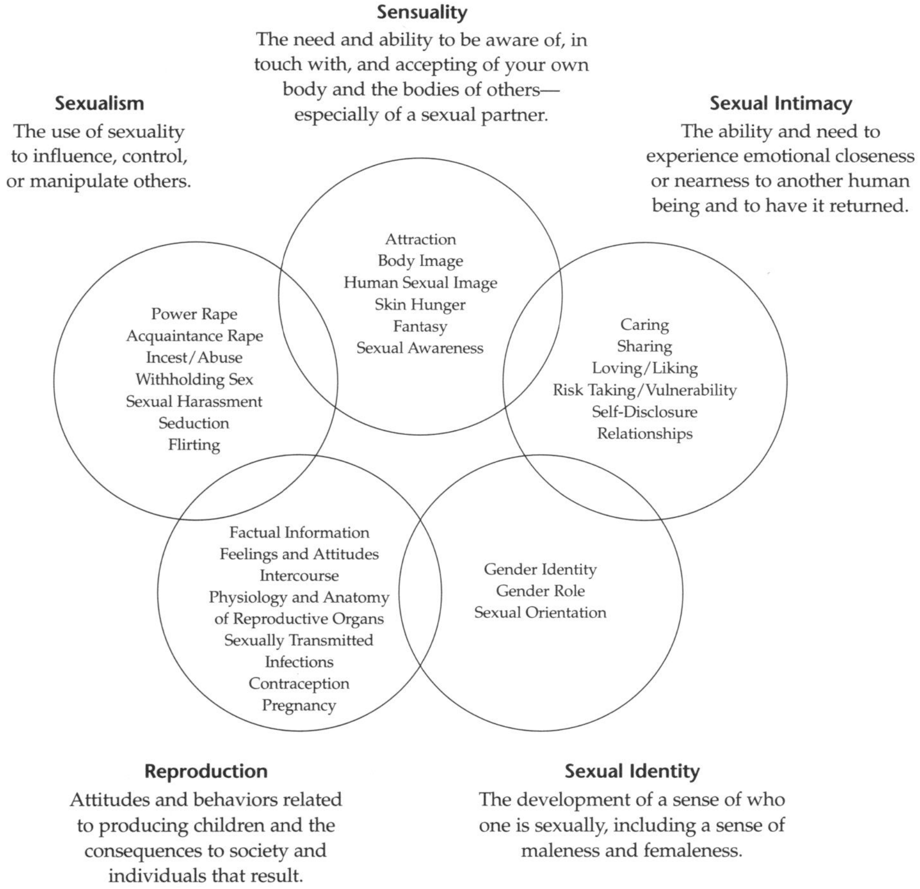

Figure 1

Intimacy is another aspect of sexuality that captures much of the richness found in our relationships with one another. Intimacy is the ability and need to experience emotional closeness or nearness to another human being and to have these feelings returned. Intimacy focuses on our closeness to others in emotional terms, whereas sensuality relates to our physical selves and physical closeness. Important components of intimacy include the following:

- Caring—having an emotional investment in the well-being of another person.
- Sharing—giving or revealing a part of oneself to another.
- Liking and loving—having strong emotional attachments to others and desiring to be with them.
- Risk taking—being willing to risk disclosing part of oneself in order to be close to another.
- Self-disclosure—risking possible exposure by another person with whom we have been open; sharing of our secret parts.

As sexual human beings we can establish intimacy without engaging in sex. Young people, especially, need the opportunity to experience intimacy without having sex. The mature expression of sexuality includes intimacy that goes far beyond mere genital sex and is expressive of the totality of human relationship.

Sexual identity, often the most complicated aspect of our sexuality, is the development of a sense of who one is sexually, including a sense of maleness or femaleness. Sexual identity develops gradually in three different areas. These include the following:

- Gender identity—a sense of maleness and femaleness that results from knowing whether one has a penis and scrotum or a vulva and breasts.
- Gender role identity—everything we do and feel that expresses our maleness or femaleness. Our development in this area often reflects society's messages about what it means to be male or female.

- Sexual orientation—whether our primary sexual attraction is to persons of the same or of the opposite gender, that is, homosexuality or heterosexuality.

All three aspects of sexual identity can have a profound effect on the well-being of a person: (1) Whether one is male or female largely determines how others perceive him or her. (2) Society's messages about gender roles, as well as how a person interprets these messages, can influence his or her feelings about self and interactions with others. (3) Sexual orientation can affect the entire quality of a person's life experience in our society.

Reproduction is the fourth and most familiar of the components of our sexuality. Reproduction includes the attitudes and behaviors related to producing children and the consequences to society and individuals that result. Human reproduction includes many recognizable aspects of sexuality, which are as follows:

- The facts of life—information about reproduction, conception, contraception, and physical development.
- Feelings and attitudes—how we feel about pregnancy, birth control, abortion, and other issues related to human reproduction.
- Physiology and anatomy—what the male and female reproductive systems are and how they actually work.
- Sexual intercourse—the human behavior that can result in pregnancy and production of a new life.
- Teen pregnancy and sexually transmitted infections (STIs)—commonly occurring, unintended consequences of sexual activity that can have profound implications for young people.

Sexualism, represented in the fifth circle, is the final element that constitutes sexuality. Sexualism is the use of sexuality to influence, control, or manipulate others. This last aspect of sexuality spans behaviors that range from harmless to sadistic and violent and includes behaviors such as flirting, seduction, withholding sexual intercourse, sexual harassment, sexual abuse, incest, and rape. In the area of sexualism we find the potentially dark and sinister side of our sexuality—therein lies the power to destroy another human being, just as in reproduction lies the ability to create life. We cannot understand ourselves as sexual beings until we acknowledge all aspects of our sexuality, including that of sexualism. In order to avoid being sexually manipulated, each of us needs to learn assertiveness skills that can protect us from sexualism.

God's Love

Having examined all five circles in Figure 1, we should have a complete definition of human sexuality. Yet something seems to be missing. Only if we draw a central circle—separate, yet connecting all the others—can we truly complete the picture (Figure 2).

This center circle is God's love, which is so essential for full realization of ourselves as sexual beings. God's love touches and influences all facets of our sexuality as represented by the five

circles. God's love fashioned the bodies housing our sensuality; God's love is reflected in our loving, intimate relationships; God's love gave us our sexual identity; God's love forged our capacity to create new life in God's image; and God's love enables us to affirm our God-given sexuality and resist the urge to exploit our sexuality.

Our sexuality is a good gift to us from God, a gift that touches all parts of us as sexual beings. In order to cherish and use this gift wisely, we need to know as much about ourselves and our sexuality as we can. The framework of interlocking circles anchored in God's love can guide our thinking and studying about our sexual selves in relation to others and to God.

As you participate in these sessions, keep these two key points in mind:

1.   All aspects of our sexuality are related.

2.   Central to our sexuality is God's love for us.

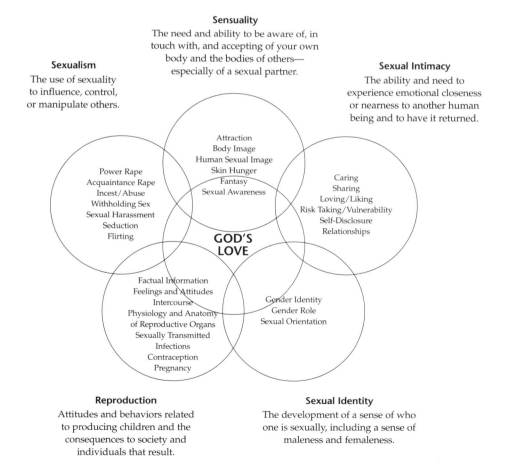

Sensuality
The need and ability to be aware of, in touch with, and accepting of your own body and the bodies of others—especially of a sexual partner.

Sexualism
The use of sexuality to influence, control, or manipulate others.

Sexual Intimacy
The ability and need to experience emotional closeness or nearness to another human being and to have it returned.

Attraction
Body Image
Human Sexual Image
Skin Hunger
Fantasy
Sexual Awareness

Power Rape
Acquaintance Rape
Incest/Abuse
Withholding Sex
Sexual Harassment
Seduction
Flirting

Caring
Sharing
Loving/Liking
Risk Taking/Vulnerability
Self-Disclosure
Relationships

GOD'S LOVE

Factual Information
Feelings and Attitudes
Intercourse
Physiology and Anatomy
of Reproductive Organs
Sexually Transmitted
Infections
Contraception
Pregnancy

Gender Identity
Gender Role
Sexual Orientation

Reproduction
Attitudes and behaviors related to producing children and the consequences to society and individuals that result.

Sexual Identity
The development of a sense of who one is sexually, including a sense of maleness and femaleness.

Figure 2

Find Someone Who . . .

Directions: Find different people in your group who match these statements and ask them to sign their names beside that statement. If the item asks for factual information, the person autographing must give the answer. Do not sign your own name.

Find someone who . . .

1. has an older brother. _____

2. sleeps with two pillows. _____

3. loves dogs. _____

4. sings in the shower. _____

5. wants to buy a car. _____

6. plans to have children someday. _____

7. knows when in her menstrual cycle a woman is most likely to get pregnant. _____

8. would like to be older. _____

9. has a parent who has talked to her or him about sex. _____

10. doesn't like to say no to good friends. _____

11. can explain what a "wet dream" is. _____

12. has a part-time job. _____

13. is on a school athletic team. _____

14. has a teen friend with a baby. _____

15. has an e-mail address. _____

16. doodles while talking on the phone. _____

17. has changed a baby's diaper. _____

18. has looked through *Playboy* or *Playgirl* magazine. _____

Session 2

Sensuality

Purpose: This session helps young people increase their awareness of their physical selves, recognize the role the media plays in developing a self-image, and become more aware of how that self-image affects behavior. The activities in this session deal with body image, touch, attraction to other people, and a theological discussion of our gift of sexuality.

Time: Two hours and ten minutes (three hours if all the activities are used)

Materials Needed

- Bibles
- Old magazines
- Tape
- Scissors
- Glue
- Newsprint and felt-tipped markers
- *Older Youth Guide*

Activities:

Body Image or Created in God's Image	30 minutes
People to People or A Touchy Subject	20 minutes
Likes/Dislikes	40 minutes
God Created Us and Gave Us the Gift of Our Sexuality	40 minutes

Background for the Leader

We believe that God created us in the image of God. This life force within us is what we call "spirit." God did not create us just as spirits or just as bodies, but God created us as total persons—body and spirit. This entire creation God called very good.

We are God's best and greatest creation, for we are God's very own image in the world. All that we are—including our bodies, including our sexuality—is God's gift to us. Our sexuality affects our thoughts, feelings, and actions. Because our sexuality is called good by God and because it is God's gift to us, we can therefore feel good about our sexuality.

Procedures

Body Image/Created in God's Image (30 minutes)
Choose to do Activity A or Activity B.

A. Body Image*
Divide the group into small groups of the same sex. Give each girls group a piece of newsprint labeled "Things Girls Don't Like about Their Bodies" and each boys group one labeled "Things Boys Don't Like about Their Bodies." Give each group a felt-tipped marker. Tell the groups to list the parts of the body that members of their sex generally don't like. Allow ten minutes for the groups to prepare their lists.

Give each group a stack of old magazines and tell them to find examples in the magazines of members of their sex they believe the opposite sex finds attractive. Have each group make a collage titled either "Attractive Men" or "Attractive Women." Display the lists and collages in the front of the room and bring the entire group together again for a discussion. Discuss questions such as the following:

- Are most women satisfied with their bodies? Are most men? Why or why not?

- Where do we get our ideas about what an "appealing body" looks like?

- Is the way we feel about our own bodies influenced by what the opposite sex finds appealing and attractive?

- Are there parts of our bodies we can change? Circle those on both lists.

- What about the parts we can't change? Do parts of our bodies affect our humor, our intelligence, our friendliness, or our ability to love and be loved?

- Are there things about our lives that are affected by our bodies? Give some examples.

*Used by permission from *Life Planning Curriculum* (Washington, D.C.: Advocates for Youth, 1985).

B. Created in God's Image
Read Gen. 1:26–27. Ask the group something like this: If you were going to meet someone for the first time, how would you describe yourself so that he or she would know who you are? Most likely you might say something about your physical characteristics. You would probably tell your height, your hair color, your size, and whether you are male or female. Our body is a part of who we are, how we see ourselves, and how others see us as a person. The characteristics of our bodies affect the way we relate to each other.

Ask participants to turn to "Created in God's Image" on page 22 of their guide. Ask them to recall each life stage and write their memories and feelings about their bodies and the way they looked at that stage. Allow fifteen minutes; then ask members to pair off and share their recollections.

Questions for discussion are as follows:

- What are some of the changes you have experienced in your body that have been the most important to you?

- How does the way we feel about our body affect the way we relate to other people?

- What are examples of body changes that teens experience that may affect their feelings about self as well as their relations with others? (Examples include breast and/or genital development that may cause embarrassment; acne and body odor that can be unpleasant; overall growth that may make other people perceive one as older and more mature.)

People to People/
A Touchy Subject (20 minutes)
Choose to do either Activity C or Activity D.

C. People to People*
Ask the entire group to stand in one area of the room and pair off, with pairs facing each other. Assure participants that it doesn't matter who their partners are because they will be changing frequently. Explain that this game is about human touch. Give these instructions: "Listen as the leader calls out a position, then assume that position with your partner. Change partners when the leader calls 'People to people,' but assume the same position."

When you are sure everyone understands, call out the first position. Once all pairs have assumed a position, call out a new one and allow time for partners to assume the new position. Start with simple, less-threatening positions and go on to those that are more complicated. Begin with nose to elbow; finger to forehead; elbow to knee; toe to toe; knee to knee; elbow to hand. Then move to neck to neck; forehead to forehead; nose to nose.

After several positions have been called, call "People to people" and have pairs change partners, then reassume the previous position. Go on to call several new positions.

After the activity, discuss questions such as the following:

- Did some of the positions cause more anxiety than others? Which ones? Why?

- Were you more comfortable with some partners than others? Why?

- Do you know anyone who would be very uncomfortable playing this game? Why?

- Make the point that it is okay to be uncomfortable with some touch. Our discomfort can be a healthy signal that another person is violating our personal space.

- Explain that parents sometimes touch their children less as the children get older. This may be a sign of parent's respect for individual space. It may mean a parent doesn't know how to be physical around his or her growing child. It doesn't necessarily mean the child has done anything wrong or is being rejected. Also, in some cultures touch is less a sign of affection than in others.

*From *The Giving Book*, by Paul Thompson and Joan Schultz, copyright 1985. Used by permission of Westminster/John Knox Press.

D. A Touchy Subject

Divide the participants into two groups and give each group one of the following tasks:

1. List the barriers that keep people from using touch to show they care.

2. List the bridges or openings that give people permission to touch.

Allow five minutes for the groups to complete their lists and then ask a member of each group to report the "bridges" or "barriers" his or her group identified. Use the sheet "Bridges and Barriers" found on page 23 in the *Older Youth Guide* to supplement the responses. Discuss why some things like alcohol and drugs might seem to be a bridge or barrier to communication. Finally, ask the whole group to rank the barriers and bridges from most significant to least significant.

Discuss more general questions, such as these:

- What messages can we give to another person with touch?

- Where do we learn to avoid touching?

- What can we do to minimize the barriers and maximize the bridges to touch as a form of physical communication?

Likes/Dislikes* (40 minutes)

Ask the group to think about the things that they like, or do not like, about members of the opposite sex. Have the males form one group, the females another. Give each group a felt-tipped marker and two sheets of newsprint. Each group is to brainstorm and make two lists. For the "Dislikes" list, they should think about the following questions: What would keep them from wanting to meet or get to know a person? What kinds of approaches bother them? For the "Likes" list, they should think about members of the opposite sex they like and why. What made them want to get to know the person? How does she or he behave?

After about fifteen minutes, have the two groups come together to share their lists. Establish these rules for reporting:

1. When the females report, the males must keep quiet and listen.

2. The males can say nothing unless they are seeking clarification.

3. After the females have reported, the males must tell the females what they heard or understood.

4. After they have demonstrated that they understand, they can comment on what the females have said.

5. The same rules apply for the males' report.

After both groups have reported, discuss the following questions:

- What have you learned about the opposite sex?

- Is everyone attracted by the same characteristics in the opposite sex?

- If you had a magic wand, what is one characteristic you would change about the opposite sex?

*Used with permission from *Life Skills and Opportunities* (Philadelphia: Public/Private Ventures, 1986).

God Created Us and Gave Us the Gift of Our Sexuality (40 minutes)

If the group is large enough, divide into small groups of three or four. On newsprint list the following Bible verses and the discussion questions. Have the group read the Bible passage and discuss the questions.

Gen. 1:26–31

Discuss the following questions:

- Why did God create human beings?
- Why did God create both males and females?
- What is God's word for creation?
- Are men and women equal or unequal as far as their authority over the things of the earth?

Gal. 3:25–28

Discuss the following questions:

- What does it mean that "there is neither male nor female"?
- How would you compare the Genesis verses to the Galatians verses?
- Do these passages give you a different view of what it means in God's eyes to be male and to be female?

Ask everyone to read "God Created Us and Gave Us the Gift of Our Sexuality" (page 24 in the *Older Youth Guide*; p. 141 in this guide). In small groups of three or four, think together about the "Questions for Bible Study" on page 24 in the *Older Youth Guide*. After the small groups have finished their discussion, come back together as a total group and compile the answers to question 7. Read the Scripture lessons again.

Ask the questions found in the "Guide for the Presbyterian Church (U.S.A.)" under the section "Human Sexuality" and the section "Equality of Men and Women." (See p. 9 in the *Older Youth Guide*; pp. 15–16 in this guide.) Have the group formulate answers for each question based on the biblical discussion. Then read the answers that the guide gives. (See p. 25 in the *Older Youth Guide* and p. 142 in this guide.) Compare the young people's answers with the answers in the guide.

Read the lines from "A Declaration of Faith" under "God Created Us and Gave Us the Gift of Our Sexuality" on page 141. Close with the following prayer:

> God, we thank you for the gifts you give us. Especially we thank you for the gift of life, the gift of our bodies, the gift of our sexuality. Help us to be grateful for your gifts to us. Amen.

Created in God's Image

Think of yourself at different stages of your life. Think about how you looked in pictures at different ages. Using words, phrases, or drawings, record what you think you looked like and how you felt about yourself. If you remember specific changes taking place, describe your feelings about those changes.

You as a baby

You as a preschooler

You as a third- or fourth-grader

You in middle school or junior high

You at your present age

You in the future (Do a little dreaming and hoping. How would you like to be someday?)

Bridges and Barriers to Physical Communication

Illness

Grief, mourning

Celebrations, awards

Alcohol or drugs

Sports events

Greetings

Partings

Pets

Status, roles

Cultural norms

Age

Gender

Race

Presence of small children

Physical disability

Appearance

Cleanliness

Lack of familiarity

Family upbringing

Posture, body language

Which are bridges? Why?

Which are barriers? Why?

God Created Us and
Gave Us the Gift of Our Sexuality

Then God said, "Let us make humankind in our image, according to our likeness; and let them have dominion over . . . the earth." So God created humankind in [God's] image, in the image of God [God] created them; male and female [God] created them. . . . God saw everything that [God] had made, and indeed, it was very good.

(Gen. 1:26, 27, 31a)

For we are what [God] has made us, created in Christ Jesus for good works.

(Eph. 2:10)

God made human beings male and female for their mutual help and comfort and joy. We recognize that our creation as sexual beings is part of God's loving purpose for us. God intends all people . . . to affirm each other as males and females with joy, freedom, and responsibility.

("A Declaration of Faith,"
ch. 2, lines 80–84, 87–88)

God has created . . . male and female and given them a life which proceeds from birth to death in a succession of generations and in a wide complex of social relations. . . . Life is a gift to be received with gratitude and a task to be pursued with courage.

(The Confession of 1967, 9.17)

God created us and called us very good. God did not create us as spirits. God did not create us as bodies. Instead, God created us as total persons—body and spirit. And this entire creation, God called very good.

Not only did God create us, but God created us to be God's very own image in the world. All that we are—including our bodies, including our sexuality—is God's gift to us.

Our sexuality is our way of being male or female in the world. Our sexuality is basic; it affects our thoughts, feelings, and actions. Because our sexuality is called good by God, because it is God's gift to us, and because we are made in the image of God, we can feel good about our sexuality.

Questions for Bible Study

1. Our sexuality is God's good gift to us. What is good for you about being male or female?

2. Do you think most people your age believe sexuality is a positive part of their lives? If not, how do they feel about their sexuality?

3. What is difficult about being female or male?

4. Do you think it is easier for males or for females to feel good about their sexuality? Why?

5. Do you think your parents feel good about your sexual development? Do they talk to you about your sexual development?

6. Are you afraid of any part of your sexuality? If so, what?

7. In one word, God described your sexuality as "good." What one word would you use?

Questions from the "Guide for the Presbyterian Church (U.S.A.)"

Human Sexuality

1. Why were we created as sexual beings?

2. Were we created as sexual beings for the purpose of having children?

3. In what ways should we express our sexuality?

4. When do we become sexual beings?

5. What is the relationship between sex and love?

6. What is our church's role in developing our understanding of sexuality?

7. Does our church believe in sex education in the schools?

Equality of Men and Women

1. In the Creation story of Genesis 2, woman is created after man. Does this mean woman is subordinate to man?

2. How was the equality of men and women understood in Old Testament times?

3. What was Jesus' treatment of women?

4. How did Paul address this issue?

Session 3

Intimacy

Purpose: There is a potential relationship with each person who touches our life. God gives us a human body. Sexuality, intimacy, and the excitement of relationships are gifts from God: "God created humankind in his image, in the image of God [God] created them; male and female [God] created them" (Gen. 1:27). Building self-confidence by understanding God's gift of sexuality is the purpose of this session. Using biblically based relationship exercises, we see how self-confidence gives youth carefree and productive teen years.

Time: Four hours (excluding optional Rathus Assertiveness Schedule)

Materials Needed

- *Older Youth Guide*
- Rathus Assertiveness Schedule (optional)
- Name books
- Newsprint, markers
- Basins, soap, water
- Towel, socks
- Oil, powder
- Timer

Activities

Rathus Assertiveness Schedule (optional)	30 minutes
Affirmation Exercise	30 minutes
Self-Esteem	30 minutes
The Family Tree	30 minutes
Friendship	30 minutes
Getting Over Embarrassment	30 minutes
Assertiveness	30 minutes
Marriage	30 minutes
God Created Us for Life in Community	25 minutes

Background for the Leader

In addition to our unique personality, we are born with three identifiers that affirm our self-worth as God's person. A name, a heritage, and a spiritual presence give us the nourishment and support to stay alive in a secular world. At the beginning of this session, the Rathus Assertiveness Schedule (RAS) found on pages 149–150 may be given as a pretest. After completing Session 10, retest with the RAS to see if individual assertiveness has increased.

Procedures

Affirmation Exercise (30 minutes)
Tell the group that in this exercise they will find out the meaning of their first name. Bring in a Bible translation of names, books on the meaning of names (baby name books are good sources), or

information from other sources, such as the Internet. Help the youth discover the positive affirmations behind their names. (For example, David is from the Hebrew for "beloved." Sobenna is a girl's name of African origin that means "Follow God.") If the youth know how and why their parents chose their name, use the following questions for discussion. If not, have them do "homework," asking their parent or parents about the reason and meaning behind their name.

- Do you know what your name meant to your parents at your birth?
- How do they feel about your name now?
- What new associations are in your name because of your personality traits and physical characteristics?
- Does your name express how you feel about yourself?

Note how many names have a Christian derivation and a positive meaning. Imagine how it feels when someone special addresses you by name. Now imagine that you make others in your family, your school, and your community feel important when you remember and address them by their name. Relationships can start with a name. Make it a challenge to remember those you meet, calling them by name as a person who is important to you.

Have all the participants focus on their last (family) name, and ask the following questions: Is your last name the same as your parent's last name? What is meant by a maiden name? Does your mother carry her maiden name? Acknowledge that, because of unique circumstances, some teens do not live with the family they were born into. Whatever their present family configuration, it is important to realize how unique their name is. "Your family supports your identity, making you an individual with characteristics you can be proud of. Not any of us have to be the same. God put us in many types of families and assures us that we and our family are important to God."

Self-Esteem (30 minutes)

In the small groups, give each person enough index cards so that he or she has one for every other member of the small group. Using a different card for each member, have each person complete the following statement about the other small group members: "I like your . . . " or "I admire you for . . . " Stress that the statements are to be affirmations only; no negative comments should be made. Suggest that they include qualities of people such as their warmth, caring, friendliness, or honesty, as opposed to something people do like play baseball or make good grades.

Once the cards are completed, pass each card to the person it is intended for. Everyone in the group should have an affirmation from every other member. Go around the circle and have each person read aloud what was written.

The small-group leader then leads a discussion with the following questions:

- How did it feel to see the comments, to read them aloud?
- Did the comments make you feel better or worse about yourself?
- Did they make you feel stronger or weaker?

The preceding exercise has helped young people feel a sense of esteem. On a sheet of newsprint, write "Esteem is . . . " Have the group complete the sentence by reflecting on the feelings they had in the previous exercise. List their answers on the sheet of newsprint. Possible answers would be "when we feel good about ourselves," "when we like ourselves," "when we trust ourselves," "when we stand up for what we believe when it is questioned by someone else," or "when we feel loved."

Discuss how in the following examples our self-esteem partially determines how we act out our sexuality:

1. If we feel good about ourselves, we are not as likely to need attention from other people or to try to find our worth in the way they treat us.

2. If we feel good about ourselves, we have less need to please others in an unhealthy way, especially if they want us to do something that we don't want to do.

3. If we feel good about ourselves, we see things in a larger perspective and are less likely to get caught up in the moment.

Ask the group to complete the "Self-Esteem Exercise" found on page 29 in their guide (p. 151 of this guide) at a later time.

Family Tree (30 minutes)

Our first nurturing relationships are those with our family. The quality of family life and relationships predicts feelings about our intimacy with one another. Becoming aware of family background is important to the self-esteem and sense of belonging of a young person. We will look at our family tree to gain insight about ourself. First have the youth look at Matt. 1:1–17 and Luke 3:23–28 to see the family tree of Jesus. Tell them that in this exercise they will trace their own family tree.

In small groups, give each person a piece of newsprint and a marker. Each will draw a tree for their father's side of the family and/or a tree for their mother's side of the family. The leaves of each tree will be made of the names of family members of each parent. Next a line will join the two tree trunks. On that line they will make a leaf named for themselves and one for each brother or sister in the family. (Be sensitive to the fact that many of the participants may come from families that are "nontraditional": single parent, divorced, step-parents, adoptive parents, living with grandparents, and so on. Give them the option of filling out their family tree with the people whom they consider their family, whether or not they are biologically related.)

There are many ways to draw a family tree. Sometimes line drawings are used to show family relationships. Other projects can include photographs of family members that make up the leaves of the tree. Use your creativity to show family relationships.

In small groups discuss the following ideas:

- Name three things about your parent or parents that you are proud of.
- Name two things about your family that are different from most families.
- Do you see physical characteristics of other family members (parents, sisters, uncles, etc.) in yourself? emotional characteristics?
- With what part of your racial-ethnic heritage do you identify most? (e.g.,

African ancestors; great-grandfather from Scotland; Korean mother.)

Friendship (30 minutes)

The "tasks" of life at the teen stage are to become more independent and to form intimate bonds with people. For teenagers, the approval of same-sex and opposite-sex friends is more important than the approval of family. However, the support a teen receives from his or her family increases self-confidence in relationships outside the family circle.

The following questions will help spark discussion in small groups:

Is your life as a teen pleasing to you?

What characteristics make a person a friend?

Which characteristics do you have?

Which qualities would you like to develop?

Are there particular experiences that help make people friends? What makes a friend different from an acquaintance?

How important is friendship to you right now?

What makes it difficult to be friends with females?

What makes it difficult to be friends with males?

Getting Over Embarrassment (30 minutes)

Presumed embarrassment inhibits teen inter-actions. This exercise challenges our comfort zone. It is created to build resilience when we would rather turn our back than deal with another person's quirks (uncoolness) or pain (or even his smelly feet).

In his final hours on earth, Jesus invited his closest friends, the disciples, to dine with him. He had prepared a banquet for them in a place that has come to be called "the Upper Room." That supper was Jesus' time of sharing his living faith. To prepare his disciples for this exchange he begin serving them in a way that was intimate—he washed their feet.

Foot washing is action-based; it is cleansing to signify helping and caring for another person without an expectation of return. It is free of gender bias, meaning that you can pair with a person of the same sex or the opposite sex and still feel comfortable after sharing.

Teens and leaders need to number off in pairs. Each pair will fill a basin with warm water.

One will have his or her feet washed first. The washing is to be done carefully, with time given for soaping, talking, massaging, and drying. Dried feet will be rubbed with oil or powder and covered with a clean pair of socks. Then have the partners wash the basins and repeat the process, exchanging places. Each pair should be separated enough so that conversations are not easily overheard. A timer in a central area can be used to set limits.

Discuss these statements about feelings when the footwashing is finished:

- "It is embarrassing to have someone else see my feet."
- "I hope my feet aren't smelly!"
- "Did I change my socks today?"
- "I refuse to do anything so dumb!"
- "I don't deserve to have anyone do this for me."
- "It felt good to have someone dry and massage my feet."
- "It feels like I could talk to this person because I have done something personal for her/him."

Could these statements, with a few changes, express how we feel in other situations of intimacy? Like the supper with Jesus and his disciples, sharing a meal or snack after foot washing is helpful for continuing closeness and nourishment.

Assertiveness (30 minutes)

As you move through exercises that promote personal growth and spiritual commitment, teen assertiveness or the ability to show self-assurance and confidence will be evident. A teen who recognizes and uses cause and effect as it applies to self will develop internal control of behaviors and actions. But the teen who is motivated by the actions and views of external forces (friends, classmates, the media, etc.) will find his or her life controlled by others.

Teens often feel that they are acting in a negative or angry manner if they assert their feelings. A common response of teens is that it is more important to comply and "appear normal" than to disagree and "appear different" from others. Teens acquire assertiveness at different levels of awareness. The teen who sees her friends smoke and feels the high when she joins them does not internalize the consequences of her behavior. However, when that same teen experiences the death of her favorite aunt from lung cancer, she may decide to change her behavior. She then is motivated by her own feelings and learns to acknowledge herself based on what comes from within.

Because it is normal for teens to begin breaking away from their family and asserting their own ideas, groups in community become a safe place to learn and talk about intimacy and friendships. Discussions can challenge unhealthy choices and support healthy ones. Honesty fosters positive attitudes and acceptance and shows love of a person even if his or her choices are not healthy.

The Jo-Hari Window (see p. 148) is a simple aid in the discussions of self in healthy relationship to others and the growth of assertiveness. It has two columns ("known to me" and "unknown to me") and two rows ("known to others" and "unknown to others"). Thus there are four distinct areas of the window. Youth should describe themselves with appropriate guidance from the window in the following categories: (1) What I know about myself that others also know about me; (2) What I know about myself that others do not know about me; (3) What I do not know about myself but others know about me; and (4) What is unknown both to myself and to others.

In the large group, draw a large-scale Jo-Hari Window and explain the meaning of each window, using the given examples or asking for examples from the group. Then have the youth break into their small groups and fill out their own window (see p. 26 in the *Older Youth Guide*). Ask each member to share examples about themselves that apply to each area, if they feel comfortable doing so. In the "Blind Spot," ask for members to share observations that they have made about a fellow member. Close with the importance of life in community by reading Matt. 22:34–40.

Marriage (30 minutes)

Ask the participants to look at the section on "Marriage" found on page 30 in the *Older Youth Guide*. Read through the questions together. Allow ten minutes for young people to jot down answers to the questions.

With those questions in mind, read together the section "Marriage" in the "Guide for the Presbyterian Church (U.S.A.)" on pages 9–10 in the *Older Youth Guide* and pages 16–17 in this guide.

Discuss the following:

- The important things to know about marriage are . . .
- The good points I see in marriage are . . .
- The difficulties in marriage are . . .

God Created Us for Life in Community (30 minutes)

Display a long sheet of newsprint on which you have listed horizontally the following terms: your mother, your father, your best same-sex friend, your best opposite-sex friend, your brother(s), your sister(s), your female teachers at school, your male teachers at school, friends.

Read "God Created Us for Life in Community" (p. 31 in the Older Youth Guide; p. 153 in this guide).

In small-group discussion, have the young people describe their relationships with each of the people listed on the newsprint (e.g., under "your mother" some might say: "happy, because we enjoy each other"; "absent, because my mom doesn't live with us"; "strained, because we disagree on quite a few issues").

In small-group discussion, have the young people think again about those relationships and describe in what sense their maleness or femaleness is expressed in each relationship (e.g., under "your father," females in the group might say: "I hide it, because my father doesn't think I'm old enough to be sexual"; "I use it to flirt, because I can get my dad to do anything I want him to if I act real cute"; "scared, because I'm afraid of my dad").

Evaluate the comments above by discussing the following questions as a group:

- Which relationships are the best at this point in your life?
- Which relationships need the most improvement?
- What is the most surprising thing you discovered in the discussion?
- How would you most like to be different?

Conclude the session by reading the Scripture passage again (Rom. 13:8–10). Close with the following prayer:

> God, we thank you for our families and friends, especially for the good way they touch our lives. Help us grow in our relationships with one another. Thank you, God, for being so close to us. Help us feel your presence and know your love. Help us share love with one another. God, we thank you for love and the possibilities of love. Help us to be open to seeing and feeling your love in the world. Amen.

What I Know/Don't Know about Myself

Common Knowledge: Things about myself that I know and others know about me as well. Information and feelings here are safe, such as "My friends and I like to drive my blue pickup to school." Discussion about changes in this area is not threatening.

Secrets: Things I know about myself but others do not know about me. For instance, an embarrassing detail would be, "My family cannot afford to buy braces for my teeth." A secret such as one about sexual abuse may be much more threatening. Items in this box may or may not be open to discussion, depending on the trust level within a group.

Blind Spots: Things about myself that I do not know but others do know about me. Others may see you as tired or unresponsive. However, you do not feel this way inside, and you do not know that others see you this way. When trust levels are high and people love each other despite discouraging characteristics, they share these observations to promote self-improvement.

Unknown Self: Things about myself that I do not know and that others do not know about me. These can be areas that are repressed because they contain disturbing revelations or demand the use of one's talents.

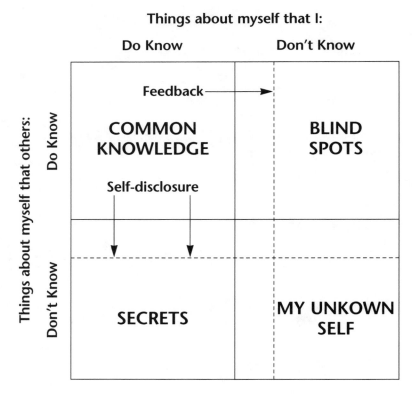

The Rathus Assertiveness Schedule (RAS)*

The Rathus Assertiveness Schedule (RAS) is a quick test of assertiveness that has reliability and validity in English-speaking countries. One can administer it just after establishing a group. Pretesting a teen as group work begins is important because assertiveness changes with modeling, rehearsal, education, and practice. Post-testing with the RAS means administering it again before group closure to see if the student has become more or less assertive or has experienced a change in attitudes toward personal goals and management of intimacy.

To administer the test, choose a quiet environment with no distractions. Before the test, review any words within the test that may cause confusion or may not be readily recognized by a student. Explain and make a display of the scale of responses at the top of the RAS test. Read each statement clearly two times, giving time for response. Then move on to the next statement until all statements have been read. Responses may be scored individually. The higher the score, the greater the level of assertiveness. Note that the asterisks that follow some statements indicate a reversed item. The process is repeated for post-testing.

Directions: Indicate how characteristic or descriptive each of the following statements is of you by using the code given below:

+3 very characteristic of me, extremely descriptive
+2 rather characteristic of me, quite descriptive
+1 somewhat characteristic of me, slightly descriptive
-1 somewhat uncharacteristic of me, slightly nondescriptive
-2 rather uncharacteristic of me, quite nondescriptive
-3 very uncharacteristic of me, extremely nondescriptive

_____ 1. Most people seem to be more aggressive and assertive than I am.*

_____ 2. I have hesitated to make or accept dates because of "shyness."*

_____ 3. When the food served at a restaurant is not done to my satisfaction, I complain to the waiter or waitress.

_____ 4. I am careful to avoid hurting other people's feelings, even when I feel that I have been injured.*

_____ 5. If a salesman has gone to considerable trouble to show me merchandise which is not quite suitable, I have a difficult time in saying "No."*

_____ 6. When I am asked to do something, I insist upon knowing why.

_____ 7. There are times when I look for a good, vigorous argument.

_____ 8. I strive to get ahead as well as most people in my position.

_____ 9. To be honest, people often take advantage of me.*

_____ 10. I enjoy starting a conversation with new acquaintances and strangers.

____ 11. I often don't know what to say to attractive persons of the opposite sex.*

____ 12. I will hesitate to make phone calls to business establishments and institutions.*

____ 13. I would rather apply for a job or for admission to a college by writing letters than by going through with personal interviews.*

____ 14. I find it embarrassing to return merchandise.*

____ 15. If a close and respected relative were annoying me, I would smother my feelings rather than express annoyance.*

____ 16. I have avoided asking questions for fear of sounding stupid.*

____ 17. During an argument I am sometimes afraid that I will get so upset that I will shake all over.*

____ 18. If a famed and respected lecturer makes a statement which I think is incorrect, I will have the audience hear my point of view as well.

____ 19. I avoid arguing over prices with clerks and salesmen.*

____ 20. When I have done something important or worthwhile, I manage to let others know about it.

____ 21. I am open and frank about my feelings.

____ 22. If someone has been spreading false and bad stories about me, I see him (her) as soon as possible to "have a talk" about it.

____ 23. I often have a hard time saying "No."*

____ 24. I tend to bottle up emotions rather than make a scene.*

____ 25. I complain about poor service in a restaurant or elsewhere.

____ 26. When I am given a compliment, I sometimes just don't know what to say.*

____ 27. If a couple near me in a theater or at a lecture were conversing rather loudly, I would ask them to be quiet.

____ 28. Anyone attempting to push ahead of me in a line is in for a good battle.

____ 29. I am quick to express an opinion.

____ 30. There are times when I just can't say anything.*

Total score is obtained by adding numerical responses to each item, after changing signs of reversed items (those followed by an asterisk). The higher the number, the greater the level of assertiveness.

*Spencer A. Rathus, "A 30-Item Schedule for Assessing Assertive Behavior," in *Behavior Therapy* 4 (1973): 398–406. Used by permission of the author.

Self-Esteem Exercise

1. The good feelings of esteem come from a variety of places—from other people, from things you do, from special times and places, such as those listed below. From what other sources might people receive reinforcement of their self-esteem? Add them to the list.

- your mother

- your father

- a grandparent

- a brother or a sister

- a teacher

- an adult at church

- God

- an accomplishment at school

- some special words of praise

- a good friend

- a celebration, such as a birthday or Christmas

- something you did for someone else

- a special skill you have

- a certain thing about your personality

- something brave you did

- a special place you like to be

- your own feelings about yourself

- _____

- _____

- _____

2. Circle the items listed above that are sources of self-esteem for you. Then, beside each one you have circled, explain exactly how it is a source of esteem.

3. Self-esteem happens when we realize:

We were created by God.
God believes we are one of God's good creations.
Others love and affirm us.
All of us make mistakes, but when we recognize and admit our mistakes, God is with us, forgiving us, no matter what we have done.

Marriage

1. The important things to know about marriage are . . .

a.

b.

c.

2. The good points I see in marriage are . . .

a.

b.

c.

3. The difficulties involved in marriage are . . .

a.

b.

c.

God Created Us for Life in Community

> Owe no one anything, except to love one another; for the one who loves another has fulfilled the law. The commandments, "You shall not commit adultery; You shall not murder; You shall not steal; You shall not covet"; and any other commandment, are summed up in this word, "Love your neighbor as yourself." Love does no wrong to a neighbor; therefore, love is the fulfilling of the law.
>
> (Rom. 13: 8–10)

> God made us for life in community.
>
> ("A Declaration of Faith,"
> ch. 2, line 61)

> The new life takes shape in a community in which men and women know that God loves them and accepts them in spite of what they are.
>
> (The Confession of 1967, 9.22)

God created us to be together. From the very beginning, God's purpose was for us to be together—with God and with one another.

One word to define this togetherness is "relationship." A *relationship* is how we describe the connection between two people. The connection might be the result of birth: We have particular relationships with our parents and brothers and sisters. The connection might be the result of feelings and commitments: We have particular relationships with acquaintances, friends, and partners. God creates us with a basic need to form relationships with others. Our relationships are answers to the loneliness we feel, and they give our lives meaning.

Another word to define this togetherness that God has in mind for us is "community." A *community* is a group of people who join together with one another. You are a part of many communities—your neighborhood, your town or city, your own particular group of friends, your church. God created us to be together in communities, which can give meaning and identity to our lives.

The very heart of what it means to be in the image of God is to be in community—joined with God and with one another. When we gather in God's name, we are God's community, the church, in the world. In the church we learn to be who God created us to be. We find our true identity with God and one another in the church.

Session 4

Sexual Identity

Purpose: In this session we explore gender identity (what it means to be male or female and how we express being male or female). We also look at what it means to be homosexual in our society. The session closes with a theological reflection, "Our Church Is a Varied Community," that looks at the variety of ways people live out relationships.

Time: Two hours (two hours and forty-five minutes if you do all the activities)

Materials Needed

- VCR and television monitor
- Newsprint
- Felt-tipped markers
- Masking tape
- Video: "On Being Gay: A Conversation with Brian McNaught" (optional)

Activities

"I'm Glad I Am . . . / If I Were . . . "	40 minutes
Homosexuality	40 minutes
Video: "On Being Gay" (optional)	45 minutes
The Church Is a Varied Community	40 minutes

Procedures

"I'm Glad I Am . . . / If I Were . . . "* (40 minutes)

Divide the group into several small groups of the same sex. Ask each group to come up with as many endings as they can for the following sentences:

Male groups: "I'm glad I'm a man because . . . "
Female groups: "I'm glad I'm a woman because . . ."

Give an example to help the groups get started. Have each small group record their responses on a sheet of newsprint.

After ten minutes, ask the groups to think of as many endings as they can for another sentence:

Male groups: "If I were a woman, I could . . . "
Female groups: "If I were man, I could . . . "

Have the groups record their responses to the second sentence on another sheet of newsprint in the same way as before. After ten minutes, discuss the following questions:

- Were any of the responses the same for both genders?
- Was it harder for males or for females to come up with reasons why they are glad of their gender?
- Was it harder for males or for females to state the advantages of being the opposite gender?

- Which of the advantages of being a man are real reasons and which are stereotyped reasons?
- Which of the advantages of being a woman are real reasons and which are stereotyped reasons?
- Is it possible to be a "man" and still have or do some of the things listed under "woman"?
- Can you think of a woman you know who has some of the traits listed under "man"?
- What is masculine? What is feminine? Are these terms different from the terms male and female? What does it mean to be "androgynous"?

Homosexuality (40 minutes)

Give the group the quiz on homosexuality found on page 32 in the *Older Youth Guide* and page 158 in this guide.

After the group has finished the quiz, read through the section on homosexuality and homophobia in the "Guide for the Presbyterian Church (U.S.A.)" on pages 13–15 in the *Older Youth Guide* and pages 20–22 in this guide. Have the young people answer the questions from "Beliefs about Homosexuality" found on page 34 in the *Older Youth Guide* and page 160 in this guide. Doing this activity helps young people translate the church's understanding of homosexuality into their own words. This is not a test. The last two questions are discussion questions. If questions are raised that you cannot answer, tell the young people that you do not know but will search for the correct answers and let them know the answers the next session. It would be especially helpful to discuss the last question. There is no right answer.

Briefly go over the answers to the quiz on homosexuality. Ask if anyone would change any answers now in light of the previous discussion.

Discuss with the young people the meaning of stereotypes. On a sheet of newsprint, list and discuss the stereotypes they have or have heard about people who are heterosexual, people who are homosexual, and people who are bisexual.

Discuss the following questions about stereotypes:

- Do you think these stereotypes are based on fact?
- Are the stereotypes positive or negative?
- Which orientations have more positive stereotypes?
- Which have more negative stereotypes?
- Why do you think this is?
- Where did you learn these stereotypes?
- Do you think they affect the way you view and feel about people of different sexual orientations? If so, how?

Have young people come forward to role play one or two of the following situations. After the role play, have the group discuss the situation and the responses of the actors.

Situation one: Two boys are good friends at school. Boy number one hears from other friends that boy number two is gay. He decides to ask boy number two if it is true. Act out the scene. Then discuss the following questions:

- How would you feel in each role?
- How would you feel about the question asked?
- What types of responses are there?
- How would you feel about other people talking about you?

Situation two: Two girls are good friends at school. Girl number one hears from other friends that girl number two is lesbian. She decides to ask girl number two if it is true. Act out the scene. Then discuss these questions:

- How was this situation different from the first?
- Were the feelings any different from the first?

Situation three: A girl and boy have been going together for three months. They have not been sexually involved on a level more intimate than hugging and kissing. The girl hears a rumor at school that her boyfriend is gay. She decides to talk to her boyfriend about it. Act out the scene. Then discuss the following:

*Used by permission from *Life Planning Education* (Washington, D.C.: Advocates for Youth, 1985.)

- What were the feelings the two people had?
- Is it easy for you to talk openly about sexual matters? Why or why not?

Situation four: A girl thinks she might be a lesbian. She needs to talk to someone. She decides she can trust her best friend. She goes to her to talk about it. Act out the scene. Then discuss these questions:

- What feelings did the two people have?
- How would the situation have been different if it were two boys instead of two girls?
- Would you remain friends if the situation happened to you?

Video: "On Being Gay" (optional) (45 minutes)

Planning Tip: This eighty-minute tape consists of two forty-minute segments: (1) introduction to homosexuality and guided fantasy: what it's like to be different; myths about homosexuals; and (2) growing up gay: a personal story; scriptural references to homosexuality; and being gay today.

Review the entire tape, select the portion of the tape you wish to use, and cue your VCR to begin there. Unless you have more than forty-five minutes for this activity, show just one of the following portions of the tape: (1) introduction and guided fantasy; (2) myths about homosexuals; (3) growing up gay; or (4) scriptural references to homosexuality. Any of these can be viewed and discussed in forty-five minutes.

Begin by introducing the concept of homosexuality as one sexual orientation, heterosexuality as another. Read the definition of each found on page 160 in this guide. Point out that we still don't know how or why people develop either sexual orientation, but it is generally believed to be due to something genetic as opposed to being learned. Explain that many people are confused about and/or uncomfortable with the topic of homosexuality, but since sexual orientation is an integral part of our sexual identity, this activity will address sexual orientation in an affirming way. Introduce Brian McNaught as a scholar, writer, speaker/lecturer who is Roman Catholic and gay.

Play the portion of the videotape you have chosen to use. Afterward, ask members of the group to do the following:

On a piece of paper, write a brief letter to an imaginary son or daughter of your own. Begin the letter in the following manner:

Dear _____

Today I met a man named Brian. One of the things I learned about him is that he is gay. More important, if you could meet him you would learn

_____
_____
_____
_____
_____

Finish the letter as if you were writing to your child.

Then discuss questions such as these:

- What new information did you learn from the tape?
- Did you experience any new feelings while watching the tape?

The Church Is a Varied Community (40 minutes)

Ask the participants to read "Our Church Is a Varied Community" (p. 35 in the *Older Youth Guide*; p. 161 in this guide).

Put up signs along a wall that say "strongly agree," "agree," "no opinion," "disagree," and "strongly disagree." Choose ten statements from the list below or make up ten of your own. Read the first statement. Ask the young people to situate themselves under the sign that represents their opinion. Discuss why they chose them. Before reading the next statement, have the group return to the middle. Continue the process until you have discussed ten of the statements.

1. The church believes there are a variety of ways in which people may choose to live out their relationships.
2. Just about everybody should be married by the time they are thirty.
3. Remaining single is a good choice for some people.
4. Total sexual intimacy should be reserved for marriage.

5. People in loving relationships who choose not to be married should also choose not to engage in sexual activity.

6. The most important consideration in choosing whether or not to marry is whether or not you are in love with the other person.

7. Marriage is intended for two people of the opposite sex.

8. I believe Jesus was a sexual being.

9. Marriage is a lifelong commitment.

10. A wedding should take place in a church.

11. Having children makes a marriage better.

12. A woman should be a virgin before marriage.

13. A man should be a virgin before marriage.

14. Men should have as much experience with sex before marriage as possible.

15. I believe that homosexuality can be a perfectly legitimate lifestyle.

16. It would be all right with me if I were homosexual.

17. Living together without marriage might be a good lifestyle choice for some people.

18. Living together without marriage is an option I would consider.

19. I believe sex and nudity in a movie can be appropriate.

20. I believe sex and nudity on TV can be appropriate.

21. I believe that extramarital sex could be morally all right.

22. If I were with a group of friends who wanted to go skinny-dipping, I would join in.

23. Masturbation is a good, healthy sexual outlet.

24. Masturbation is all right for me.

25. Sexual intercourse with another person could be all right, even if you are not in love with that person.

26. Sexual intercourse is best if you are in love with the other person.

Close the session with prayer.

Planning Note: Ask the young people to fill in the "Family History" and "Personal History" forms on pages 42 and 43–44 in the *Older Youth Guide* and bring them with them to the next session.

Homosexuality Quiz

Directions: Answer each statement True (T), False (F), or do not know (DK).

1. _____ Homosexuality is feeling attracted to or turned on mostly by members of one's own sex.

2. _____ We know homosexuality is caused by an imbalance of hormones.

3. _____ Homosexuals are born that way.

4. _____ More males than females are homosexual.

5. _____ You can easily tell homosexuals by the way they dress or act.

6. _____ Most homosexuals are child molesters.

7. _____ Once a person has a homosexual experience, then he or she is a homosexual.

8. _____ Most churches see homosexual behavior as sinful.

9. _____ About one-third of all males engage in homosexual behavior at some point in their lives.

10. _____ Almost all people have homosexual feelings at one time or another, but they usually won't admit it.

11. _____ Women who are successful in their careers are often lesbians (a term for female homosexuals).

12. _____ Homosexuals are more creative than heterosexuals.

13. _____ A male can do things traditionally considered feminine and not be a homosexual.

14. _____ A female can do things traditionally considered masculine and not be a homosexual.

Homosexuality Quiz—Answer Key

1. Homosexuality is feeling attracted to or turned on mostly by members of one's own sex. **True.**

2. We know homosexuality is caused by an imbalance of hormones. **False.**

3. Homosexuals are born that way. **Do not know.**

4. More males than females are homosexual. **True.**

5. You can easily tell homosexuals by the way they dress or act. **False.**

6. Most homosexuals are child molesters. **False.**

7. Once a person has a homosexual experience, then he or she is a homosexual. **False.**

8. Most churches see homosexual behavior as sinful. **True.**

9. About one-third of all males engage in homosexual behavior at some point in their lives. **True.**

10. Almost all people have homosexual feelings at one time or another, but they usually won't admit it. **True.**

11. Women who are successful in their careers are often lesbians (a term for female homosexuals). **False.**

12. Homosexuals are more creative than heterosexuals. **False.**

13. A male can do things traditionally considered feminine and not be a homosexual. **True.**

14. A female can do things traditionally considered masculine and not be a homosexual. **True.**

Beliefs about Homosexuality

1.   What do people believe the causes of homosexuality might be?

2.   What does it mean to say that "homosexuality is a sin"?

3.   What does our church say about the relationship between membership in the church and being homosexual?

4.   What does our church say about the relationship between ordination and being homosexual?

5.   What is homophobia?

6.   What additional information would help you better understand homosexuality?

7.   How would you express your feelings about those who are homosexuals?

Definitions

Usually, people are attracted to someone of the opposite gender—males to females, and females to males. We don't know why. It's the way God created them. It's just a part of who they are deep inside. A word used to describe people who are sexually attracted to people of the opposite gender is *heterosexual.*

Some people are sexually attracted to people of the same gender—males to males, and females to females. We don't know why. Most of the people who are this way think it's because God created them this way. A word used to describe people who are sexually attracted to people of the same gender is *homosexual.*

Our Church Is a Varied Community

For just as the body is one and has many members, and all the members of the body, though many, are one body, so it is with Christ. For in the one Spirit we were all baptized into one body—Jews or Greeks, slaves or free—and we were all made to drink of one Spirit. . . . Now you are the body of Christ and individually members of it.

(1 Cor. 12:12–13; 27)

There is no longer Jew or Greek, there is no longer slave or free, there is no longer male and female; for all of you are one in Christ Jesus.

(Gal. 3:28)

The young need to see in the church role models of both sexes who communicate by life, even more than by words, the goodness of our femaleness and maleness and the equal opportunity of both for service, responsibility, and authority in the life of the church. They need to see the varied responsible ways in which one can live out one's maleness and femaleness and be helped to affirm the goodness of their own sexuality.

("The Nature and Purpose of Human Sexuality," lines 469–475)

The many ways in which people choose to live out their relationships include casual acquaintances, friendships, and marriage. In all our relationships we are to relate to one another lovingly and responsibly.

Some people remain single all their lives. They have friendships and close loving relationships without necessarily having sexual intercourse. Sometimes people are widowed or divorced and must renew friendships and other relationships as a single person.

Marriage is a covenant of love and responsibility in which a couple makes a commitment of faithfulness. Sexual intercourse is the ultimate expression of this mutual and lasting covenant. Some people choose to become parents, making commitments to love, protect, and support their children.

The ways we live out our relationships are influenced by many factors: our families, our friends, our early sexual experiences, and the sex education we receive. Other factors that influence us are the particular economic, racial, and ethnic group to which we belong and the community and neighborhood in which we live. Sometimes we live out our relationships in sexist ways—stereotyping males and females in particular ways and assigning them superior or inferior status simply because they are males or females. Sometimes we live out our relationships in homophobic ways—stereotyping homosexual men and women because of their sexual orientation. Sometimes we live out our relationships in racist ways—stereotyping particular groups of people simply because of their race. In our own church, we have held and sometimes still hold sexist, homophobic, and racist views. To avoid these views, we must embrace the diversity within our community and strive toward a good, positive, and healthy view of our sexuality as God has intended.

Whether we are children, youth, or adults; single, divorced, married, or widowed; male or female; heterosexual or homosexual; and whatever our economic status or racial/ethnic heritage, we are all loved by a God who is faithful and just.

Session 5

Good Health Habits

Purpose: This session is designed to help young people become aware of their responsibility to God for their good health. The session begins with a short quiz on anatomy. Health history forms are used to help young people look at their general health. Male and female reproductive tract examinations are explained. The session ends with the Myth Information game, which helps dispel common reproductive health myths.

Time: Two hours and twenty minutes ("Family History" and "Personal History" forms should be completed before this session begins. For instance, retreat participants should do this with their parents before the retreat and bring the forms to the retreat with them. Suggest that the forms be filled in in pencil so they can be changed easily if necessary.)

Materials Needed

- *Older Youth Guide*
- Box or paper bag
- Newsprint
- Felt-tipped markers
- Manila folders

Activities:

Anatomy and Physiology Review   20 minutes
General Health   30 minutes
Reproductive Health   60 minutes
Myth Information Game   30 minutes

Procedures

Note: Before this session begins, make a copy of the "Myth or Fact" sheet. Cut the statements on the copy into strips and put them in a container.

Teenagers need to realize that the responsibility for their health and well-being is shifting from their parents to themselves. Therefore, getting accurate health information is important.

Some of the information presented here is very clinical. If possible, invite a practitioner (an obstetrician, a gynecologist, a family practice doctor, a nurse practitioner, or a family planning specialist) to present this material to your group. Ask the person to bring a speculum, pap stick, gonorrhea culture kit, and so on to show young people.

Some people may prefer to divide into groups of the same sex to discuss examinations of their respective reproductive tracts. However, being informed about the examinations of the opposite sex is important; therefore, it is better not to divide the group.

Anatomy and Physiology Review
(20 minutes)

Have the group work on the male and female anatomy pages in their guides (pp. 36–38 in *Older Youth Guide*). Allow them eight to ten minutes to complete the pages. Review the correct answers and terminology. Ask them to put the correct answers on their papers.

General Health (30 minutes)

A healthy person possesses physical, emotional, spiritual, and sexual health. These four areas are interdependent, and a balance in all areas is desirable. Problems with a person's emotional health can lead to poor spiritual health just as being physically ill can alter a person's sexual health. If a person seeks physical health through proper nutrition and exercise, but neglects emotional health, spiritual health, or sexual health, he or she is not considered healthy as a whole person.

Brainstorming

Brainstorm for five minutes about what the young people think are the leading causes of death for their age group in the United States. Have in mind the five categories: (1) accidents, (2) homicide, (3) suicide, (4) cancer, and (5) other. As the young people respond, write down their answers exactly as they give them but try to place them in one of the five categories. Label the categories at the end of the brainstorming activity.

Because the belief that "nothing will happen to me" is very common among teenagers, to openly confront the concept that they, too, are mortal beings is important. Help them also see that deaths of people in their age group are largely preventable.

Prevention

The leading causes of death for the age group 15 to 24 in the United States are as previously listed in rank order: (1) accidents, (2) homicide, (3) suicide, and (4) cancer. Accidents are the leading cause of death for teenagers. And 50 percent of all teenage deaths resulting from motor vehicle accidents are associated with alcohol use. When combined with other factors, such as not having driver's education, not using seat belts, and speeding, the risk of death is greater. Other accidents such as sports injury, accidental drug overdose, and gun accidents also fall under this category.

Briefly discuss how all four of these leading causes of death in their age group can be prevented. List means of prevention such as the following:

- Driver's education
- Seat belt use
- Not drinking and driving or not riding with one who is drinking and driving
- Sports safety
- Firearms safety
- Being familiar with the signs and symptoms of depression and reporting or taking seriously any threat of suicide
- Not getting involved with gang activity
- Routine physical examinations
- Breast self-exams (BSE)
- Testicular self-exams (TSE)
- Not smoking
- Not using recreational drugs
- Using alcohol in moderation, if at all.

Family and Personal Health Histories

Each person should be aware of his or her own health needs and risks. This is best determined by knowing one's family health history and personal health history.

The family history and personal history forms (see pp. 172 and 173–174 in this guide) are written in a way to help a teenager who may be thinking and writing about his or her health for the first time. Some of the information must be obtained from family members. Each person's form is confidential. Give each participant a manila folder and ask him or her to begin a self-health file with these forms and keep them as part of his or her permanent health record. This information can be valuable later in life.

Discuss questions such as these:

- What did you find out about your family health history that you did not know before?
- Did you see any patterns in your family health history that are important for your own health?
- How healthy are you? Rate yourself from 1 to 5 (5 is top).
- What is one health habit you want to change now?

Reproductive Health (60 minutes)

Pretest

Have each person take the pretest on page 47 in the *Older Youth Guide*. Allow only a brief time for completion so that the young people will give their initial responses; then ask them to share their answers and reasons for selecting those answers. The correct responses and discussion points are listed below.

Key to Pretest and Discussion

1.   A Pap smear test will detect cancer of the cervix. **True**

Discussion: The cervix is the end of the uterus and can be seen during the pelvic exam. A small wooden stick is used to obtain a sample of cells to be examined under a microscope to detect if cancer cells are present. A Pap smear is recommended for females eighteen years old and older and for those who become sexually active prior to age eighteen.

2.   There is no way to know if a male has cancer of the testicle. **False**

Discussion: A testicular self-exam (TSE) done once a month can reveal changes in the testicle. If a lump or nodule is felt instead of the usual smooth contour, see a doctor right away.

3.   An X ray of the breasts should be done once a year after age eighteen. **False**

Discussion: Mammography (X ray of the breasts) is not recommended until age 40 unless you are at very high risk (i.e., mother or sister has had breast cancer).

4.   Girls who use tampons probably have had sexual intercourse. **False**

Discussion: A virgin (someone who has never had sexual intercourse) may use tampons. A tampon is inserted in the same opening through which menstrual fluids leave the body.

5.   Some very absorbent tampons can be used through the night while you sleep. **False**

Discussion: Tampons should be changed every three hours. Since this cannot be done without disturbing sleep, it is recommended that sanitary pads be used at night. This will help prevent toxic shock syndrome (TSS) from tampon use. The incidence of menstruating girls and women who get TSS is very small (approximately 9 to 14 out of 100,000).

6.   A good health habit is to douche once a week. **False**

Discussion: The vagina is self-cleansing (rids itself of old menstrual blood). A douche is not necessary after a menstrual period, after sexual relations, or on any routine basis. The vagina has a natural pH balance that prevents infection. Douches can alter this balance and leave the vagina dry. Douches with fragrances can cause allergic reactions. Douching is not necessary unless a medicated douche is prescribed by a doctor. Most important, douching after sexual intercourse is not an effective form of birth control.

7.   Females are much more likely to get an infection in the urinary tract than males. **True**

Discussion: The urethra (opening for urination) on the female is very close to the vagina and rectum. Therefore, bacteria can enter the urethra easily. Also, the female urethra is shorter than the male urethra so it is a much shorter trip for bacteria to get to the bladder and set up an infection. The following are ways to prevent urinary tract infections:

- After urination or defecation wipe away from the vaginal area (where the urethra is); wipe from front to back.
- Keep the perineum clean and dry.
- Drink a lot of water.
- Do not use any unprescribed creams or powders in the perineal or vaginal area.

8.   A female is most likely to get pregnant about two weeks before her next menstrual period. (When the cycle is twenty-eight days, this is usually about the fourteenth day, counting the first day of menstruation as the first day of the cycle.) **True**

Discussion: Many teenagers have irregular menstrual cycles, and the time of ovulation (when they are most likely to get pregnant) is very unpredictable. An egg is usually released in the middle of the cycle but may be released at other times. Although the ovum (egg) usually lives only about one or two days, the sperm commonly lives at least three days, and sometimes longer. Therefore, there are many days each month when intercourse may result in pregnancy.

9.   A discharge of fluid from the urethra at the end of the penis could be a sign of a urinary infection or a venereal disease. **True**

Discussion: Any discharge of fluid from the male urethra (the tube that carries urine and semen out of the body) is always significant and infection is likely. A male who experiences this should see a urologist.

10.   A female's genital area has a bad odor, especially when she is on her period. **False**

Discussion: Some odor is noted by the female when she is on her period, but usually it is not noticed unless she is changing a tampon or sanitary pad. Menstrual blood does have an odor when exposed to the warmth of the body and air. Others cannot smell when a woman is on her period. The best way to control the odor is to bathe or shower with soap and water and to change tampons and sanitary pads frequently. Perfumed sprays and deodorant pads may cause an allergic reaction, are more expensive, and are not necessary.

Self-Examination

Discuss the examination of the reproductive tract for the male and female. Use the sections "The Exam for the Female Reproductive Tract" and "The Exam for the Male Reproductive Tract" (pp. 48–49 in the *Older Youth Guide*), and highlight the general procedures used in each exam.

Ask everyone to turn to "Testicular Self-exam Instructions" and "Breast Self-Exam Instructions" found on pages 51 and 52 in the *Older Youth Guide*. Review the procedure as outlined and have the females sign the BSE form and keep it for their health file and the males sign the TSE form and keep it for their health file.

Myth Information Game (30 minutes)

Note: You will need to make a copy of the questions found on page 183 of this guide. Cut up the copy and put the strips in a bag or other container before this part of the session begins.

Begin by talking with youth about how messages about sex can be found in so many aspects of our society—TV, movies, music, magazines, the Internet. But often there is little correct information attached to these messages. Myths, rumors, and superstitions are passed off as fact. This game will help dispel some of the myths related to sexuality.

Divide the group into two teams and have them sit on opposite sides of the room. The first player on team A should choose a statement from the bag and, with the help of teammates, answer whether it is a fact or myth. If they are right, give them a point. Then team B does the same, getting a point if they are right. Continue until all the statements have been discussed Allow time for giving additional information as needed.

Reassure the group that most people believe some myths, but that open-minded people are willing to admit it when they find they have been misinformed.

Close with prayer.

Anatomy Drawing (Male)

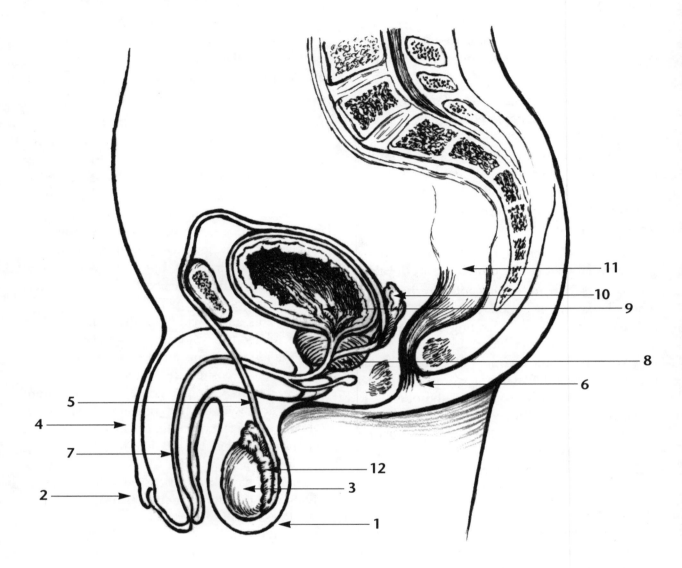

Scrotum   Penis   Anus
Vas deferens   Prostate gland   Glans penis
Testis   Urethra   Epididymis
Bladder   Rectum   Seminal vesicle

1. _____   7. _____
2. _____   8. _____
3. _____   9. _____
4. _____   10. _____
5. _____   11. _____
6. _____   12. _____

Anatomy Drawing (Female-Internal)

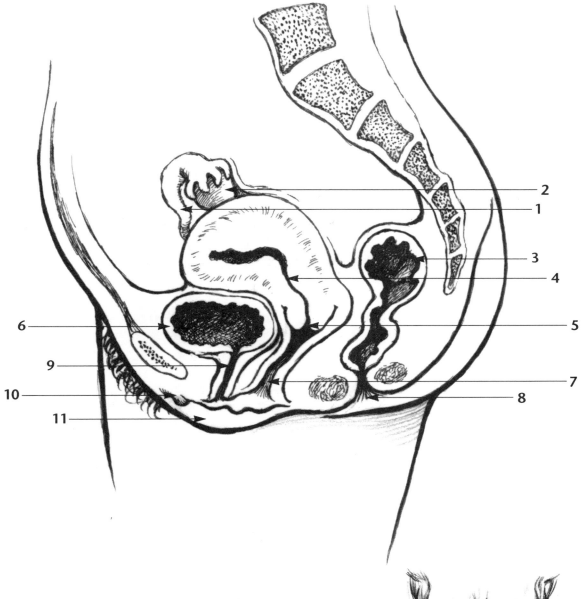

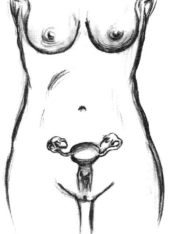

Urethra	Vagina	Anus
Bladder	Fallopian tube	Rectum
Labia	Uterus (womb)	Clitoris
Cervix	Ovary	

1. _____   7. _____
2. _____   8. _____
3. _____   9. _____
4. _____   10. _____
5. _____   11. _____
6. _____

Anatomy Drawing (Female-External)

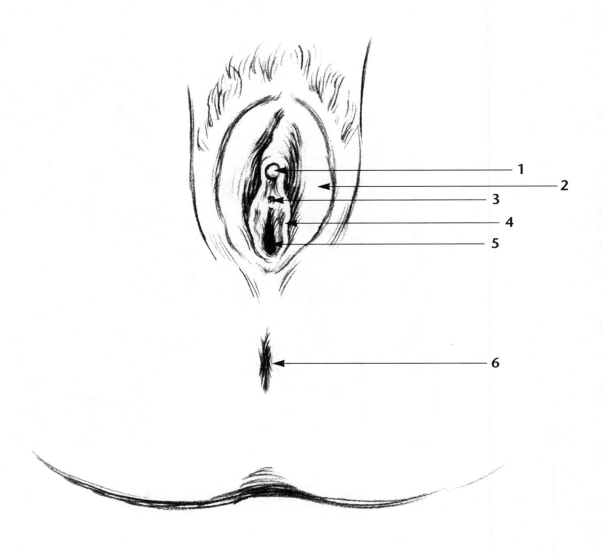

Labia minora (inner lips)   Anus (opening)   Labia majora (outer lips)
Urethra (opening)   Clitoris   Vagina (opening)

1. _____   4. _____
2. _____   5. _____
3. _____   6. _____

Anatomy Drawings—Answer Key

Male

1. Scrotum
2. Glans penis
3. Testis
4. Penis
5. Vas deferens
6. Anus
7. Urethra
8. Prostate gland
9. Bladder
10. Seminal vesicle
11. Rectum
12. Epididymis

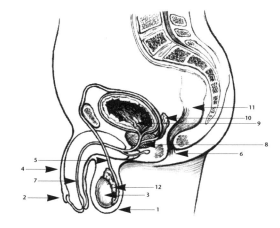

Female (Internal)

1. Fallopian tube
2. Ovary
3. Rectum
4. Uterus (womb)
5. Cervix
6. Bladder
7. Vagina
8. Anus
9. Urethra
10. Clitoris
11. Labia

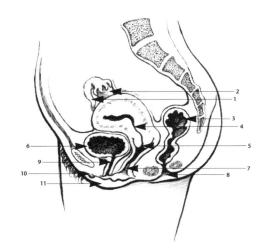

Female (External)

1. Clitoris
2. Labia majora (outer lips)
3. Urethra (opening)
4. Labia minora (inner lips)
5. Vagina (opening)
6. Anus (opening)

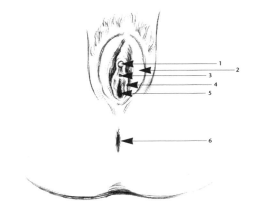

Male Anatomy and Physiology

External Parts and Functions

Penis: The male organ for sexual intercourse.

Circumcision: The removal of the foreskin that covers the head (glans) of the penis; usually done in the first two days of life; does not affect sexual functioning. Physicians are currently debating the advantages and disadvantages of circumcision. The American Academy of Pediatricians recommends that the decision whether to circumcise be made by the parents in consultation with their pediatrician.

Erection: The process by which the penis fills with blood and becomes hard in response to thoughts, fantasies, temperature, touch, or sexual stimulation.

Scrotum: The pouch located behind the penis that contains the testicles; provides protection to the testicles; controls temperature necessary for sperm production and survival.

Testes: Two round glands that descend into the scrotum following birth; produce and store sperm starting in puberty, and produce male sex hormone, testosterone.

Anus: The opening for the expulsion of feces (not a part of the reproductive system).

Internal Parts and Functions

Vas deferens (sperm tube): Passageway for sperm leading from each testicle and joining with the urethra.

Seminal vesicles: Two saclike structures lying behind the bladder; they secrete a thick fluid that forms part of the semen.

Prostate gland: A gland located in the male pelvis; secretes a thick, milky fluid that forms part of the semen.

Cowper's glands: Two small glands that secrete fluid released from the penis soon after erection; may contain sperm; neutralize the acid in the urethra.

Urethra: The tube through which urine passes from the bladder to the outside of the body; closed to urine during ejaculation.

Sperm: The male sex cells; too small to be seen without a microscope; shaped like tadpoles; movement aided by lashing their tails; production

begins usually between age 12 to 14; total number per ejaculation is 200 to 500 million; may survive in the fallopian tubes seven days but rarely cause fertilization after seventy-two hours.

Ejaculation: The release of semen from the penis.

Semen: The sperm-containing fluid that passes out of the penis at the time of ejaculation; produced and stored in the seminal vesicles and prostate gland; clear color in young males due to low sperm count; whitish color develops as sperm count increases. Regardless of the color of their semen, males are still capable of impregnating females.

Nocturnal emissions (wet dreams): Erection of the penis and subsequent ejaculation during sleep; related to the individual's level of sexual awareness and interest, usually triggered by sexual dreams and fantasies. Occurs most frequently in males who do not engage in masturbation or sexual intercourse.

Female Anatomy and Physiology

External Parts and Functions

Labia majora and labia minora: Outer and inner folds of skin and fatty tissue on either side of the vagina; provide protection to the clitoris and the urethral and vaginal openings; referred to as vaginal lips.

Clitoris: A highly sensitive structure located above the urethral opening at the point where the inner labia (lips) meet; function is for sexual stimulation for the female.

Urethral opening: A small opening above the vagina for the passage of urine.

Vaginal opening: Located between the urethral opening and the anus; often covered by a thin membrane (hymen) prior to first experience of intercourse; opening in which penis is placed during sexual intercourse; outlet for the menstrual flow.

Anus: The opening for the expulsion of feces (not a part of the reproductive system).

Internal Parts and Functions

Pelvic region: The part of the body located between the waist and the thighs.

Bladder: A saclike structure in the pelvic region; responsible for storing urine (not a part of the reproductive system).

Urethra: A tube through which urine passes from the bladder to the outside of the body (not a part of the reproductive system).

Vagina: Passageway extending from the uterus to the outside of the body; canal through which a baby passes during delivery; passageway for the menstrual flow to the outside of the body; place where intercourse occurs. Capable of expanding during intercourse and childbirth. Lubricates during sexual arousal; females often experience vaginal lubrication and possibly orgasm during sleep.

Cervix: The mouth or opening into the uterus; protrudes into the uppermost part of the vagina.

Uterus: A pear-shaped, muscular organ located in the pelvic region; beginning at puberty, the lining sheds periodically (usually monthly) during menstruation; baby develops in the uterus during pregnancy.

Fallopian tubes: Passageway for the egg from the ovary to the uterus; place where fertilization or conception occurs.

Ovaries: Almond-shaped structures located in the female pelvic region; contain 300,000 to 500,000 egg cells at birth; produce female sex hormones, estrogen and progesterone; begin release of eggs, one each month, at time of puberty.

Ovum or egg: About the size of a pinhead; if not fertilized, dissolves and is absorbed. Usually one is released monthly; if more than one egg is released and fertilized, may result in twin or multiple births.

Menstruation

Function: Monthly shedding of the uterine lining which has formed in preparation for a fertilized egg.

Age of onset and termination: Varies from age 9 to 17, ends at menopause, about forty-five to fifty-five years of age.

Length of cycle: Varies, average is twenty-eight days. Intervals may be irregular in young girls.

Duration of flow: Varies, average is two to seven days. Amount of flow also varies. Some females experience cramps caused by uterine contractions.

Hygiene: May be necessary to bathe more frequently; use sanitary protection; change frequently.

Common myths: Males can tell when a female is having her menstrual period; bathing and washing one's hair is harmful while menstruating; males get venereal disease if they have intercourse at the time of partner's menstrual period; bathing causes menstrual cramps.

Reproductive Process

Ovulation: During ovulation, an ovary releases a mature egg that then becomes available for fertilization; occurs approximately fourteen days before the next menstrual period begins but is frequently irregular in young females. The first ovulation may or may not coincide with the first menstrual period; a female may begin to ovulate before, at the same time, or sometime after she first menstruates. Multiple ovulation may result in twin or multiple births if fertilization occurs.

Fertilization: The union of an egg with a sperm in the fallopian tube. Sperm are capable of fertilization three to seven days after intercourse.

Family History

Instructions:

1. Put an "A" for every family member who is alive and a "D" for each family member who is deceased. Under "Explanations" give cause of death for deceased; type of cancer, type of allergy, and so on.

2. Put a check for each person listed if they have had or now have any of the illnesses listed.

	Mother	Father	Sister(s)			Brother(s)			Maternal Grand-mother	Maternal Grand-father	Paternal Grand-mother	Paternal Grand-father	Explanations
A=Alive													
D=Deceased													
Allergies													
Asthma													
High Blood Pressure													
Stroke													
Heart Attack/Disease													
Glaucoma													
Cancer													
Diabetes													
HIV/AIDS													
Kidney Disease													
Epilepsy													
Obesity													
Tuberculosis													
Arthritis													
Gout													
Jaundice (yellow skin)													
Migraine Headache													
Sickle Cell Anemia													
Cystic Fibrosis													
Hemophilia													
Depression													
Manic-Depressive Disorder													
Alcoholism													
Suicide													
Other													

If you don't know all the answers, keep this form and ask your family members. Update this as changes occur, and keep this as part of your permanent health file.

Note: This form may be duplicated to hand out to parents.

Personal History

Instructions: Answer all questions as completely as possible. Examples are given for guidance.

Name _____ Age _____ Sex _____

List any medical problems you have had in the past (e.g., mononucleosis, hepatitis, diabetes, asthma, etc.). Give the date.

Were you ever in the hospital to be treated for any of these medical problems? List the problem and give the date (e.g., in the hospital with pneumonia in 1995):

List surgery you have had and give the date (e.g., appendix removed, 1994):

List any injuries or emergency room treatment you have had. Give the dates (e.g., broken left wrist, 1992):

List medications, foods, chemicals you are allergic to (e.g., penicillin, shellfish):

List all immunizations you have had to date. (You will need your "baby shots" record. At age 12 to 14, a booster for polio (TOPV) should be given; tetanus shots should be up to date.)

List dates of dental checkups (should be every six to twelve months):

Last date of last complete physical exam. (A complete exam is recommended at age 13, including blood test for cholesterol, complete blood count, urinalysis, and a tuberculosis (TB) skin test.)

Females: Last pelvic exam and Pap smear _____
         Age of first menstrual period _____
         Date of last menstrual period _____
         Did your mother take DES during pregnancy? Yes ____ No ____ (risk for cervical cancer)
         Do you do a breast self-exam once a month? Yes ____ No ____

Males: Did your mother take DES or birth control pills during pregnancy or were you treated for undescended testicles as a child? Yes ____ No ____ (risk for a tumor of the testicle)

         Do you do a testicular self-exam once a month? Yes ____ No ____

What is your blood type? _____
Childhood diseases you have had (e.g., chicken pox, measles, German measles, mumps, etc.):

_____

_____

_____

Evaluate Your Habits

Instructions: Check the box that applies.

	Frequently	Occasionally	Never
Exercise			
Sleep six to eight hours; feel rested after sleeping			
Eat nutritious meals			
Have a couple of good, close friends			
Have at least one person to confide in			
Feel unusually sad			
Feel anxious or nervous			
Use over-the-counter drugs (OTC) (e.g., aspirin, sinus medication, vitamins, diet pills, etc.)			
Use prescribed medications (e.g., antibiotics, allergy medications, insulin, birth control pills)			
Use alcohol			
Use tobacco/cigarettes			
Use illegal drugs (marijuana, cocaine, heroin, etc.)			
Use caffeine (coffee, tea, colas)			

Note: This form may be duplicated to hand out to parents.

Past and Present: Review of Systems

Instructions: Go through this list carefully and note any problems you have ever had or still have that pertain to the systems listed. (Again, examples are given as a guide.)

System	Examples	Your Response
Skin	Frequent sunburns, change in color or size of mole (increased risk for skin cancer)	
Head	Concussion, knocked unconscious, sinus infection	
Neck	Swollen glands, thyroid gland enlarged	
Throat	Tonsillitis, strep throat	
Mouth	Ulcers, sores	
Teeth	Cavities, gum disease	
Eyes	Poor vision corrected with glasses or contact lenses	
Ears	Hard of hearing, ear infections	
Nose	Broken nose, nose bleeds	
Breasts	Lump in breast, pain, infection	
Axilla (armpit)	Lump, rash	
Chest/Lungs	Bronchitis, pneumonia	
Heart	Pericarditis, pain, rheumatic heart disease	
Blood vessels	Blood clot, varicose veins	
Abdomen/Stomach	Ulcer, constipation	
Intestines	Diarrhea	
Muscles	Injury, pain	
Urinary Tract/Bladder/Kidney	Infection, blood in urine	
Uterus/Fallopian Tubes/Ovaries	Infection, cyst	
Vagina	Infection	
Penis, Testicles	Lump in testicle, rash, or irritation	
Anus	Hemorrhoids, painful defecation	

Menstrual Calendar

Instructions: Put an "X" on the day your period began and an "X" for each day that you were menstruating. *Example:* Menstruation began on January 11 and ended on January 15.

Month	1	2	3	4	5	6	7	8	9	10	11	12	13	14	15	16	17	18	19	20	21	22	23	24	25	26	27	28	29	30	31
January											x	x	x	x	x																
February																															
March																															
April																															
May																															
June																															
July																															
August																															
September																															
October																															
November																															
December																															

Month	1	2	3	4	5	6	7	8	9	10	11	12	13	14	15	16	17	18	19	20	21	22	23	24	25	26	27	28	29	30	31
January																															
February																															
March																															
April																															
May																															
June																															
July																															
August																															
September																															
October																															
November																															
December																															

Pretest

Instructions: Working quickly, circle either "T" (true) or "F" (false) after each statement.

1. A Pap smear test will detect cancer of the cervix.   T   F

2. There is no way to know if a male has cancer of the testicle.   T   F

3. An X ray of the breasts (mammogram) should be done once a year after age 18.   T   F

4. Girls who use tampons probably have had sexual intercourse.   T   F

5. Some very absorbent tampons can be used through the night while you sleep.   T   F

6. A good health habit is to douche once a week.   T   F

7. Females are much more likely to get an infection in the urinary tract than males. T   F

8. A female is most likely to get pregnant about two weeks before her next menstrual period occurs T   F

9. A discharge of fluid from the urethra at the end of the penis could be a sign of a urinary infection or a venereal disease. T   F

10. A female's genital area has a bad odor, especially when she is on her period.   T   F

Exam for the
Female Reproductive Tract

The bones of the hip region are called the pelvis. The pelvic bones surround the female reproductive organs (pelvic organs), which is why the examination of the female organs is called a pelvic exam. It is also called a gynecological exam or a "female exam." The exam is routinely performed by a practitioner who has specialized in the female reproductive tract, such as an obstetrician/gynecologist (OB/GYN), a nurse practitioner, or a family planning practitioner.

A pelvic exam should be done once a year beginning at either age 18 or whenever sexual relations begin. That is, if a sixteen-year-old is having sexual relations, a pelvic exam should be done at age 16. Another example of when a pelvic exam should be done at an earlier age is if there is any abnormal bleeding from the vagina (other than during the menstrual period) or if there is a discharge of abnormal fluid from the vagina (fluid of unusual color or odor) that might indicate a vaginal infection.

Schedule the exam for a time when you expect that you will not be having a menstrual period. Expect some questions about your menstrual cycle, such as when your last period was. The way to answer this accurately is to give the date your last period began. You may want to keep this marked on a calendar so you will not have to guess.

If it is your first pelvic exam, it is wise to tell the practitioner. Usually, he or she will go a little slower and explain each step of the procedure to you. Also there are different-sized speculums, and you can request that a small (pediatric) speculum be used for your first exam.

Routine tests will be done, such as checking height, weight, and blood pressure; testing urine for sugar or protein; and testing blood for anemia. Expect that the thyroid gland in front of your neck will be felt as you swallow. The practitioner will listen to your heart and lungs with a stethoscope. A breast exam will be done as well as a review of how a breast-self exam should be done. (If you are unsure of the procedure, this is a good time to get clarification or ask questions.)

You will be asked to remove all your clothes but will be given a gown and a sheet for a drape to protect your modesty. Then you will be asked to lie down on an examining table and to put your legs on rests or your feet on stirrups. This enables the practitioner to see the perineum. The entire pelvic exam can be done in three to four minutes. There are four parts: (1) inspection of the area, (2) speculum exam, (3) bimanual exam, and (4) rectal exam. A chart is included on page 180 to explain to you what is being examined, how, and why.

1. *Inspection:* The practitioner touches the area around the perineum, separating the folds of skin around the vagina to detect any abnormalities.

2. *Speculum exam:* The instrument used to view the cervix and inside the vagina is called a speculum, a stainless steel instrument that is gently placed just inside the vagina and then moved inside and back toward the cervix. The speculum is then opened up enough to allow the practitioner to see the cervix while the Pap smear and culture are done. You can expect that it will be left in place about thirty to forty-five seconds. This may be slightly uncomfortable but should not be painful because the muscles around the vagina are very stretchable and the instrument is not sharp. A bright light is turned on and directed toward the vaginal area so the practitioner can see the cervix and walls of the vagina. A small wooden or plastic stick and/or cotton-tip applicator (like a Q-tip) is touched to the cervix to obtain a Pap smear (test for cancer of the cervix) and gonorrhea culture (test for venereal disease). Again, you will be able to feel that this is being done, but it is very quick and should not be painful. The speculum is removed. Many girls, after the first pelvic exam, make comments like "Is that all?" or "That wasn't that bad!" or "That was fast!"

3. *Bimanual exam:* This part of the exam can be a surprise to a female on her first visit for a pelvic exam and can cause unnecessary anxiety unless you know about it ahead of time and understand why it is being done. It takes about fifteen to thirty seconds. The practitioner will put some lubricant on a gloved hand and insert one or two fingers in the vagina and, at the same time, press down on the lower abdomen with the

other hand. Again, this need not be painful. This is the only way to examine the uterus, the fallopian tubes, and the ovaries. Since they cannot be seen with the speculum, these body parts must be felt (palpated) to determine if the size is normal and to ensure there are no growths or tumors. The uterus, for example, can be felt between the two fingers inside the vagina and the examining hand on the outside of the lower abdomen.

4. *Rectal exam:* A lubricated gloved finger is inserted in the rectum and rotated to palpate the back side of the uterus and the space between the vagina and the rectum. This procedure usually lasts about five to ten seconds.

Exam for the Male Reproductive Tract

The examination of the male reproductive tract should be part of a complete physical exam and can be done by a family doctor. However, if you are having any symptoms, you may need to see a urologist, a specialist for the male genito-urinary tract.

After routine tests (height, weight, blood pressure, etc.) are done, you will be asked to stand in front of the practitioner, who will be seated to inspect the penis and the scrotum. The left testicle will appear lower than the right.

First, the penis will be inspected. If uncircumcised, the foreskin of the penis should be able to be retracted (moved back) easily. At this time instructions will be given about how to retract the foreskin to clean it daily when bathing. The urethra will be inspected for drainage or any abnormalities. If there is discharge or an unusual fluid, a cotton-tip applicator will be used to do a gonorrhea culture.

Next, the testicle and epididymis (a group of microscopic tubes where sperm are stored) will be palpated between the thumb and first two fingers, and the spermatic cord will be identified. At this time instructions for testicular self-exam will be given. If there is any swelling or growth, a flashlight will be directed from behind the scrotum. This procedure, called a transillumination, will help delineate a solid mass (tumor) from a fluid mass (swelling). Each testicle will be examined and palpated separately.

To check for a hernia, the practitioner will insert a finger in the scrotal area above the testicle where there is loose scrotal skin and move it into the linguinal canal in the groin. If there is a hernia, a mass can be felt during coughing or straining. You will then be asked to cough or bear down (strain). Next, you will lie down on your side or stand up and bend over at the waist for a rectal exam. The prostate gland, which surrounds the male urethra, is near the urinary bladder. The gland itself projects into the rectum and is examined by doing a rectal exam, a procedure that lasts five to ten seconds. If there is swelling, infection, or a tumor, it can be detected during this procedure.

Examination of the Reproductive Tracts

Female

What is examined?	How?	Why?
Perineum Vaginal opening Urethra	Inspection	Inspect for redness, signs of irritation, sores, swelling, or nodules
Cervix Walls/Inside of vagina	Speculum	To detect vaginal infections; to inspect cervix and obtain Pap smear and gonorrhea culture
Uterus Fallopian tubes Ovaries	Bimanual	Palpate to detect swelling, abnormal growths, or unusual pain
Area behind uterus	Rectal	To detect tenderness or swelling in the area between the vagina and the rectum and the posterior (back) portion of the uterus; to detect pilonidal cyst or hemorrhoids

Male

What is examined?	How?	Why?
Penis Urethra	Inspection	If uncircumcised, foreskin should be able to be retracted; inspect for redness, signs of irritation, sores, swelling, or nodules
Testicles Epididymis	Inspection and Bimanual	Palpate for swelling, abnormal growths, or unusual pain
Prostate gland Anus	Rectal	To detect enlarged prostate, pain, or tenderness due to infection; to detect pilonidal cyst or hemorrhoids
Inguinal area (groin)	Palpation	To detect hernia

Testicular Self-Exam Instructions (TSE)

Purpose: Early identification of tumors of the testicle. (When diagnosed early, there is a very high cure rate.)

Who is at risk?

Young males (age 15 to 34) who have a previous history of undescended testicles or a mother who took DES or birth control pills during pregnancy.

Who should be involved in this self-screening program?

All males. This is a positive health habit to acquire as a teenager and continue throughout life.

When?

Once a month. Best done during or just after a shower or bath because warm water causes the testicles to descend further in the scrotum so they are easier to examine.

How?

Inspection: Look at testicles in mirror to detect swelling or unusual appearance. Left testicle will be lower than right.

Palpation: Hold the scrotum in the palm of the hand and use the thumb and fingers of both hands to palpate (feel).

- The testicle should feel somewhat rubbery with a smooth surface and free of lumps.
- The epididymis and spermatic cord are also located in the scrotum and should be felt for growths.
- Most tumors are located at the front or the sides of the scrotum.

  For more details and information contact your local American Cancer Society office. You can also call 1–800–4CANCER.

  I have read these instructions and understand that I should do a testicular self-exam once a month.

_____

(Signature)   *(Date)*

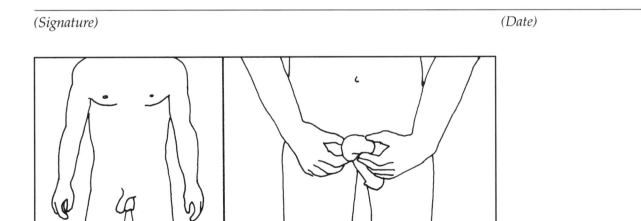

Used by permission of the American Cancer Society.

Breast Self-Exam Instructions (BSE)

Purpose: Early identification of tumors (or lumps) in the breast.

Who is at risk?

Any age woman but especially one who has a strong family history of breast cancer (grandmother, mother, or sister with breast cancer that occurred before menopause). One in ten women will develop breast cancer.

Who should be involved in this self-screening program?

All females. This is a positive health habit to acquire as a teenager and continue throughout life.

When?

Once a month. Best done a few days after the menstrual period because the breasts are less likely to be tender or have swelling at this time.

How?

Inspection: Look in the mirror at breasts with arms at your side, then with hands pressed against your hips, and then with both arms above your head. See if both breasts look the same (for one breast to be slightly larger than the other is normal), and check for unusual signs such as swelling or an indentation.

Palpation: Lie down flat on a bed. Put your left arm behind your head, which stretches the breast tissue out and allows for an easier examination, and use your right hand to examine the left breast. The breast feels generally "lumpy" because it is so glandular. A mass in the breast may feel like a marble, a pea, or a small rubber ball. Place the flat part of your fingers (not finger tips) over the nipple and areola area and palpate (feel) by pressing down in a slight circular motion from the nipple area out to edge of the breast.

When approaching the axilla be sure to palpate all the way to the edge of the breast tissue (the tail). Compress the nipple gently; there should not be any discharge from the breasts. Then switch. Put your right arm behind your head and use your left hand to palpate the right breast. If breasts are extremely large or pendulous, place one hand underneath the breast so the breast rests in the palm of the hand, and use the other hand to palpate.

For more details and information contact your local American Cancer Society office, or call 1-800-4CANCER.

I have read these instructions and understand that I should do a breast self-exam once a month.

_____

(Signature)   *(Date)*

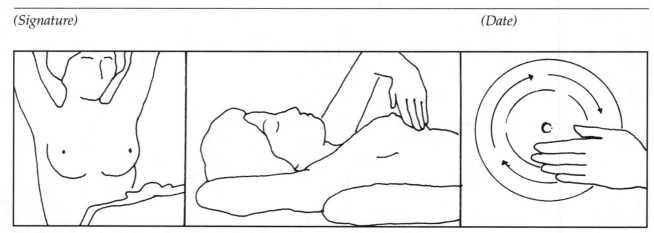

Used by permission of the American Cancer Society.

Myth or Fact?

1. Most teenagers have had sexual intercourse.

2. Once a female has had her first period, she can become pregnant.

3. Before a female has had her first period, she can become pregnant.

4. For a female to bathe or swim during her period is unhealthy.

5. The sperm cell from the male determines the gender (sex) of a baby.

6. A teenager does not need parental consent to get birth control from a clinic.

7. Females or males can have sexually transmitted infections (STIs) without having any symptoms.

8. If a female isn't menstruating by the time she is sixteen, there's something wrong with her.

9. A female can get pregnant if she has sex during her period.

10. Birth control pills cause cancer.

11. Only homosexuals and drug users are at risk for AIDS.

12. By age 18 one in four young women (24 percent) in the United States will have a pregnancy.

13. In order for sperm to be manufactured, the temperature in the testicles must be slightly cooler than body temperature, but not too cool.

14. Teenagers can be treated for sexually transmitted infections without their parent's permission.

15. Alcohol and marijuana are sexual stimulants.

16. There is one absolutely safe time between menstrual periods when a female cannot get pregnant.

17. All males have wet dreams.

18. When a rape occurs, the rapist is usually a stranger.

19. Once a male gets really excited and gets an erection, he has to have intercourse or he will be harmed.

20. A female can get pregnant even if a boy doesn't ejaculate or "come" inside her.

21. If a female misses her period, she is definitely pregnant.

22. You can't get HIV/AIDS from touching things that a person with HIV/AIDS has used.

23. A male can tell whether or not a female is a virgin.

24. Females who start having sexual intercourse before age 16 are more likely to get pregnant than those who wait until they are eighteen or nineteen to have sex.

25. Females are born with all their eggs in their ovaries.

26. Cancer of the testicle is more common among teenage males than among males over thirty-five.

27. You can get HIV/AIDS from deep (French) kissing.

Myth or Fact? Answer Key

1. Most teenagers have had sexual intercourse. **MYTH.** While it is true that about one-half of all teenagers have had sexual intercourse, it is also true that about one-half have not had intercourse while in high school.

2. Once a female has had her first period, she can become pregnant. **FACT.** When a female starts having menstrual periods, it means that her reproductive organs have begun working and that she can become pregnant. It doesn't mean, however, that she is necessarily ready to have a baby.

3. Before a female has had her first period, she can become pregnant. **FACT.** Because a woman's ovaries release an egg before the onset of her menstrual period, it is possible for a female to get pregnant before her first period.

4. For a female to bathe or swim during her period is unhealthy. **MYTH.** There is no reason that a woman should need to restrict any activity during her period.

5. The sperm cell from the male determines the gender (sex) of a baby. **FACT.** The father's sperm cell provides the genetic message that tells the developing fetus whether it will be male or female.

6. A teenager does not need parental consent to get birth control from a clinic. **MYTH** and **FACT.** Family planning clinics in most states don't have to tell anyone in order to provide birth control to teenagers. However, in some states parents do have to give their consent in order for teenagers to get birth control. Be sure you know what the law is in your state.

7. Females or males can have sexually transmitted infections (STIs) without having any symptoms. **FACT.** While some STIs may have quite recognizable symptoms, others may not. Gonorrhea and chlamydia, for example, typically display no symptoms in females and often are undetectable in males. To be examined by a doctor is important if a person thinks he or she may have an STI.

8. If a female isn't menstruating by the time she is sixteen, there's something wrong with her. **MYTH.** Absolutely not! For a female to begin having her period as early as age 8 or as late as age 16 or 17 is perfectly normal. If a female is sixteen and is worried because she hasn't started menstruating, she can always see a doctor just to be sure that everything is okay.

9. A female can get pregnant if she has sex during her period. **FACT.** For a female to get pregnant at any time during her menstrual cycle, including during her period, is possible.

10. Birth control pills cause cancer. **MYTH.** Though there can be side effects associated with using the pill, there is no conclusive evidence that the pill causes cancer.

11. Only homosexuals and drug users are at risk for AIDS. **MYTH.** While sex between two men and intravenous drug use remain the largest exposure categories, people infected through heterosexual contact comprise the fastest-growing segment of the AIDS population.

12. By age 18, one in four young women (24 percent) will have a pregnancy. **FACT.** Eighty-five percent of these pregnancies are unplanned. But this does not mean that females can't avoid pregnancy if they want to.

13. In order for sperm to be manufactured, the temperature in the testicles must be slightly cooler than the body temperature, but not too cool. **FACT.** Sperm cells can only be manufactured in the testicles when they are slightly cooler than body temperature. The scrotum acts like a temperature gauge and when a man is warm, allows his testicles to hang away from the body. When it is cold (cold air or cold water), the scrotum draws the testicles up closer to the body to keep them from being too cool.

14. Teenagers can be treated for sexually transmitted infections without their parent's permission. **FACT.** Laws vary, but most states do not require parental permission to provide treatment for STIs to teenagers.

15. Alcohol and marijuana are sexual stimulants. **MYTH.** These substances have exactly the opposite effect. Alcohol and marijuana may increase desire and reduce inhibitions (make you feel freer), but they decrease the flow of blood to the genital area and can decrease sexual performance by making it difficult to maintain an erection (for males) or to experience an orgasm.

16. There is one absolutely safe time between menstrual periods when a female cannot get pregnant. **MYTH.** Even a female who is using

techniques to monitor her menstrual cycle cannot be absolutely sure when she ovulates.

17. All males have wet dreams. **MYTH.** Many males do have wet dreams (when the penis spurts out semen while a male sleeps). But some males don't have wet dreams; those males who have regular ejaculations may not have wet dreams.

18. When a rape occurs, the rapist is usually a stranger. **MYTH.** A woman is four times more likely to be raped by someone she knows (an acquaintance, date, friend, or relative) than by a stranger. Many more unreported rapes are thought to be in this category. Fifty percent of all rapes occur in the victim's home.

19. Once a male gets really excited and gets an erection, he has to have intercourse or he will be harmed. **MYTH.** There is no harm in not acting on every sexual urge; semen cannot get backed up, and it is not necessary to ejaculate. Occasionally a male might feel some discomfort if he is sexually excited for an extended period of time. This will disappear when he is able to relax.

20. A female can get pregnant even if a male doesn't ejaculate or "come" inside her. **FACT.** Even if a male just ejaculates near a female's vagina, sperm can still find their way inside and make her pregnant.

21. If a female misses her period, she is definitely pregnant. **MYTH.** In fact, teenage girls often have irregular cycles and may even skip a month at times. However, if a female has had sexual intercourse and she misses a period, she could be pregnant. She should see a doctor right away.

22. You can't get HIV/AIDS from touching things that a person with HIV/AIDS has used. **FACT.** Doorknobs, bed linens, clothing, towels, toilets, telephones, showers, swimming pools, and eating utensils are all safe. They cannot transmit HIV. HIV is transmitted only through the exchange of blood, semen, breast milk, and vaginal fluids.

23. A male can tell whether or not a female is a virgin. **MYTH.** No one can tell by looking, and because the hymen can be stretched through physical activity, a male cannot tell during sexual intercourse whether or not a female has ever had intercourse before.

24. Females who start having sexual intercourse before age 16 are more likely to get pregnant than those who wait until they are eighteen or nineteen to have sex. **FACT.** Younger teenage girls are twice as likely to get pregnant because they don't usually use contraception. When young teenage girls have sex, they are also more likely to get sexually transmitted infections (STIs) and certain kinds of cancer.

25. Females are born with all their eggs in their ovaries. **FACT.** Baby girls are born with thousands of eggs in each ovary. They begin to ripen at puberty, and one egg leaves its ovary each month. This is one way females' bodies are different from males' bodies. Males' testicles begin making sperm cells only at puberty, not before.

26. Cancer of the testicle is more common among teenage males than among males over thirty-five. **FACT.** Most males don't know this, but cancer of the testicle is most common among young adult and teenage males. The first sign is a lump on a testicle; therefore, young males should check their testicles regularly for lumps and report anything suspicious to a parent or a doctor.

27. You can get HIV/AIDS from deep (French) kissing. **MYTH.** There have been no reported cases of HIV/AIDS due to kissing.

Session 6

Contraception

Purpose: This session provides practical and factual information about contraception. It stresses that abstinence is the church's teaching for teenagers. Read the guidelines for leaders carefully. You may want to invite a health professional to meet with your group during this session.

The session begins with a factual discussion of birth control methods, then moves to a discussion of who is at risk for getting pregnant. An exercise to help people understand the risks of getting pregnant and to help them begin to get comfortable talking about birth control is included. The session ends with a theological discussion of responsibility.

Time: Two hours (two hours and thirty minutes if you do all the activities)

Materials Needed

- Birth control kit
- *Older Youth Guide*
- 3" x 5" index cards
- Newsprint
- Felt-tipped markers
- Pens or pencils
- Magazine ads depicting couples in romantic situations
- Construction paper of several different colors
- Tape or glue
- 8½" x 11" paper
- 100 wrapped candies (yellow or other color) and 100 wrapped candies (white or other color). These must be exactly the same shape and size; they must feel alike but differ only in color.
- Two containers (shoe boxes or paper bags)

Activities

Presentation on Birth Control Methods	45 minutes
Who's at Risk? or Bringing Up Contraception	30 minutes
Pregnancy Game	15 minutes
Our Church Is a Community of Love and Responsibility	30 minutes

Guidelines for Teaching about Contraception

Planning Note: If you do not feel prepared to conduct this session, invite a health educator or family planning professional from your neighborhood health or family planning clinic. Be sure to request someone who is comfortable working with adolescents. Ask the person to spend about an hour reviewing the methods of birth control, giving special emphasis to the nonprescription methods (abstinence, condoms, foam, jelly, etc.). You may choose to divide the material and present two sessions on contraception if your group seems very interested and/or seems to need more of this information.

The topic of contraception or birth control is one of the most sensitive areas of any sexuality education curriculum. There are two specific questions that you as a church educator need to be aware of and prepared to deal with in a manner sensitive to the needs of both young people and their parents.

1. How can church educators teach about birth control without seeming to approve of premarital sex or imply that young people need birth control information right now?

- Present abstinence as the most appropriate decision for young people based on their religious background.

- Stress that abstinence is the most effective method of birth control because it prevents both unwanted pregnancy and the spread of sexually transmitted infections.

- Do not assume, and do not let teens assume, that anyone in the group is or should be sexually active. Suggest that information about contraception is something that almost all people need at some time in their lives, but not necessarily now.

- When discussing birth control methods or community resources, use the third person. For example, say "If *a couple* goes to a birth control clinic" instead of "If *you* go to a birth control clinic."

- Affirm the concerns of parents and adults about teenage sexual activity.

2. How can church educators teach about birth control without imposing their values on the students?

- Before you begin teaching this session, think about your own values related to premarital sex, teenage sexual behavior, and birth control. Talk with other adults, friends, and peers if needed. Be careful not to teach your personal values. Emphasize that everyone has to make his or her own decisions regarding birth control.

- Get up-to-date information about birth control methods and effectiveness.

- Make sure that your presentation on birth control is factual, balanced, and up to date.

- Discuss the various religious, moral, and community values related to birth control issues. Stress that there is no "right" point of view for everyone.

- Clearly articulate what the church's teachings are regarding premarital sex, teen sexual behavior, birth control, and sexual responsibility. Use the "Guide for the Presbyterian Church (U.S.A.)" (pp. 14–22 in this guide) as a basis for your presentation.

Procedures

Presentation on Birth Control Methods (45 minutes)

Begin the discussion of birth control by reiterating the issues discussed above. Make it clear that you are not assuming that the youth are, or should be, sexually active. Explain that the purpose of this discussion is to present factual information about birth control, and although some group members do not need it now, they may need it some time in the future. Thinking about birth control in advance will help them make a better decision when the need arises.

Finally, make it clear to the youth that values about sexuality vary. Some religions and some individuals do not approve of any use of birth control; some approve of using only a few specific forms of birth control. Again, use the "Guide for the Presbyterian Church (U.S.A.)" (pp. 14–22 in this guide) to help you clarify what you want to present.

Have the group name as many methods of contraception as they can. Write the list on newsprint. Add to the list, if necessary, so it includes all of the following:

- abstinence*
- coitus interruptus (withdrawal)*
- condoms*
- contraceptive foams and suppositories*

- diaphragm/cervical cap
- contraceptive creams and jellies*
- intrauterine device (IUD)
- fertility awareness methods (natural family planning)*
- oral contraceptives (the pill)
- Norplant®
- Depo-Provera®
- Vaginal pouch (female condom)*

Indicates nonprescription methods

For each method, discuss the following:

- how it works
- advantages
- disadvantages
- how to use it
- where to get it

If you brought a birth control kit, pass around the items for the group to examine. Allow the group time to react to each method. Find out their real concerns. Be sure to dispel myths.

Give the verbal quiz that follows, randomly calling on group members for answers. When appropriate, show an illustration or an example of the method that is being discussed. Allow group members to participate in discussing each method. Add relevant facts when needed, using "Birth Control Methods" (pp. 56–59 in the *Older Youth Guide*; pp. 192–195 in this guide) for additional information.

Verbal Quiz

Q. Which birth control method blocks the entrance to the uterus and must be used with cream or jelly that has chemicals to kill sperm?

A. Diaphragm

Q. Which methods prevent an ovum, or egg, from being released from the ovaries?

A. The pill, Norplant®, Depo-Provera®

Q. Which method does not help prevent pregnancy?

A. Douching

Q. Which methods prevent semen from entering the vagina?

A. Condom, vaginal pouch (female condom), abstinence

Q. Which is the only 100 percent sure method of birth control?

A. Saying no (abstinence)

Q. Which method requires that couples plan to avoid intercourse around the time the woman's egg is released?

A. Fertility awareness (natural family planning)

Q. Which methods fill the vagina with a substance that kills sperm?

A. Contraceptive foams, jellies, creams, and suppositories

Q. Which methods prevent the spread of diseases such as AIDS?

A. Condoms, abstinence

Q. Which contraceptive consists of matchstick-sized capsules inserted under the skin of the woman's arm?

A. Norplant®

Q. Which contraceptive methods provide protection against most STIs (including HIV/AIDS)?

A. Only condoms (male and female) and abstinence

Questions for Discussion

- Do most teenagers know this information on birth control?
- What effect does having information about birth control have on teenagers?
- Are teenagers who know about birth control more likely to have sexual intercourse?
- Are knowledgeable teenagers more likely to use birth control if they are having sex?

Make the point that, in most states, teenagers do not need parental consent to obtain any method of contraception or to visit a clinic. (Make sure you know the law in your state.) However, all clinics strongly encourage teenagers to discuss this important decision with their parent or parents.

Emphasize again that no method of birth control is effective unless used each time a couple has sexual intercourse. The only 100 percent effective method is abstinence.

Who's at Risk? (30 minutes)

Begin this activity by asking teens to think carefully about comments that follow.

If a couple does have sexual intercourse:

- the number-one risk they have to worry about is pregnancy. (The likelihood of contracting AIDS is far less than the risk of pregnancy.)

- they have to answer the question, "How bad would it be if we had a pregnancy now?"

- they need to know how big a risk of getting pregnant they're taking.

Explain that some teens take a much greater risk than others, and often don't recognize how big a risk they are taking. In this activity you will look at sexual behaviors that put teens in different categories of risk.

On newsprint or a chalkboard list the following categories and explain that each column represents a different level of pregnancy risk:

HIGH RISK   LOW RISK   NO RISK

Beginning with the "No Risk" category, ask the group to brainstorm about the question, Which people are at no risk for getting pregnant? Allow plenty of time and accept all answers from the group. Continue with "Low Risk" and "High Risk" in the same way. After the group has suggested responses for each level of risk, use "Who's at Risk for Pregnancy?" (p. 59 in the *Older Youth Guide*; p. 195 in this guide) for discussion.

Put the behavior of the following couples in one of the three risk categories:

1. Helen and Mike see each other every summer when Helen visits her grandmother. They usually have intercourse only three to five times and don't use any birth control.

2. Malcolm and Asha spend a lot of time together. They kiss a lot and have touched each others' genitals until they both reach orgasm. They have never had sexual intercourse.

3. Tyler and Kathy have intercourse regularly. She is on the pill, but she hates taking them. Often she misses two or three pills during the month.

4. Emily and Pedro are in love. They kiss and touch a little, but that is it. They don't feel comfortable doing more.

5. Min and Tommy kiss and touch each other. They have never had sexual intercourse or reached orgasm together. Sometimes they each masturbate alone at home.

Add other situations if time permits.

Bringing Up Contraception* (30 minutes)

Before this session begins, find five or six ads depicting couples in romantic situations. Liquor, perfume, and mouthwash ads usually work well. Cut out each ad so that you've included only the picture of the man and woman, making sure that any script has been cut away. Tape each picture onto newsprint. Using construction paper of a contrasting color, cut out "balloons" to tape next to the heads of the man and the woman on each page. In essence, you will have created uncaptioned cartoons.

Introduce this activity by telling the group that there are ways couples who plan to have sex must talk about the issue of contraception. Sometimes this is difficult. Ask the group to form several small groups (no more than you have ads for) and give them the following instructions: "Imagine couples who are planning on pursuing careers and can't afford a pregnancy now. How do they bring up the topic of birth control? I'm going to distribute pictures of couples. Your assignment is to write a brief script in which each couple brings up the subject of birth control and discusses the method they plan to use."

First complete one picture together to give the group a sense of what they need to do. Choose one of the pictures and show it to the group. As a whole group, brainstorm a dialogue for the couple. In the dialogue, include the choice of birth control method and why the couple chose that method.

Distribute one ad and a sheet of paper to each small group. Tell the groups they will have ten minutes to create a conversation, after which a reporter from each group will present its picture and conversation.

After each presentation, ask the following questions:

- What did you think of the way the couple brought up the topic of birth control? Could real teenagers discuss the topic the same way?
- What does this couple have to do to obtain their chosen method of birth control?
- How is the method used?
- What could go wrong with the method?
- How can these potential problems be avoided or overcome?
- Did any group choose abstinence? Why or why not?

*Used by permission from *Positive Images: A New Approach to Contraceptive Education,* by P. Brick and C. Cooperman (New Jersey: Planned Parenthood of Bergen Co., 1987).

Pregnancy Game (15 minutes)

Note: Before the session, put eighty-five yellow candies and fifteen white candies (two different colors may be substituted) in one container marked "Sex with No Contraception." Put eighty-five white candies and fifteen yellow candies in a second container marked "Sex with Contraception." (Yellow = pregnant; white = not pregnant)

This activity will visually and concretely show the probability of pregnancy when couples use no birth control versus when they use various methods. Introduce the activity by telling the group that you want to show them how easy it is for a young woman to get pregnant if a couple does not use any method of birth control.

This activity has two parts. For part one, you will demonstrate the chances of getting pregnant if a couple has sexual intercourse regularly during one year without using any method of birth control. Set out on the table the container with eighty-five yellow candies and fifteen white candies. Explain that the yellow candies represent the number of women who would probably become pregnant in one year of intercourse with no birth control. They illustrate the fact that a woman has an 85 percent (85 women out of 100) probability of becoming pregnant in one year of unprotected intercourse (not using any method of birth control). Tell students to close their eyes and pick a candy from

the container. A yellow candy represents one of the women having sex with no birth control who would be pregnant; a white candy represents one of the women having sex with no birth control who would not be pregnant. How many had yellow candies?

Now repeat the activity using eighty-five white candies and fifteen yellow candies. This part of the experiment demonstrates the chances of getting pregnant if a woman has sexual intercourse for one year but does use some form of birth control. Again have all participants close their eyes and pick a candy from the second container. How many picked yellow candies this time?

The second container (eighty-five white candies and fifteen yellow candies) represents those people trying to avoid a pregnancy by using some form of birth control. Some methods are more effective than others, but overall, an average of 15 women out of 100 would be pregnant after one year. The failure rates of various birth control methods are listed on the table "Birth Control Failure Rates" (p. 59 in the *Older Youth Guide*; p. 195 in this guide).

Our Church Is a Community of Love and Responsibility (30 minutes)

In order for the goodness of our sexuality to continue to be a good part of our lives, it must be used responsibly. Have everyone read "Our Church Is a Community of Love and Responsibility" (p. 60 in the *Older Youth Guide*; p. 196 in this guide). Then have the young people write the phrases that they believe are important in helping them define "responsibility." As a group, write a definition of "responsible." The statement your group develops should be similar to the following:

> An act can be described as "responsible" if it is motivated by love and is within the boundaries understood by our community.

In this session and the session on good health habits, three facets of responsibility have been mentioned: responsibility to self, responsibility to others, and responsibility to God. Tell the participants: "Using Gal. 5:22–23a and Matt. 22:34–40, write a letter to yourself about what you believe your responsibility is to yourself, to others, and to God in terms of your total health."

Divide your group into three smaller groups to explore the following three areas of concern about responsibility. Have each group prepare to report to the total group their common understanding. (If your group is not large enough to divide, explore these areas as a whole group.)

A. The Meaning of Responsibility

- Does "responsibility" when applied to sexuality have the meaning of "don't use your sexuality at all"?
- Is it possible to be both sexual and responsible at the same time?
- Is it easy to be both sexual and responsible?
- In what sense do you think God cares how we use our sexuality?

B. Responsible Actions

- Could you describe what you believe is responsible behavior in terms of sexual intimacy? in terms of contraception? in terms of a healthy body?

C. Responsibility and Loving

- Do you think it is enough to say that responsible sexuality is loving sexuality?
- What situations would be loving that would not be responsible?
- What kinds of sexual expression are not loving?
- In order to be responsible, does our sexuality need to have more guidelines than just "loving"?

Close with prayer and read together the section from *A Declaration of Faith* found in the theological statement "Our Church Is a Community of Love and Responsibility" (p. 60 in the *Older Youth Guide*; p. 196 in this guide).

Birth Control Methods

Note: The starred (*) methods are nonprescriptive methods of birth control.

Abstinence (No Sexual Intercourse)*

How it works: Prevents sperm release into the vagina.

How it is used: Mutual agreement or an independent decision by either partner.

Effectiveness: Almost 100 percent. (Ejaculation outside but close to the opening of the vagina can still result in pregnancy.)

Myths: Causes "blue balls" in males; a female who abstains is "hung up" or frigid.

Additional information: Abstinence is readily available to both males and females without cost, medical side effects, risks, worry, or conflicts with adults. This is the method that the church has said is right for all persons who are not married.

A person who has had sex in the past may decide to abstain at any time in any relationship.

Abstinence protects one's later ability to have children by reducing or eliminating the risk of sexually transmitted infections (STIs), pelvic inflammatory disease, abortion, and contraceptive-related health problems.

Coitus Interruptus (Withdrawal)*

How it works: Prevents the ejaculation of sperm into the vagina.

How it is used: Requires the penis to be removed before ejaculation.

Effectiveness: 75 to 80 percent (based on actual use).

Additional information: Even though the penis is withdrawn before ejaculation, some sperm may have been released and could cause pregnancy.

Using this method requires control and motivation. Couples often find this method physically and emotionally unsatisfying. It is not recommended but is definitely better than using no method at all.

Condom (Rubber)*

How it works: Prevents sperm passage into the vagina.

How it is used: Before sexual intercourse begins, a condom is placed over the erect penis; space must be left at the end to collect the sperm (some condoms have a special tip for sperm collection). After ejaculation, the condom should be held in place on the penis while the penis with the condom is withdrawn so sperm do not spill into the vagina.

Condoms should be used for each act of intercourse and thrown away after one use; they should never be reused.

Effectiveness: 90 percent; 95 percent if used with spermicidal foam or jelly.

Where to obtain it: Drug stores; many supermarkets, convenience, and department stores; family planning clinics; and some public rest rooms.

Additional information: Vaseline may destroy the condom; also, the condom may deteriorate over time.

The condom is a relatively inexpensive contraceptive method and is the only available method for males.

Condoms prevent the spread of most sexually transmitted infections, including HIV.

Depo-Provera®

How it works: Depo-Provera is a synthetic hormone that keeps ovaries from releasing eggs. It also thickens the cervical mucus to keep sperm from joining with an egg.

How it is used: Depo-Provera is injected into the woman's buttock or arm every twelve weeks.

Where to obtain it: Family planning clinic or private physician

Effectiveness: Depo-Provera is one of the most effective methods of birth control. Of every 1,000 women who use it, only 3 will become pregnant during the first year (99.7 percent effective rate).

Diaphragm/Cervical Cap

How it works: Prevents sperm from passing into the uterus and kills sperm with spermicidal cream or jelly.

How it is used: Should be inserted within six hours before intercourse. The woman places a sperm-killing cream or jelly into the cap and around the rim of the diaphragm or cervical cap, then puts the diaphragm or cervical cap into the vagina, completely covering the cervix. After intercourse the device should be left in for six to eight hours; if intercourse is repeated within six hours, the diaphragm or cervical cap must be left in and more jelly or cream inserted into the vagina with an applicator. After each use, the diaphragm or cervical cap should be washed with soap and water, dried, and stored in its case.

Effectiveness: Approximately 82 percent (based on actual use). Studies have shown wide differences in effectiveness rates for users of the diaphragm/cervical cap. One study shows that the diaphragm or cervical cap can be 94 percent effective among young women who are highly motivated to use it.

Where to obtain it: Private physician or family planning clinic

Myths: It always destroys the spontaneity of sex; it is uncomfortable to wear for six to eight hours; it can get lost in the body.

Additional information: The diaphragm must be kept readily available and used each time intercourse occurs. If the diaphragm is inserted incorrectly, it may not protect the woman from conceiving.

Foam, Jelly, Cream, and Suppositories*

How they work: Temporarily block the opening into the uterus with spermicide that immobilizes the sperm, preventing it from joining the egg.

How they are used: Placed with an applicator into the vagina immediately before intercourse.

Effectiveness: 79 percent (actual use); 95 percent if used together with condoms

Where to obtain them: Drug store; many supermarkets, convenience, and department stores; family planning clinic.

Additional information: Foam, jellies, creams, and suppositories must be available and used each time intercourse occurs. Douching is unnecessary, but if used, should be delayed at least six to eight hours after intercourse. They are an inexpensive method but cause irritation in some women; they can be fairly messy.

Intrauterine Device (IUD)

How it works: There are several theories. Some hypothesize that the IUD prevents the fertilized egg from implanting in the uterus. One IUD, the Progestasert®, secretes a hormone believed to interfere with conception.

How it is used: A trained medical person inserts it

into the uterus with an attached string left hanging into the vagina. The string should be checked after each menstrual period to make sure the IUD is in place. You should have a checkup within three months of insertion.

Effectiveness: 95 percent (based on actual use).

Where to obtain it: Private physician or family planning clinic.

Myths: An IUD can travel to the heart and cause a stroke; the IUD strings can cut a man's penis.

Additional information: The IUD is one of the easiest birth control methods to use but is not recommended for women who have never had a child. Some IUDs have to be removed after one to three years.

Possible side effects include cramps, heavier menstrual flow, irregular bleeding, infection, expulsion of the IUD, and rarely, uterine perforation. Occasionally, the partner can feel the string during intercourse.

Note: In the late 1980s most IUDs were taken off the market because of lawsuits brought by patients who suffered from complications. The cost of insurance to protect manufacturers from liability became too expensive for some companies to make profits from the sale of IUDs. As of this writing there are only two brands of IUDs available in the United States: Progestasert® and ParaGard®. Check with your physician or family planning clinic for more detailed information about the benefits and risks of IUDs.

Fertility Awareness Methods (Natural Family Planning)*

Types of fertility awareness methods: Calendar (rhythm), basal body temperature, and cervical mucus.

How it works: Prevents the release of sperm into the vagina during the time when the egg can be fertilized.

How it is used: The time of ovulation is determined by changes in the female's body temperature or cervical mucus. Intercourse is then avoided for a specific number of days before and after ovulation.

Effectiveness: 60 to 75 percent (based on actual use).

Where to obtain instructions: Physician or family planning clinic.

Additional information: Fertility awareness is difficult for some couples to use. It requires training from a qualified professional and is often unreliable, particularly in females younger than twenty whose cycles may be irregular. It requires the couple to refrain from intercourse for several days during each cycle and, therefore, demands motivation and control. Fertility awareness methods may be used with another method of contraception if intercourse occurs close to the time of ovulation.

Norplant®

How it works: Six soft capsules are inserted under the skin of the female's upper arm. They release a small amount of hormone that keeps the ovaries from releasing eggs.

Effectiveness: Of every 10,000 women who use Norplant, only 4 become pregnant in the first year. Left in place, it can protect against pregnancy for five years.

Where to get it: Physician or family planning clinic.

Oral Contraceptives (The Pill)

How it works: Prevents release of an egg from the ovary (ovulation). Prevents implantation of the fertilized egg in the uterus if ovulation should occur.

How it is used: One type is taken daily for twenty-one days and a new package is started after seven days. Another type is taken continuously for a twenty-eight-day cycle; the last seven pills are placebos designed to keep the woman in the habit of taking a pill every day. Pills should be taken at a convenient and consistent time each day.

If a woman misses a pill, she should take the one she missed as soon as possible, take the next pill at the regular time, and use a backup method to prevent pregnancy through the rest of that menstrual cycle. The backup is necessary for most women because of the low dosages of estrogen in the pill. The woman should ask her doctor for specific instructions for using pills.

Effectiveness: 97 percent (based on actual use, including those who skip days).

Where to obtain it: Private physician or family planning center.

Myths: Pills cause deformed babies; you take the pill only on the days that you have intercourse; pills cause sterility.

Additional information: Ordinarily, women with certain physical problems such as high blood pressure, history of blood clots, cancer of the breast or uterus, and heart disease should not use the pill. Women over the age of thirty-five and women who smoke are not good candidates for the pill. Possible side effects of taking the pill include reduced menstrual flow, swollen or tender breasts, headaches, slight weight gain or loss, depression, and nausea. Serious but rare side effects include hypertension, stroke, and blood clots. Warning signals of serious side effects include severe abdominal pain, chest pain, severe headaches, eye problems, or severe leg pain.

Vaginal Pouch (Female Condom)*

How it works: A polyurethane sheath that is inserted into the vagina. The ring at the closed end holds the pouch in place. It collects semen before, during, and after ejaculation and prevents sperm from entering the vagina.

Effectiveness: 76 percent; if used regularly.

Where to get it: Drugstores; family planning clinics; some convenience stores and supermarkets.

Factors Affecting Personal Choice of a Contraceptive

- *Methods:* Effectiveness, convenience, risks, side effects, availability.
- *Users:* Age, frequency of intercourse, motivation, religious beliefs and values, partner's preference, family knowledge and support, experience with various methods.
- *Relevant state and local regulations:* Parental consent for contraception is unnecessary for minors in most states. However, in some states written parental consent is required. Family planning services must provide confidentially. Voluntary sterilization for minors is ordinarily not available.
- *Availability:* Health centers, Planned Parenthood clinics, hospital family planning clinics, private physicians, drugstores, vending machines.

- *Protection from diseases:* Remember, latex condoms and the vaginal pouch are the birth control devices that provide the most protection against STIs, including HIV.

Who's at Risk for Pregnancy?

Possible Responses

High Risk

Couples using no contraception

Couple using contraception occasionally or infrequently

Couples using withdrawal as their only method

Couples using rhythm as their only method

Couples having sexual intercourse infrequently but with no contraception

Couples having sexual intercourse when the woman is breast-feeding but using no contraception

Low Risk

Couples using one of these methods of contraception every time they have intercourse: condoms, pill, sponge, IUD, diaphragm

Couples having unprotected intercourse only when the woman is having her period

No Risk

Couples not having sexual intercourse

Couples expressing their feelings in sexual ways other than intercourse (e.g., petting, oral sex)

Couples of the same sex

Couples who masturbate to relieve sexual feelings

Points to Remember

High Risk

Couples having infrequent sexual intercourse without contraception are high risk. It only takes one time to get pregnant.

Couples having sex regularly but using no method are going to be taking the greatest risk—nine of ten will get pregnant in one year.

Couples using a risky method of contraception, such as withdrawal or foam, can decrease their risk by choosing another method.

Low Risk

Couples who use an effective method of contraception each time they have sex are still taking a risk with pregnancy.

Low-risk couples who cannot afford to take any risk because pregnancy would alter their plans for the future can move into the no risk category if they stop having intercourse.

No Risk

Couples who do not have sexual intercourse can still experience an intimate and satisfying relationship.

Couples who can't afford to take any risk with a possible pregnancy (e.g., they want to finish school; they aren't financially secure; pregnancy would hurt their relationship, etc.) should make sure they are in this category.

Birth Control Failure Rates

Method	User Failure Rate (percent pregnant within one year)
Continuous Abstinence	0
Norplant®	0.04
Depo-Provera®	0.3
IUD	2.6
Birth Control Pill	3.0
Condom	12.0
Diaphragm/Cervical Cap	18.0
Withdrawal	18.0
Fertility Awareness Methods	20.0
Contraceptive Foams, Creams, Jellies, Suppositories	21.0
Vaginal Pouch (female condom)	24.8
No Method of Birth Control Used	85.0

Our Church Is a Community of Love and Responsibility

By contrast, the fruit of the Spirit is love, joy, peace, patience, kindness, generosity, faithfulness, gentleness, and self-control.

(Gal. 5:22–23a)

[God] has told you . . . what is good; and what does the Lord require of you but to do justice, and to love kindness, and to walk humbly with your God?

(Micah 6:8)

We believe that we have been created to relate to God and each other in freedom and responsibility.

We may misuse our freedom and deny our responsibility by trying to live without God and other people or against God and other people.

Yet we are still bound to them for our life and well-being, and intended for free and responsible fellowship with them.

("A Declaration of Faith," ch. 2, lines 66–73)

The Church, as the household of God, is called to lead men [and women] out of this [sexual] alienation into the responsible freedom of the new life in Christ. Reconciled to God, each person has joy in and respect for his [or her] own humanity and that of other persons.

(The Confession of 1967, 9.47)

Sexuality is a good and positive part of our lives created by God. In order for our sexuality to continue to be a good part of our lives, it must be used responsibly.

Some people define responsible sexuality by saying that certain actions are wrong and others are right and that responsible behavior is simply a matter of following these rules. At the other extreme, some say deciding for yourself what is right and wrong is an individual matter.

Our understanding of responsible sexuality is not found at these two extremes. We are a part of a community of faith. Joined together, we read and study God's Word, pray and listen for God's guidance for us, study the beliefs of our church in the past, and then, being guided by all this, we make statements together that express our beliefs. Presbyterians do take definite stands on issues. At the same time, we uphold the right of each person to maintain the dignity of his or her own conscience in the light of Scripture.

To belong to the church means to share in the values of the church. The guiding principle that defines the church is love. Within the boundaries of the church, there is freedom, but this freedom is bounded by love. We are free to use our sexuality, and yet, we are limited in this freedom because of our commitment to God to live a life of love and obedience. We care about the effects of our actions on others as well as on ourselves. Therefore, our sexuality is to be expressed lovingly, responsibly, and obediently.

We know we are expressing our sexuality lovingly, responsibly, and obediently when we work for love and justice in the world. We also know that God's Spirit is present when there is love, joy, peace, patience, kindness, goodness, fidelity, gentleness, and self-control. We can be sure that we are acting responsibly when we keep God's Spirit as the guide of our lives.

Session 7

Sexually Transmitted Infections (STIs)

Purpose: This session deals with sexually transmitted infections (STIs). One activity shows how easily STIs can spread. Another deals with facts and feelings about STIs. The session also includes information about HIV/AIDS that is current as of the date of the revision of this course. The session ends with a theological discussion of what it means to be a community of love and responsibility.

Time: Two hours

Materials Needed

- Container
- Pens or pencils
- Fact/Feeling Spinners (one for each small group)
- Twelve 3" x 5" index cards in one color and twelve cards in a different color for each small group; an additional index card for each participant
- Video: "A Million Teenagers"
- VCR and television monitor

Activities

STI Handshake	15 Minutes
Fact/Feeling Spinner	30 Minutes
Video: "A Million Teenagers"	45 minutes
Our Church Is a Community of Love	30 minutes

Procedures

STI Handshake (15 minutes)

In advance: Count out enough 3" x 5" index cards and pencils so that each member of the group gets just one. Mark the back of one of the cards with a very small *x*.

Gather the group in the middle of your room, and have the participants pass around the cards and pencils, one for each participant. (One person will receive the card with the *x* on the back, but should not notice it since everything is being passed out and you are giving directions.) Instruct the group to shake hands with three different members of the group. After each handshake, the two people sign each other's cards. Tell the participants to sit down as soon as they have three signatures on their card.

When the participants have finished shaking hands, announce that one card has an *x* on the back, representing a sexually transmitted infection. Ask the person with the *x* to stand up and read the three names on the card, disclosing those who have contracted the infection.

Instruct these three to stand as their names are read. Then have them read the names of those with whom they shook hands after shaking person x's hand, with each of those people standing. Continue until all infected people are identified. If someone's name reappears, that person raises a hand to demonstrate reinfections. For a large group, you might have everyone get five signatures instead of three.

Be sure to emphasize that you do not get STIs by shaking hands. The purpose of the game is to demonstrate graphically and personally how quickly and widely STIs can spread. Ask the person with the x how he or she felt about having the x, and about spreading it to so many in the group. Ask all group members to discuss the following questions:

- How did you feel about having been given an infection without any intention on your part?

- Was the infection more widespread than you would have expected?

- If you'd known it was possible to get an infection in this way, how might you have protected yourself from the infection?

- What might you have done if you had known in advance that someone was carrying the infection?

Next ask the participants to look at "Types of Sexually Transmitted Infections" (pp. 62–64 of the *Older Youth Guide*; pp. 201–203 of this guide) and discuss the following questions:

- What is an STI? (A contagious infection that typically is acquired as a result of close sexual contact. Reemphasize that STIs are not contracted by shaking hands.)

- How are STIs spread? (Almost always through sexual contact. However, any STI-infected area or discharge touching broken skin or mucous membranes [mouth, eyes, anus, vagina, or penis] can result in an STI. In the case of AIDS, intravenous (IV) needle use is a major source of transmission of the disease.)

- How do people know they have an STI? (Symptoms include genital soreness; pain at urination; cloudy or strong-smelling urine; unusual discharge from penis or vagina; sores or blisters on or near genitals, anus, or inside the mouth; excessive itching or rash; abdominal cramping; fever; and overall sick feeling. Another indication that a person might have an STI is a sexual partner with symptoms.)

- How can STIs be prevented? (All STIs can be prevented by not having sexual contact or having only one partner, who is healthy; some STIs can be prevented by using condoms or spermicidal foams and jellies.)

- How does sex with more than one partner affect the STI rate?

- How are STIs affecting sexual behavior?

Fact/Feeling Spinner* (30 minutes)

Note: To make a spinner, draw lines on a paper plate, dividing it into pieces like the slices of a pie. Using the same two colors as the index cards, color half of the "pie wedges" one color and the other half a different color, alternating colors. Write "Fact" on the wedges with the first color and "Feeling" on the other half. Attach a movable cardboard arrow to the center of the spinner with a brass brad; make sure the arrow spins easily. Write the "Fact" questions (not the answers) on index cards of the first color and "Feeling" questions on cards of the second color. These questions are found on pages 200–201 of this guide. Or make a copy of "Fact/Feeling Questions," cut out each question (not the answer), and paste them onto a card. You will need a spinner and a set of questions for each small group.

Introduce this activity by telling the group that you want to review information about sexually transmitted infections (STIs). This activity will give them an opportunity to discuss feelings as well as facts about these infections.

If possible, divide into groups of four to six persons. Provide a spinner and set of Fact/Feeling index cards for each group. Participants should take turns spinning the arrow and drawing a card that matches the color the arrow stops on. A participant who does not want to answer the particular question she or he has drawn may put the question at the bottom of the pile and draw again. Encourage participants to answer all the questions, but also make it clear that no one has to answer.

After all participants have had at least one turn, bring the full group together and review the "Fact/Feeling Questions" by discussing these questions:

- Which questions were easier to answer, fact or feelings?
- Did you learn anything about yourself?
- Do you have any additional questions?

Make the point that fear is a common feeling regarding STIs. While it is normal to be afraid, people should not let fear control their lives. Instead, they should use their energy to get as much information as possible about STIs and do everything they can to prevent getting or giving diseases.

*Used by permission from *Life Skills and Opportunities* (Philadelphia: Public/Private Ventures, 1986).

Video: "A Million Teenagers"* (45 minutes)

Note: Before the session, find out the local phone number that teens can call for more information about AIDS.

Introduce the video by telling the group that getting a sexually transmitted infection (STI) is one of the risks a person takes when he or she has sexual intercourse. AIDS is a unique STI because it can be sexually transmitted, and it can be transmitted in other ways as well. AIDS is incurable and almost always results in death. People have many questions about AIDS, and much of the information people receive is confusing. This video should help answer some of the questions about AIDS.

Show the video and then discuss the following points:

1. AIDS is a disease caused by a virus that can be transmitted from an infected person to an uninfected person only by an exchange of blood, semen, vaginal mucus, urine, or feces.

2. AIDS is hard to get. Transmission of the disease by touching, hugging, sharing a pizza or a drink, and so on is not possible.

3. AIDS is not a "homosexual" disease. In recent years, HIV infection has been decreasing in the gay population due to increased education and awareness. AIDS among heterosexuals now is increasing faster than in homosexuals. Other high-risk groups include intravenous drug users, hemophiliacs, and other people who had frequent blood transfusions before April 1985, and sexual partners of all these risk groups. Babies born to women with AIDS are also at risk of being infected with the AIDS virus from their mothers before they are born.

4. Ways to protect yourself from AIDS are to
- avoid having sexual intercourse, or always use or have your partner use condoms if you do have any kind of sexual intercourse (anal, vaginal, or oral).
- avoid having sex if your partner has AIDS or is a member of one of the high-risk groups.
- avoid having several sexual partners.
- avoid using IV drugs. (Never share needles with anyone.)

5. Persons with AIDS haven't done anything wrong; they just have a terrible, deadly disease, and they need our love and support.

6. Many teenagers believe that they don't have to be worried about AIDS because they aren't gay and they don't use drugs. However, one should remember that if a person has sex, she or he probably won't know everything about the partner, such as whether or not the partner has ever used drugs. Also, the partner might have been infected by the AIDS virus and not even know it. A couple should always be sure they use a condom if they have sex. If either partner is infected with the virus, the other partner could get it.

*Used by permission from *Life Skills and Opportunities* (Philadelphia: Public/Private Ventures, 1986).

Our Church Is a Community of Love (30 minutes)

The primary value defined by the church is love. Read "Our Church Is a Community of Love" (pp. 3–4 in the *Older Youth Guide*; p. 205 in this guide). As the statement is read, have the young people underline the phrases they believe are important in helping them define "love." The statement that your group develops should be similar to the following:

An act can be described as "loving" if it remembers love for God, is loving of the other person, and is respectful of oneself.

Discuss with the young people the following questions in order to define the particular actions they believe are "loving."

1. Whom do you know who loves God?
2. What does this person do to express this love?
3. Whom do you know who loves others?
4. What does this person do to express this love?
5. Whom do you know who loves himself or herself?
6. What does this person do to express this love?

One way to determine the appropriateness of the physical expression of our sexuality in relation to another is by the level of committed and faithful love in the relationship. Describe the level of love that would have to be present for you to engage in one of the following acts:

* touching "safe" body parts (back, arm, etc.)
* kissing
* French kissing
* touching sexual body parts
* disrobing with a partner
* oral sex
* intercourse

Is there agreement in the group about what is appropriate and what is not? Read the section on premarital sex in the "Guide for the Presbyterian Church (U.S.A.)" (pp. 10–11 in the *Older Youth Guide*; pp. 17–18 in this guide) for further help in making decisions about physical expression.

Tell the participants: "Love and responsibility go together. We were created to love God, our neighbor, and ourselves. From your participation in the three sessions on good health, contraception, and STIs, write a sentence or two about what you believe to be the most responsible and loving expression of your sexuality."

Fact/Feeling Questions

Facts

Q. True or False. Gonorrhea is the most common STI in the U.S.

A. False. Chlamydia, a disease that is similar to gonorrhea, is most common. Doctors need to do a special test to find out if a person has chlamydia. If a person has the disease, it can be cured with antibiotics, but not penicillin.

Q. Which STIs cannot be cured?

A. At this time, there are no known cures for AIDS and herpes.

Q. What is the best way to keep from getting an STI?

A. Using abstinence or condoms

Q. What is the worst thing that can happen to a person who has gonorrhea and doesn't get treatment?

A. He or she could get an infection in the reproductive organs (fallopian tubes or vas deferens). The result is usually sterilization, inability to get pregnant or to get someone pregnant.

Q. What are common symptoms of STIs?

A. Sores or blisters on genitals, burning sensation when urinating, unusual discharge from the vagina or penis, severe weight loss (only with AIDS).

Q. What are unsafe sex practices?

A. Sexual intercourse (anal or vaginal) without condoms; allowing semen to enter the mouth, anus, or vagina; having more than one sexual partner

Q. What are safe sex practices?

A. Always using condoms; having no exchange of bodily fluids (semen, vaginal fluids, saliva); limiting sexual contacts to one person

Q. What should people do if they find out they have gonorrhea or chlamydia?

A. Go to a doctor; abstain from sex; inform partner(s); take all medication

Q. Which STIs can cause death?

A. AIDS and sometimes syphilis

Q. Can teenagers get AIDS?

A. Yes. If they have unsafe sex or share needles

to shoot drugs, getting HIV/AIDS is very possible.

Q. Can people who are not gay and don't use drugs get AIDS?

A. Yes. If they have sexual contact with someone who has the virus, they can contract the disease. Heterosexuals, particularly young women, are the fastest growing group of people with HIV/AIDS.

Q. Can warts on the genitals be spread through sex?

A. Yes, venereal warts can be passed to a sexual partner. The warts are usually pink or brownish and grow in little clusters. In moist areas like the vulva, they are usually soft. In dry areas like the penis, they are usually hard. They are normally painless and can be removed.

Feelings

1. Do you think most teenagers who are having sex worry about getting an STI? Why or why not?

2. How do you feel about the disease AIDS?

3. How do you think you would feel if you got herpes?

4. What should a person who has herpes say to a new sexual partner?

5. Should couples who are thinking about having sexual intercourse discuss their past sexual experiences? Why or why not?

6. How do you think a young man would react if a woman asked him to use a condom?

7. What do you think about young women keeping condoms on hand?

8. Do you think young women who are on the pill should also use condoms? Why or why not?

9. What do you think it would be like to tell a sexual partner that you have gonorrhea?

10. Do you think condoms should be advertised on TV? Why or why not?

11. How would you react if a sexual partner told you he or she had an STI?

12. What would you tell your sixth-grade child about sex and sexually transmitted infections?

Types of Sexually Transmitted Infections

Chlamydia

The most prevalent STI in the United States today. There are four million new cases of chlamydia in the United States every year. Chlamydia is difficult to diagnose because it often coexists with other diseases.

Symptoms: Twenty-five percent of infected males are asymptomatic. When they have symptoms, men may experience a painful or burning sensation when they urinate and/or a watery or milky discharge from the urethra. Seventy-five percent of infected females are asymptomatic. Symptoms for women who have them may include abnormal vaginal discharge, irregular vaginal bleeding, and pelvic pain accompanied by nausea and fever. Chlamydia can also cause painful urination, blood in the urine, or a frequent urge to urinate. Eyes of men and women may become infected, producing redness, itching, and irritation. Infection of the eyes does not require sexual contact.

Damage: If left untreated, chlamydia may cause severe complications such as nonspecific urethritis (NSU) in men and pelvic inflammatory disease (PID) in women.

Treatment: Chlamydia is caused by bacteria that are effectively eliminated by tetracycline or erythromycin; penicillin will not eliminate chlamydia.

Gonorrhea

One million cases of gonorrhea are reported in the United States every year.

Symptoms: Males have a cloudy (thick, grayish-yellow) puslike discharge from the penis and a burning sensation during urination. Symptoms appear two to ten days after contact with an infected person; 10 percent or more of males show no symptoms. Females usually show no symptoms. Some women do have a puslike vaginal discharge, vaginal soreness, painful urination, and lower abdominal pain two to ten days after contact.

Damage: Sterility; pelvic inflammatory disease (PID) in women, which can recur even after the gonorrhea and original PID have been cured.

Diagnosis: The patient should inform the physician of all points of sexual contact (genitals, mouth, or anus). For males, the medical practitioner examines genitals, mouth, or anus for signs of irritation, soreness, or discharge, and takes a bacterial culture from the infected area. For females, the medical practitioner examines genitals, mouth, lymph glands, and cervical discharges, and takes a bacterial culture.

Treatment: Oral antibiotics that kill the bacteria within one to two weeks.

Genital Herpes

Each year 500,000 to 1 million cases are reported in the United States.

Symptoms: Painful blisterlike lesions on or around genitals or in anus; symptoms appear three to twenty days after contact with the infected person. Some people have no symptoms.

Damage: Recurring outbreaks of the painful blister occur in one-third of those who contract herpes. Herpes may increase the risk of cervical cancer, can be transmitted to a baby during childbirth, and can promote psychological problems such as social withdrawal, lowered self-esteem, anger, and stress.

Diagnosis: Microscopic examination of blister tissue.

Treatment: Genital herpes is caused by a virus and has no cure. Treatment is aimed at relieving the pain, burning, and itching of active sores by bathing with soap and water or other drying agents. Immediate treatment by a doctor can reduce the severity.

Syphilis

The incidence of syphilis is increasing among teenagers.

Symptoms: Painless chancre sore on or in genitals, anus, mouth, or throat. Appears ten days to three weeks after contracted. If left untreated, a skin rash will develop, often on the hands and soles of feet, about six weeks after the chancre appears.

Damage: Loss of hair in patches. If left untreated after the rash appears, it can eventually cause heart failure, blindness, and damage to the brain and spinal cord.

Diagnosis: Medical practitioner examines chancre site, eyes, throat, heart, lungs, and abdomen; performs a microscopic examination of chancre pus and a blood test.

Treatment: Oral antibiotics that kill the bacteria within one to two weeks.

Pelvic Inflammatory Disease (PID)

A bacterial infection of the fallopian tubes. PID can be caused by the gonococcal bacteria or contamination by bacteria from the rectum or other foreign sources.

Symptoms: Abdominal cramps
Treatment: Antibiotics

Nonspecific Urethritis (NSU)

Symptoms: A bacterial infection of the urethra causing inflammation, painful urination, and a discharge.

Treatment: Antibiotics

Monilia

A yeast infection caused by an imbalance of the vaginal organisms.

Symptoms: Females may have itching, burning, a whitish lumpy (cottage cheese–like) discharge that smells like yeast, and dryness of the vagina.

Males have inflammation of the penis.
Treatment: Locally applied cream

Trichomoniasis

A vaginal infection caused by a single-cell organism present in the bladder of some people; in rare cases it can be transmitted by wet clothing, washcloths, or towels.

Symptoms: Females may have a burning sensation at urination and an odorous, foamy discharge, along with a reddening and swelling of the vaginal opening. Males usually have no symptoms or only a slight discharge.

Treatment: Oral medication

Venereal Warts

Warts are the result of a virus spread during sexual contact.

Symptoms: In moist areas like the vulva, they are usually pink or red and soft. They often grow together in little clusters. In dry areas such as the penis, the warts are small, hard, and yellowish grey.

Treatment: A locally applied treatment easily destroys the warts.

Pubic Lice (Crabs)

Symptoms: About the size of a pin head, the lice live and breed in the pubic hair, causing an intense itching. Can be spread through bodily contact as well as bedding, clothing, toilet seats, or towels.

Treatment: Wash the affected area with a preparation that kills the adult lice and their eggs.

Scabies

Symptoms: An infection caused by a tiny mite that burrows under the skin, causing intense itching and redness of the skin.

Treatment: A topically applied lotion, cream, or shampoo containing an insecticide usually kills the mites in one application.

Hepatitis B Virus (HBV)

Hepatitis B is the only STI that is preventable with vaccination. But about 200,000 Americans get HBV every year because they have not been vaccinated.

Symptoms: Extreme fatigue, headache, fever, nausea, vomiting, tenderness in lower abdomen, yellowing of skin and whites of the eyes (jaundice)

How it is spread: In semen, saliva, blood, and urine by sexual contact (kissing, vaginal, oral, and anal intercourse); use of unclean needles. Hepatitis B is *very* contagious.

Damage: Although 90 to 95 percent of adults with HBV recover completely, the virus can cause severe liver disease and death.

Diagnosis: Blood test

Treatment: None. In most cases the infection clears within four to eight weeks. Some people, however, remain contagious for life.

HIV/AIDS (Human Immunodeficiency Virus/ Acquired Immune Deficiency Syndrome)

HIV infections weaken the body's ability to fight disease and can cause acquired immune deficiency syndrome (AIDS)—the last stage of HIV infection. HIV is transmitted through an exchange of bodily fluids (blood, semen, vaginal fluids) either through sexual contact, intravenous drug use, or blood transfusions. People who suffer from AIDS become susceptible to a variety of rare illnesses not found in people whose immune system is working correctly.

Symptoms: Early signs are similar to those of other illnesses such as colds or flu: night sweats or swollen glands. These generally continue, along with unexplained weight loss, yeast infections, persistent cough, and fatigue.

How it is spread: Exchange of bodily fluids through unprotected sexual intercourse, sharing needles or syringes, receiving a transfusion of HIV-infected blood, receiving tissue or organs transplanted from a donor with HIV/AIDS.

Damage: HIV breaks down the immune system and causes people to develop harmful infections that don't usually affect people. These are called opportunistic infections and include a number of unusual cancers, pneumonia, tuberculosis, and various viral, bacterial, fungal, and parasitic infections.

Diagnosis: Blood test, available from Planned Parenthood health centers, most physicians, hospitals, and from local, state, and federal health departments. Over-the-counter tests are also available at many drug stores.

Treatment: Various drugs are being researched, but at this time there is no vaccine or cure.

General Information on HIV/AIDS

What exactly is AIDS?

AIDS is an acronym for acquired immune deficiency syndrome. This is a viral disease that occurs in people months to years after infection with the HIV virus. A person with this condition is unable to fight off a variety of infections and rare illnesses.

What are the symptoms?

While the symptoms of AIDS vary, they usually remain for long periods. The person may have repeated infections that result in persistent diarrhea, swollen glands, fatigue, fevers, or a persistent cough that the body is unable to fight off. Months or years from the time an individual is infected with HIV, more severe and life-threatening illnesses develop, usually pneumonia or uncommon cancers.

How can AIDS be transmitted?

The HIV virus is found in blood, semen, vaginal fluids, and breast milk of people with AIDS and can be spread through anal, vaginal, and oral intercourse, and through sharing contaminated needles, through transfusion of contaminated blood products, through childbirth from an infected mother to her child.

Can children get HIV/AIDS from adults or other children?

Children, like adults, can only catch this disease from intimate sexual contact or blood-to-blood contact with a person who has the AIDS virus. Most of the children who are known to have the disease received the infection from exposure to their mother's blood during pregnancy or childbirth, from breast milk from their infected mother, from a blood transfusion, or from blood products used in treating hemophilia.

Can you get rid of AIDS? If not, are there any developments in that direction?

There is no known cure or vaccine. Several drugs have been developed to help control and contain the infections that occur with AIDS, but none of these get rid of AIDS.

Do all people with AIDS die?

In the early years of the HIV epidemic most people diagnosed with AIDS died within two years. However, some people have now lived with AIDS for more than ten years. New treatments and increased knowledge may help many more people live with AIDS even longer.

Can you get AIDS from donating blood?

No, not if you donate blood to the Red Cross or a medical center.

Is it certain that AIDS can't be caught from toilet seats, drinking out of the same cups, and so on?

HIV cannot be transmitted through casual contact, including: being sneezed on, coughed on, or breathed on by someone with HIV/AIDS; crying with, sweating with, kissing, or hugging anyone who has it; touching things that an HIV/AIDS infected person has used, including doorknobs, bed linens, towels, toilets, telephone, swimming pools, eating utensils, and drinking cups.

Can heterosexuals really get AIDS?

Yes, heterosexuals can get AIDS if they are exposed to the AIDS virus. Heterosexuals can get AIDS if they share a contaminated needle to shoot drugs or if they have sex with a partner who has been exposed to the AIDS virus. Heterosexuals, young people, people of color, and women have the fastest-growing rates of infection. It is foolish to think that you cannot get AIDS if you are not gay or bisexual.

Our Church Is a Community of Love

Beloved, let us love one another, because love is from God; and everyone who loves is born of God and knows God. Whoever does not love does not know God, for God is love. . . . Beloved, since God loved us so much, we also ought to love one another. No one has ever seen God; if we love one another, God lives in us, and God's love is perfected in us.

(1 John 4:7–8; 11–12)

And one of them, a lawyer, asked [Jesus] a question to test him. "Teacher, which commandment in the law is the greatest?" He said to him, "'You shall love the Lord your God with all your heart, and with all your soul, and with all your mind.' This is the greatest and first commandment. And a second is like it: 'You shall love your neighbor as yourself.' On these two commandments hang all the law and the prophets."

(Matt. 22:35–40)

Q. 42. What is the sum of the Ten Commandments?

A. The sum of the Ten Commandments is: to love the Lord our God with all our heart, with all our soul, with all our strength, and with all our mind; and our neighbor as ourselves.

(The Shorter Catechism, 7.042)

We are created to be in community, in relationship, with God and with one another. Above all else, God has loved us, does love us, and will love us faithfully. In the same way, we should love God and one another.

The summation of the law by Jesus—to love God and to love your neighbor as yourself—indicates that the love of oneself is included in the love of others. Clearly our sexual attitudes and relationships should be motivated by love both for our neighbors and for ourselves. Our sense of identity and our way of acting should affirm others as well as affirm ourselves and should respect others as well as respect ourselves. We are to be concerned for others' needs and feelings without discounting our own.

Because we are total persons, we express our maleness or femaleness in all our relationships. Physical intimacy progresses from the simple affirmation of a handshake or hug to the total intimacy of marriage. Different levels of physical intimacy are appropriate to different kinds and stages of relationships. Often in a relationship, we find ourselves asking what is appropriate. One way to determine the appropriateness of the physical expression of our sexuality is by evaluating the level of committed and faithful love in the relationship.

Session 8

Parenthood

Purpose: This session deals with the impact on teenagers' lives when they become parents and looks at the decisions that they have to make in relation to teenage pregnancy. This session provides young people with the opportunity to study what the Presbyterian Church (U.S.A.) has said about abortion. The last activity helps young people explore adoption.

Time: Three hours (The adoption session can be done in two parts.)

Materials Needed

- Audiocassette recording of Dee Ann's Story
- Cassette tape player
- Extension cord (if necessary)
- Newsprint
- Felt-tipped markers
- *Older Youth Guide*

Activities

Dee Ann's Story	30 minutes
Facing an Unplanned Pregnancy	45 minutes
Understanding Abortion	45 minutes
Adoption	60 minutes

Procedures

Dee Ann's Story (30 minutes)

Note: You will need to tape the story before this session. Be sure you have a tape player with good quality sound, preferably a large one with speakers rather than a small portable tape player. Set the tape so it is ready to begin with Dee Ann's first words.

Introduce the tape as a story one girl tells about becoming a teenage mother. Tell the group that Dee Ann is fifteen and a real person; this is really her story.

Play the tape; then ask the group to comment. Divide a piece of newsprint into two columns, labeling one column "Pluses (+)" and the other "Minuses (-)." Ask the group to list the things Dee Ann said that were pluses about being a teenage mom or were positive things in her life. Do the same for minuses or the negative things in her life. Use the questions that follow for discussion:

- Why did Dee Ann have sex without using any protection? (She thought girls on the pill "fooled around." She didn't have sex often, so she didn't think she needed to use contraception.) Do you know any girls or guys who think that girls who are on the pill or use another method of contraception "fool around"?

- Rob, the father of the baby, hasn't been much help to Dee Ann. How do you feel about him? How does Dee Ann feel about him?

- Did Dee Ann plan to have this baby? Do you think she would do things the same way again?

- How do you think things will turn out for Dee Ann and her baby?

*Used by permission from *Family and Community Health Through Caregiving* (Newton, MA: Education Development Center, 1978).

Dee Ann's Story

I first discovered I was pregnant when I was four months along. I was fifteen years old. I kept telling everybody, "I'm going to get pregnant," so I thought I might be. However, when I found out, I just couldn't believe it. I wasn't using any protection. I figured that if somebody's going to take the pill, they're the ones that fool around. And if you're not going to do it all the time, then why take them. I didn't see any reason, but I guess that's the time it happens.

I went to the local clinic, and the doctor really didn't say much of anything. Just told me I had to tell my mom. And he gave me all the choices. Doesn't seem like there's very many. So I finally decided to keep the baby myself. I figured I took the responsibility of letting it happen, and I was going to accept the responsibility now.

I hid it from my mom the whole time I thought I might be pregnant. But when I finally found out for sure and told her, she said, "Where did I go wrong?" The same thing they always say. And my dad doesn't live with me, but when I told him, he flipped out, too. Nobody wanted me to keep the baby. All my friends told me to give it up or I wouldn't be able to run around like I did. I was really scared and I cried a lot. And Rob— he's the father—didn't want to talk about it.

I had known Rob for about five or six months, off and on. I was serious about him, but he wasn't about me. When he first found out, he denied it. But he knew it was his. And then he called me every once in a while to see how I was doing—and to give me a bunch of lies. He always said he'd be around, but he never came back. He kept in touch, and whenever he called, he acted concerned. But I figure that if he really was concerned, he would have done something about

it instead of just calling on the phone. It would have been easier if he had been there.

Once my family knew I was pregnant, they babied me. It drove me nuts. They seemed to care, but when my mom talked about it, she didn't seem to care because she wanted me to give the baby up. Once I realized that I was actually going to have a baby, my biggest fear was that I wouldn't be able to raise him by myself. That aspect is still the biggest fear. I still have it. And that I might not make a good mother and things like that. And I figure, by the time he's old enough to know what a father is, I should be married. I hope.

Things are a lot different than before, especially at home. I have more responsibilities than I did. My mom works, so that means I have the house, the baby, my little sister, and the cooking to do. My mom helped out with the baby in the beginning, but now she won't even hold him. Maybe she'll hold him for five seconds and then give him back. And she worries about things, and she cries a lot.

I feel I don't have as many friends as I used to because I can't go out. Old friends talk to me, but just to be nosy. You lose a lot of friends. Either they're not wanting to hang around 'cause you can't do anything, or else their mothers and fathers are saying not to. But a few stay close.

The only regret I have is that he looks just like the father. He looks just like him, and it drives me nuts. The father called me one time, and he said he wanted to see the baby. My mom told me he wasn't allowed to see him. But I told him that if he really wanted to, I'd find some way. But he never called again. He called once while I was in the hospital, but he wouldn't go to the hospital. He called the week after I got home, but it's been two months since I've heard from him. He doesn't write, so I figure he didn't care about that either.

My baby's ten weeks old now. He rolls over already, and I can't believe it because it's just too early. He laughs a lot. He smiles every time you look at him. I've gotten him spoiled. He only goes to sleep if I'm lying down and he's lying on my chest. But then I can put him in his bed and he won't wake up. He's growing so fast, I just wish—the only thing I wish is that Rob would be around to see it.

Facing an Unplanned Pregnancy (45 minutes)

Explain to youth the following facts: Each year more than one million teenage women in the United States become pregnant. Eighty-five percent of those pregnancies are unplanned. Every one of the teenagers involved in these pregnancies is faced with a decision that has no easy solution. The decisions of the couple in this story will involve religious, moral, ethical, and practical considerations.

Then ask the group to read the story "Lisa and Mike" (p. 210) and answer the questions on the worksheet. Assure them that they will not have to share their answers to question A.

Divide the youth into groups of five or six and have them discuss questions B and C for about ten minutes.

Gather the large group together and discuss these questions:

- What religious, moral, and ethical values do people need to take into consideration when making a decision about an unplanned pregnancy?
- What information do these people need about their options?
- Who could a couple like Mike and Lisa turn to as they make this important decision?

Emphasize that making a decision about an unplanned pregnancy is a very complex issue. The couple needs to take into account how their decision will impact the other people in their lives, such as parents and other family members. Support from these people, as well as from clergy, is very important at this time.

Understanding Abortion (45 minutes)

Ask the group to turn to "Abortion" (p. 67 in the *Older Youth Guide*; p. 211 in this guide) and to spend a few minutes writing their first response to the questions there. Tell them their answers are just for themselves and to be shared only as they choose.

When they are finished, read together the section on abortion in the "Guide for the Presbyterian Church (U.S.A.)" (pp. 12–13 in the *Older Youth Guide*; pp. 19–20 in this guide). As you read each question and answer, have the young people write beside their original answers their understanding of the position stated in the "Guide."

Discuss their findings in this exercise as they choose to share their responses. Use questions such as the following:

- On what question did your response most agree with the "Guide"?
- Were you surprised at how much your responses were similar to or different from the "Guide"?
- Did any answer given in the "Guide" really surprise you?
- How much are you going to be influenced by the positions stated in the "Guide?"
- Are there any statements that you would like to research further by looking in the original documents from which the statements in the "Guide" were taken?
- What did you learn from this exercise?

Adoption (60 minutes in this session; 40 minutes in the next session)

Note: This exercise will carry over into the next session and will require time outside of class. It may not be appropriate for a retreat setting. You might want to use this activity at another time or do only part 1.

Getting interviews is a sensitive issue. This activity should only be done if there is a family willing to talk about adoption and if the young people in the group are mature enough to be aware of the feelings of others, especially birth parents who have given up a child for adoption.

Part 1

Within your group of young people there will probably be one or more who have been adopted. At least, members of the group will know relatives or friends who are adopted. For about twenty minutes, brainstorm together the questions the group would like to have answered about adoption. The following questions might be included:

A. For Those Who Have Been Adopted

- How has the experience of adoption affected you?
- What feelings have you had toward your birth parents?
- How have you used your adoption positively and negatively with your adoptive parents?
- How do you feel about siblings who have also been adopted?
- What kinds of questions would you like answered about your birth parents?
- How have your adoptive parents handled talking with you about your adoption?
- Have you communicated with your birth parents? Would you want to? How would your adoptive parents feel about it?
- How do you understand God's presence in the adoption process?

B. For Adoptive Parents

- How has the experience of adoption been for you?
- What have been your regrets?
- What feelings have you had toward the birth parents?
- Do you communicate with the birth parents? If not, would you want to? Would you want your children to?
- How do you understand God's presence in the adoption process?

C. For Birth Parents

- What are reasons that someone would choose adoption?
- What are the reasons for not choosing adoption?
- What are the difficult times for the birth parents?
- What kinds of regrets are there?
- What kinds of questions do you have after adoption?
- Do you want to see the children later in their lives?
- Do you ever feel guilty?
- How do you come to terms with the decision to choose adoption and know it was the best decision?
- How often is the birth father involved in the decision?
- How many birth parents communicate with the adoptive parents?
- How has this experience affected your faith?

Part 2

Have each young person choose someone to interview. They might want to choose a friend who has been adopted, the parents of an adopted friend, someone in the community who deals with adoption, or someone referred by your pastor. Refine the questions developed in the previous activity for an interview. Talk about how to set up an interview and carry it out, paying particular attention to questions of sensitivity and confidentiality. Have each young person interview someone before you get together again.

When you meet next, spend about forty minutes letting each person share what was learned in the interview. Discuss the following questions:

- What are some common findings?
- What differences were there?
- Is there any one understanding you can come to about adoption as a result of the interviews?
- How is faith related to adoption?

Close with prayer.

Facing an Unplanned Pregnancy

Directions: Read the story below and answer the questions following it.

Lisa and Mike

Lisa and Mike are like many high school couples, maybe even a couple you know. Mike cheers for Lisa at her soccer games; Lisa cheers for Mike at his basketball games. They are both good students, and Mike, a senior, has just been offered a scholarship to a good university in a neighboring state.

They have been going together for a year and a half, and recently they started having sexual intercourse. Lisa, a sophomore, just found out that she is pregnant. They are both confused and frightened, and unsure about what to do. Mike could get a job to support them, but he wouldn't be able to go to college. Lisa is mature for a sixteen-year-old, but she had hoped to play soccer in college. Neither one feels ready to be a parent.

They have four options: (1) get married and have the baby; (2) have the baby outside of marriage; (3) give the baby up for adoption; (4) terminate the pregnancy by abortion.

- In the context of your own religious, moral, and ethical values, what do you think about each of the four options?

1. Getting married and having the baby _____
2. Having the baby outside of marriage _____
3. Giving the baby up for adoption _____
4. Terminating the pregnancy by abortion _____

- What are the practical considerations of each decision?

1. Marriage _____
2. Single parenting _____
3. Adoption _____
4. Abortion _____

- Where should Mike and Lisa go to get help in making this decision? _____
_____
_____
_____
_____
_____
_____
_____
_____

Abortion

Questions from the "Guide for the Presbyterian Church (U.S.A.)"

1. Can the choice of abortion be a responsible Christian choice?

2. What is our primary guide in decision making?

3. Who has the responsibility for deciding about abortion?

4. When should a decision about abortion be made?

5. Should abortion be available to anyone who chooses it?

6. Should a woman feel guilty for considering an abortion?

7. Should abortion be considered a form of birth control?

8. What does our church believe the public policy on abortion should be?

9. What does our church believe about violence at women's health clinics?

10. Is there a variety of beliefs about abortion within our church?

Session 9

Sexual Violence

Purpose[1]

In this session, participants will

- understand that sexuality and violence are two different things.

- grasp that sexual violence is a misuse of power.

- understand that power comes from resources.

- increase their understanding of rape and sexual harassment.

- recognize their own power and vulnerability and how they might use them responsibly.

Time: About three hours

Materials Needed

- Newsprint and markers, chalkboard and chalk or overhead projector, transparencies, and markers

- Two newspaper articles describing an assault

- VCR, TV, and video "Scoring: Date Rape" (order in advance and preview)

- Contact person at a local sexual assault center or battered women's shelter

Activities

Introduce the Session	15 minutes
Discuss Sexuality	15 minutes
Domestic Violence	15 minutes
When Violence and Sexuality Are Mixed	20 minutes
Power and Resources	40 minutes
Break	10 minutes
Sexual Harassment	30 minutes
Rape	30 minutes
Conclusions	15 minutes

Background for the Leader[2]

This session has as its core understanding the belief that sexuality is a gift from God. It relies on the rest of the course to help participants come to a greater understanding of what that means. We will look specifically at sexual violence. There are three concepts we want to convey:

1. Sexuality and violence are two very different things.

2. When talking about sexuality and violence, it is important to understand power and resources.

3. Sexual violence is an example of the misuse of power.

---

1. In preparation, it is recommended that you contact the Center for the Prevention of Sexual and Domestic Violence, which is an interreligious organization working on issues of sexual and domestic violence prevention. In order to obtain a list of resources, please write to the following address: CPSDV, 936 North 34th Street, Suite 200, Seattle, WA 98103, (206) 634-1903.

2. Much of this information is taken from *Sexual Abuse Prevention: A Course of Study for Teenagers*, by Rebecca Voelkel-Haugen and Marie Fortune (Cleveland: United Church Press, 1996), pp. 1–8.

1. Sexuality and violence are two very different things.

God blessed us with the gifts of bodiliness and sexuality. God created us with longings for intimacy and connectedness with one another. A sexual relationship can be one expression of deep intimacy and love. But our sexuality is more than what we do genitally. Our sexuality is "the divine invitation to find our destinies, not in loneliness, but in deep connection."[3]

Contrasted to this is violence. Violence is the antithesis of connection and intimacy; for it not only destroys trust, but it also violates and degrades another's humanity.

Although sexuality and violence have often been viewed as opposites, they were still seen as related. Rape/sexual violence was at one end of the spectrum; "normal" sexual activity was at the other. In other words, rape was seen as sex that just "got out of hand."

Normal sexual activity	Rape

In this session, we want to suggest a different model. In this model, healthy sexuality and sexual abuse/violence are on different continuums. They are completely different.

Continuum I: Healthy Sexual Activity = Consensual

Receptive Sexual Activity	Proactive Sexual Activity

Continuum II: Sexual Abuse/Violence = Nonconsensual

Coercion	Use of Physical Force

Although this may seem obvious to *us* that sex and violence are completely different, our society constantly confuses the two. In music videos, advertising, movies, magazines, the Internet, and much of the culture that young people have contact with, we are taught that "good" sex is violent and violence is sexy. We are taught that our sexuality is about dominance and submission. For men this means that, to be a man, we need to be in control and get what we want, no matter what. For women, this means that, to be feminine, we need to let others take control, give up choices and whatever someone does to us is okay.

This session takes as its first premise the belief that this intermingling of sex and violence is wrong. It is harmful and it leads to sexual harassment and sexual violence that deeply hurts and can destroy its victims.

2. When talking about sexuality and violence, it is important to understand power and resources.[4]

In order to understand sexual violence, it is necessary to understand power and the way in which we choose to use the power we have. However, it is important to define what we mean by power because it may differ from the common understanding.

Power, as used here, has two very important components: relational and contextual.

- *Power as Relational*—Power is not an absolute trait, like skin color or height; it is relative. Person A may have power in relation to Person B but not in relation to Person C. That is why it is inaccurate to simply say that someone "has power" or "is powerful." For example, a business executive may have power in relation to those she manages, but in relation to her doctor who is older and male, she has less power.

- *Power as Contextual*—A person's power or lack of it is not a constant but varies with the context. A twenty-year-old walking down the street may be more powerful than a thirteen-year-old he meets, but when the twenty-year-old is in class, his professor is more powerful than he.

Both of these concepts rest on the idea that power is a measure of one person's (or group's) resources as compared to another person's (or group's) resources. Those who have greater

---

3. From *Sexuality and the Sacred: Sources for Theological Reflection*, edited by James B. Nelson and Sandra P. Longfellow (Louisville: Westminster/John Knox Press, 1994), xiv.

4. Much of the information on power and resources is taken from *Clergy Misconduct: Sexual Abuse in the Ministerial Relationship—Trainer's Manual* (Seattle: Center for the Prevention of Sexual and Domestic Violence, 1992), IV-62 to IV-66.

resources than others have power relative to them; those who command fewer resources are vulnerable relative to them.

It is important to note that resources can be anything that can be a source of strength, anything that can be drawn on to take care of a need or be used to one's advantage. The chart on page 219 clearly illustrates this idea.

The other important distinction about power is how we use it. Power can be used to control or manipulate. We define this as "Power Over." Power is also defined as the capacity to do things or make things happen, to act, including on behalf of others. This is "power to do/make" or "Power With." Examples of this distinction are as follows:

Power Over	Power With
To control others (e.g., a coach who uses his/her role to coerce his/her player into a sexual relationship)	To provide leadership (a coach who uses his/her role to guide the team with genuine care for the players)
To preserve privilege and power of gender, race, body size, etc. (e.g., a teenaged boy harassing a classmate who is a girl)	To respect and protect the vulnerable, i.e., those who have less power

3. Sexual violence is an example of the misuse of power.

As seen in the two examples of "Power Over," sexual violence is an example of one person using his/her power to hurt another. In this session we will look at two examples of sexual violence—harassment and rape.

For our purposes, we use the U.S. Federal Equal Employment Opportunity Commission's definition of sexual harassment:

> The use of one's authority or power, either explicitly or implicitly, to coerce another into unwanted sexual relations or to punish another for his or her refusal; or the creation of an

intimidating, hostile or offensive . . . environment through verbal or physical conduct of a sexual nature.

The definition we use for rape in this session is as follows:

> . . . [T]he most comprehensive definition [of rape] refers to forced penetration by the penis or any object of the vagina, mouth or anus against the will of the victim.[5]

In the above-mentioned definition, we see that rape is usually perpetrated by a man against a woman. However, about 10 percent of rape victims are men. In these cases, nearly all the perpetrators are also men. But women can rape, too, and it is important to share this fact. Regardless of the circumstances, rape is a crime.

In this session, we will look at date/acquaintance rape, which we will define as follows:

> In acquaintance rape, the rapist and the victim may know each other casually—having met through a common activity, mutual friend, at a party, as neighbors, as students in the same class, at work, on a blind date, or while traveling. Or they may have a closer relationship—as steady dates or former sexual partners. Although largely a hidden phenomenon because it is the least reported type of rape (and rape, in general, is the most underreported crime against a person), many organizations, counselors, and social researchers agree that acquaintance rape is the most prevalent crime today.[6]

In both acquaintance/date rape and sexual harassment, the perpetrator uses his/her power over another. Therefore, it is important to recognize that in any case of harassment or rape, it is the perpetrator's responsibility. It is never the victim's fault. The particularities of what the victim was wearing, what she/he had done in the past, whether or not she/he had been drinking, and so forth do not matter. Abuse of power through sexual harassment or date/acquaintance rape is the perpetrators choice. It is his/her responsibility.

5. *Sexual Violence: The Unmentionable Sin*, by Marie M. Fortune (New York: The Pilgrim Press, 1983), 7.
6. *Never Called It Rape: The Ms. Report on Recognizing, Fighting, and Surviving Date and Acquaintance Rape*, by Robin Warshaw (New York: Harper & Row, 1988), 12.

Procedures

Introduce the Session (15 minutes)

Begin by asking participants what they've heard about this session and this topic. What are their expectations? As individuals respond, be aware of their answers. For males, note if they discount the importance of this information or if they say they don't need to know about harassment and rape. Be prepared to share examples that will help focus their awareness on the fact that males can also be victims. (One such example is that one in seven boys is sexually abused before they reach age eighteen and that 10 percent of reported rapes are of boys and men.)[7]

In addition to noting resistance, be aware that there is a high likelihood that at least one of your students will be a survivor. Tell the group that you will be available to talk if anyone needs to. (Reread the section "Recognizing and Reporting Abuse" on pp. 6–7 in this guide.) Be prepared with names and phone numbers of local resources, such as the sexual assault clinic, the battered women's hotline, the YWCA, or the local women's center.

Go over the session plans briefly. Identify which expectations they have raised that you plan to cover. Be clear with the students that the subject matter is very important and can be painful and difficult. Lay out some ground rules. Because this is painful and difficult material, it is very important that everyone respect one another. This means listening to others, not making fun of what another person has said, paying attention to whoever is speaking, and keeping confidential things that are said in the group. Ask participants if they have other ground rules that they would like to follow.

Discuss Sexuality (15 minutes)

Ask participants to define sexuality. On a sheet of newsprint, on an overhead transparency, or on the chalkboard, make a list of their definitions.

Using these words and the definition provided in the "Background for the Leader" (pp. 212–214 in this guide), identify sexuality as being essentially about connection, with God and with one another. Note where this may be different from what they have listed and clarify what the difference is.

Discuss Violence (15 minutes)

Ask participants to define violence. List the words and phrases they provide on newsprint, an overhead, or on the chalkboard.

Bring two articles from newspapers or magazines that describe an assault or other form of physical violence. Have several members of the group, both males and females, read the articles aloud.

Ask the group to discuss the articles. (You may want to acknowledge that it's hard to do this because it's hard to talk about people getting hurt.) What is the relationship described in the articles?

Using the words the group listed above, the discussion about the articles, and the information provided in the "Background for the Leader" section, discuss what violence is.

Put the list of words that define sexuality next to the list of words that define violence. Ask the participants to compare them. What do they notice? What is the difference between sexuality and violence?

Note: The most important difference to note is the element of choice and consent. Violence is the use of power over someone else. It is against her or his will. It is against her or his choice or consent. It harms because it inflicts physical pain, but it also harms because it degrades and violates another's humanity. Sexuality is a gift from God that is based on respect for the other, mutuality, equality, and honesty. It is based on the ability to choose.

Draw on newsprint or chalkboard the two continuums found in "Background for the Leader" (p. 213 in this guide). Point out to the youth that one of the main things that you hope they will remember from this session is that sexuality and violence are two very different things.

When Violence and Sexuality Are Mixed (20 minutes)

If you can find someone who would be willing and think that it would work with your group,

---

7. Cited in *The Courage to Heal*, by Ellen Bass and Laura Davis (New York: Harper & Row, 1994).

have someone who is a survivor of harassment or sexual assault come to the class and tell her or his story. (If a woman speaks of her experience, be prepared to share a man or boy's story, such as "Johnny." If the survivor is a man, be prepared to read a woman's or girl's story, such as "Luisa.") If a visitor is not possible, read the stories "Luisa" and "Johnny" on page 220. Acknowledge that it is difficult to hear stories like these. Remind them that you are available if they want to talk privately afterward.

Note: Any story about a male either sexually abusing or harassing another male usually brings up reactions from participants about the offender or the victim being gay. (In fact, this is one of the biggest barriers for boys who have been victimized by other boys or by men to report the incident. They are afraid that people will think they are gay.) It is important to remind participants that most men who molest children, either boys or girls, are heterosexual. And just because a boy experiences harassment or assault by another male does not make him gay. Being gay is a sexual preference, and is not related to violence. Being molested or harassed by someone does not necessarily influence your sexual orientation. If someone molests or harasses you, they perpetrate violence against you.

Ask participants if they know people like Luisa and Mark or like Johnny and Tony, or if they know of other stories. Ask them how they think Luisa and Johnny felt. If they had experienced something like this, what could they do in response? Who could they tell? Do they think that either Luisa or Johnny had a choice? Why or why not?

Power and Resources (40 minutes)

Ask participants to define both power and vulnerability, and list their responses on newsprint, the chalkboard, or an overhead. Using the information provided in the "Background for the Leader" on pages 212–214 of this guide, emphasize with participants the importance of context and relationship. Clarify with them the importance of resources in terms of power and relationships.

Discuss the chart "Sources of Power and Sources of Vulnerability" on page 219. If participants have questions about race or gender, talk

with them about how our society discriminates against people of color and women and this is why white people have a resource in their race and their gender. (Point out that just because this is the situation, doesn't make it right.)

Have the group do two role plays. In each role play, ask two members of the group to stand up in front of the group. Then ask the group to describe the following relationships:

- One in which one person has more power than the other
- One in which the power seems relatively equal between the two

Have the group describe to the two actors the roles they are about to play. For example, "Antoine, pretend that you are Mr. Smith, the earth science teacher. Jane, pretend you're in Mr. Smith's class." Then ask Antoine, as Mr. Smith, to say something to Jane that illustrates his power in relation to her. For example, he might tell her to do a homework assignment. Ask Jane to respond to Mr. Smith in a way that illustrates his power in relation to her. For example, she goes home and does it and turns it in.

To illustrate the relationship where the power is equal, you could ask two people to pretend they are best friends of the same age and race going to a movie together.

After the role plays, ask participants for more examples from their own lives that illustrate equal power relationships and ones in which someone has more power than another.

Use the following examples and ask participants to discuss who is more powerful and who is more vulnerable in each and the reasons why:

- A 15-year-old African American girl and an 18-year-old Asian American boy who are dating
- A 14-year-old white boy and his 25-year-old coach who is male
- A 16-year-old Latina girl and her 15-year-old Native American best friend
- A 14-year-old white boy who is "popular" and a 14-year-old white boy who isn't

In the first situation, the resources of race are equal, but the boy has both gender and age as resources to make him more powerful. In the second example, two white males have equal resources in these areas, but the coach has both age and role as resources so his is more powerful. In the third situation, both are girls, both are people of color and, although their age is somewhat different, their resources are almost equal; therefore their power is equal. In the fourth situation, both boys are white and male, but the "popular" boy has the resource of his standing within the community, therefore he holds more power in this situation.

Introduce the concepts of "power over" and "power with." On a piece of newsprint, a chalkboard or on an overhead, ask them to list examples from their own lives of people using their power "over" another person and people using their power "with" someone.

Break (10 minutes)

Sexual Harassment (30 minutes)

Introduce the concept of sexual harassment. Ask participants what they think it means. Share the definition given in the "Background for the Leader" on page 214. Point out the fact that harassment is an example of someone using his or her power over another. It is an example of one person with more resources using them over and against another in order to control, manipulate, or humiliate them.

Reread Johnny's story from earlier in this session. Ask participants to talk about Johnny and other people they know (without using their names) who have experienced sexual harassment. Discuss the following:

- How is harassment an example of the misuse of power?
- How do you think Johnny felt when he was harassed? How would you feel if you were harassed?

Rape (30 minutes)

Ask participants how they would define rape. Add any information from the "Background for the Leader" on page 214. Point out that rape is another example of someone using their power over another. Rape is about force, power, and violence, and takes place against the will of the victim. Remind participants again that anyone can be a victim, including boys and men.

Ask the group to define date/acquaintance rape. Write the definition on a piece of newsprint, an overhead, or the chalkboard. Clarify the definition using the information provided in the "Background for the Leader" on page 214.

Note: Be sure to highlight that the relationship between the rapist and the victim is irrelevant. Regardless of whether the couple has had sex before, just met, or has been dating for a while, if one person forces another to have sex against her or his will, it is considered rape.

Show the video "Scoring: Date Rape." After the video, divide the group into two, with one group for males; the other for females. Try to have a discussion leader for each group who is of the same sex as the rest of the group. Discuss the following questions in small groups and then gather the groups together to share reactions.

- Was this situation believable for you? Does this happen at your school? Do you know anyone who has had this happen? (Do *not* give names.)
- Are there things that Jimmy believed that made him do the things he did? Can you give examples? Can you think of someone you know like Jimmy? (Do *not* give names.)
- What were some of the things that Jimmy did that Lionel and Tim told him were wrong? Has that ever happened to anyone you know? (Do *not* give names.)
- Why didn't Jimmy stop when Jesse told him "no"?
- Do you understand why Jesse felt the way she did after Jimmy raped her? Explain.

Conclusions (15 minutes)

Ask if participants have any questions or comments, then recap the three main areas covered in this session:

1. *Sexuality and violence are two very different things.*

    - Sexuality is a gift from God; it is about connection with God and with other people.
    - Violence degrades and separates us from one another and from God.

2. *When talking about sexuality and violence, it is important to understand power and resources.*

    - Power is based on our resources.
    - Each of us has a choice how we use our power and how we use our resources.
    - We can use our power "with" another or "over" another.

3. *Sexual violence is an example of the misuse of power.*

    - When we use our power over another we can abuse them.
    - Sexual harassment and rape are two examples of using power over another to control and degrade them. It is a misuse of our power and it is wrong.

Ask participants what they think they need to know in order to help themselves and others from becoming a victim or prepetrator of sexual violence. See "What We Need to Know" on pages 220–221.

End with a prayer of your own or use the following:

> Gracious and Loving God, You have created each of us in Your image and we give you thanks. For our sexuality that is a gift, we rejoice. But sometimes we get confused. And sometimes your gift of sexuality gets mixed up with violence. Sometimes we hurt someone else or we get hurt. So we ask for your guidance and healing. Help us to use our power responsibly. Help us to respect and love each other. In Your Holy name we pray. Amen.

Sources of Power and Sources of Vulnerability

	Sources of Power	**Sources of Vulnerability**
Age	older (or adulthood)	younger (or youth)
Gender	male	female or transgender
Race	Caucasian	Asian/Pacific Islander, African American, Native American, Latina/o, and other people of color
Role	teacher, coach, parent	student, player, child
Sexual Orientation	heterosexual	lesbian, gay, bisexual
Physical Resources	ability, large physical size, physical strength	disability, small size, physical weakness
Economic Resources	wealth, job skills	poverty, lack of job skills
Intellectual Resources	knowledge, access to information	lack of these
Psychological Resources	breadth of life experience	inexperience, lack of coping skills, mental illness
Social Resources	support, friends, family	isolation
Community Resources	high standing/respect within a community/group	lack of these

Sexuality and Violence

Luisa

Luisa had had a secret crush on Mark ever since he started school last spring. He had transferred from another school district and immediately became one of the most popular kids. He was the star of the basketball team, vice-president of the senior class, and drove a really cool car. On top of that, she thought he was really cute.

One Friday afternoon he stopped by her locker and asked her if she wanted to go out that night. She was so surprised and excited. He had barely spoken to her before that. Of course she said yes. On the walk home it felt like her feet barely touched the ground.

He picked her up at her house that night and they drove to the mall. But when they got there, Mark went straight to the arcade and started playing video games. He hardly paid any attention to her. Luisa just watched him, hoping that he'd stop soon so they could see a movie or something. Then some of his friends came by and he didn't even introduce her. When he finally stopped playing, she asked him to take her home. On the ride home, Mark drove to a deserted street and forced Luisa to have sex with him.

Johnny

Johnny was not the most popular kid in his class. He was tall and thin and had acne. He sang in the choir and played computer games after school with his friends. He tried out for the basketball team but didn't make the final cut.

One day he was late for math class and rounded a corner too quick. He bumped into Tony, one of the most popular kids in school, and knocked his books to the floor. Tony shoved him against the lockers and said "Watch where you're going, gay-boy."

After that, whenever Tony saw Johnny in the hall he would make a fist and pretend that he was going to hit him. When Johnny flinched, Tony and his friends would laugh and call him a "skinny gay-boy."

What We Need to Know*

Males

Regarding Rape

- Understand that "no" means "no."
- Know that it is never okay to force yourself on a girl, even if you think she's been teasing you and leading you on.
- Know that it is never okay to force yourself on a girl, even if you've heard that women say "no" when they really mean "yes."
- Know that it is not "manly" to use force to get your way.
- Know that it is never okay to force yourself on a girl, even if you feel physically that you've got to have sex.
- Know that it is never okay to force yourself on a girl, even if she is drunk.
- Know that whenever you use force to have sex you are committing a crime called rape even if you know her or have had sex with her before.
- Be aware of peer pressure to "score," and work against it by listening to what your date is saying.
- Be aware of what society may tell you it means to be a "real" man, and work against it by forming your own values based on respect, honesty, good listening skills, and so forth.
- Recognize that you can be raped too.

Regarding Harassment

- Be aware of what your peers may be telling you about being "cool"; avoid putting other boys down who may not act like you.
- Work on your own self-image, which is based on respect for other people rather than being better than someone else.

Females

Regarding Rape

- Say "no" when you mean "no"; say "yes" when you mean "yes"; stay in touch with your feelings to know the difference.

- Believe in your right to express your feelings and learn how to do so assertively.

- Be aware of stereotypes that prevent you from expressing yourself, such as "anger is unfeminine," "being polite, pleasant, and quiet is feminine."

- Be aware of specific situations in which you do not feel relaxed and "in charge."

- Be aware of situations in which you are vulnerable and have fewer resources.

- Be aware that if you are raped, it is not your fault, you didn't deserve it, and you can get help.

Regarding Harassment

- Remember that you have the right to your feelings and your space.

- If you have experienced harassment, remember that you are not alone, you can report it and get help.

*Excerpted from *Sexual Abuse Prevention: A Course of Study for Teenagers*, by Rebecca Voelkel-Haugen and Marie Fortune (Cleveland: United Church Press, 1996), 22. Used by permission.

Session 10

Decision Making

Purpose: This session helps young people learn a process for making decisions. Good decision making takes place when one is calm and can think, not when passions are high. Making decisions about sexual behavior before getting into dating situations will help young people avoid trouble. The activities include decision-making models, a theological discussion on decision making, and a quiz on what our church believes about sexuality.

Time: Two hours

Materials Needed

- *Older Youth Guide*
- Newsprint
- Felt-tipped markers
- Masking tape

Activities

Decision Making	45 minutes
Have You Weighed Your Options?	30 minutes
God Gives Us Responsibility for Our Own Decisions	45 minutes

Procedures

Decision Making* (45 minutes)

Ask for volunteers to role play the following scenarios. Allow a maximum of three minutes for each role play. Engage the group in discussion following each scenario using the following questions as guides:

- Do you agree with how this situation in the role play was handled?
- Do you think anything should have been done differently? What?
- How did your faith inform the situation?

Scenario 1

Mary and Alice are talking Friday afternoon after school about their plans for the evening. Mary, who has been dating Jake for most of the school year, tells Alice that he is putting a lot of pressure on her to have sex. Mary admits she's leaning toward having sex with Jake because she "doesn't want to lose him." Alice says that she thinks Mary should carry condoms, and Mary is appalled at Alice's suggestion.

Scenario 2

Jim and Tom go to a party together where alcohol is being consumed. Many people are "coupling off," appearing to be under the influence of alcohol. Tom has too much to drink and seems to be getting "seriously" close to a girl he met earlier in the evening. As Tom and the girl are walking up the stairs, Jim stops them, concerned.

Scenario 3

Matt and Susan spend a great deal of time together and are growing very close. One evening the two of them are lounging on the floor watching a movie. Matt reaches over and hugs Susan. Rather than taking his arm away, Susan moves closer. Matt asks Susan if she would like to go to bed.

In closing, talk about the importance of making wise decisions and, as a result, behaving responsibly.

*Adapted from *The Congregation: A Community of Care and Healing,* by Sharon Youngs. Louisville: Presbyterian Church (USA)/ Presbyterian AIDS Network, Social Justice and Peacemaking Unit, Office of Human Services, Health Ministries (USA), © Presbyterian Church (U.S.A.), 1992. Used by permission.

Have You Weighed Your Options? *(30 minutes)*

Introduce this activity by pointing out that the failure to make good decisions about sex is one of the reasons that young people experience an unplanned pregnancy. Explain to the group that they are going to look at the specific decision to have sexual intercourse. Use the figure on page 225, or draw a picture of a scale on newsprint. The scale represents the two choices a teenager can make—to have sex now or to wait until later to have sex.

Ask the group to brainstorm all the reasons a young person might give for saying yes to sex. List all of their reasons on the left side of the scale. Next, ask the group to list all the reasons why a young person might say no to having sex. Record all of the group's responses on the right side of the scale. You may want to supplement their reasons with those found at the end of this session.

Ask the group to look again at the left side of the scale picture, where all of the reasons why someone might say yes to sex are listed. Ask the group to eliminate all the reasons that are not good reasons for having sex. Help them evaluate the reasons, but accept all those that they think are good reasons.

Repeat the same process for the right side, where the reasons why a young person might choose to say no to sex are listed. Eliminate the bad reasons. Again, help them evaluate the reasons, but accept all those that they think are bad.

Now add up the reasons on each side of the scale. Tell the group that each good reason weighs one pound. Which way does the scale tip? (It should always tip to no. If necessary, you can suggest additional reasons not to have sex.)

Then discuss these questions:

- Are there pressures that influence our decision whether or not to have sex? What are they? (sex drive; media messages; wanting to be grown up; peer pressure; lack of communication about sex from parents and other adults; lack of assertiveness skills)
- Is a sexual decision more difficult to make than another kind of decision? Why or why not?
- Is it difficult to stick to the decision not to have sex? What can you do to follow through with that decision?
- What does a person need to know or do if he or she decides to have sex in a responsible fashion? Point out that teens who say yes to sex must plan ahead so they can avoid all the consequences that are given as reasons for not having sex (pregnancy, STI, etc.).
- Can you change a yes decision to a no decision the next time you have to decide about having sex? How?

Optional Activities*

1. Use the scale and a similar procedure to "weigh" other decisions that young people in the group might be making or facing.

2. Have group members construct a list of possible barriers that might prevent them from following through with their decisions. Then have them come up with ways to overcome each possible barrier and have them role play several of the decisions, barriers, and actions to overcome the barriers. For example:

Decision: I will never take drugs.

Barrier: My girlfriend calls me a "chicken."

Action: Tell her it sometimes takes more nerve not to do something.

Discuss how to avoid barriers before they occur and what elements barriers have in common (e.g., peer pressures, conflicting values).

*Used by permission from *Life Planning Education* (Washington D.C.: Advocates for Youth, 1985).

God Gives Us Responsibility for Our Own Decisions (45 minutes)

Have everyone read the section "God Gives Us Responsibility for Our Own Decisions" (p. 6 in the *Older Youth Guide*; p. 226 in this guide).

Have the participants imagine an important decision they have to make, such as whether or not to become sexually involved with another person. While thinking about this decision, each one should list on a sheet of newsprint all the things he or she believes would influence the decision. Help them make their lists as inclusive as possible, being sure to include such things as particular people, advertising, parental teachings, church teachings, school teachings, conscience, prayer, community standards, peer pressure, the influence of the community, economic factors, time factors, and so forth.

Have the young people rank those factors from most to least important for them in their decision making. Gather the group back together and discuss the similarities and differences in the lists.

Ask the group to complete the quiz "Our Church's Understandings" (pp. 72–73 in the *Older Youth Guide*; pp. 227–228 in this guide). Give people ten minutes to answer the questions and then go over the quiz.

Discuss the lists and the quiz. Include the following questions in the discussion:

- Which things influence you positively?
- What person has the most influence on you at this point in your life?
- How influential are your family's beliefs?
- Peer pressure is supposedly the most important factor in your life at this point. Would you agree that most of what you do is in line with what your friends are doing?
- Which of the influences could be defined as racist?
- Which of the influences could be defined as sexist?
- How free do you think you are at this point in your life to make your own decisions?
- Would you want to have more freedom to make your own decisions, or are you comfortable with the amount of freedom you have?
- Our church believes that there can be conscientious disagreement on moral issues. Would you like it better if we took stands that were final decisions for all the church?
- Do you find sexual issues complex, or are you clear about your answers to questions related to sexuality?
- Do you find yourself in agreement with your parents on most issues relating to sexuality? Your friends? Your teachers? Your church? What you perceive as our society's values?

Close with a prayer, asking for God's guidance as we live out our lives and giving thanks for this course.

Have You Weighed Your Options?

Reasons to Have Sex

Reasons to Wait Until Later to Have Sex

Which Way Does the Scale Tip?

Pros and Cons of Teenage Sexual Activity

Reasons that Some Young People Become Sexually Involved

- They are pressured by peers.
- They want to communicate warm, loving feelings in a relationship.
- They want to keep from being lonely.
- They want affection.
- They seek pleasure or fun.
- They want to show independence by rebelling against parents, teachers, and other authority figures.
- They want to hold on to a relationship.
- They want to show that they are adults.
- They want to become a parent.
- They want to satisfy curiosity.

Reasons that Young People Postpone Sexual Involvement

- It violates their religious beliefs.
- It violates their personal values.
- They are not ready for a sexual relationship.
- They like the relationship with a boyfriend or girlfriend as it is.
- A pregnancy could harm their health and alter their plans for the future.
- They fear getting a sexually transmitted infection.
- They might jeopardize their future goals.
- The relationship with their parents might be hurt.
- Their reputation with friends might be changed.
- They want sexual relations to be warm and open, not making them feel guilty about having sex.

God Gives Us Responsibility for Our Own Decisions

I appeal to you therefore, brothers and sisters, by the mercies of God, to present your bodies as a living sacrifice, holy and acceptable to God, which is your spiritual worship. Do not be conformed to this world, but be transformed by the renewing of your mind, so that you may discern what is the will of God—what is good and acceptable and perfect.

(Rom. 12:1–2)

If the people of the church are to be given the resources to live out their lives responsibly as sexual beings, the enabling leadership of the church must . . . assist people in their problems of identity and moral choice. This assistance will, however, have deprived people of the chance to grow and of the need to wrestle with their own choices if it consists predominantly of handing out prescriptions and passing judgment. What is more, the counsel of the church will be sought more if people see in its stance not only a convinced perspective which orients its approach but also a willingness to recognize the complexity of sexual problems, the possibility of conscientious disagreement on moral decisions, and the opportunity for renewal of life for forgiven sinners.

("The Nature and Purpose of Human Sexuality," lines 689–700)

In our decision making, we are instructed by God's Word to us. We are to be influenced by our Christian beliefs. We are aware of other influences—what our friends believe, how we feel, and what we have learned about our sexuality. We need to learn to sort out those different factors because some may be sexist, or homophobic, or racist, or the result of pressures from others.

The guiding principles that define the church are love, responsibility, obedience, and forgiveness. Keeping these principles in mind and exploring their meanings within our community will lead us to make responsible decisions for our own lives.

To talk about how we make decisions for ourselves and how we communicate those decisions to others is important. Our decisions, based on love, responsibility, and forgiveness, are discovered in relationship with God, with one another, and with ourselves.

Quiz: Our Church's Understandings

In order to make decisions, we must be informed by the understandings of our church. The following is a quiz to help you test your knowledge of our church's beliefs. Try to answer each question. If you do not know, or are unsure, then look up each question in the "Guide for the Presbyterian Church (U.S.A.)."

1. What is the purpose of statements the General Assembly makes about social issues?

a. The statements are guides to help us understand issues and make up our own minds.

b. The statements are official pronouncements of what Presbyterians believe.

c. The statements tell us what to believe.

2. What is the purpose of our sexuality?

a. Primarily for creating new life

b. Primarily for relating to one another

3. Does our church advocate sex education?

a. Yes, in the family and church

b. Yes, in the family, church, and school

c. Yes, in the family, church, school, and private and public agencies

4. What does our church believe about the relationship of men and women?

a. They are equal.

b. The woman is to be subordinate to the man.

c. The man is to be subordinate to the woman.

5. Does our church believe a married couple should have children?

a. Yes, after they have been married long enough to know each other well

b. Yes, because it completes their relationship and makes them a family

c. Not necessarily, because every couple must decide for themselves

6. What does our church believe about contraception?

a. Contraception should not be used by a married couple because it interferes with the natural process of reproduction.

b. Contraceptives should be made available and used by any married couple who does not want to reproduce.

7. What does our church believe should be done about infertility?

a. Infertility is the result of a natural process, and we should not interfere with the reproductive process.

b. We believe medical intervention should be used if necessary, including the use of artificial insemination and in vitro fertilization.

c. We believe medical intervention should be used if necessary, but not if it requires artificial impregnation, such as with artificial insemination and in vitro fertilization.

8. What does our church believe about premarital sex?

a. The level of sexual intimacy before marriage is a matter of responsible behavior as defined by the couple.

b. The level of sexual intimacy before marriage is a matter of responsible behavior as defined by the couple, but sexual intercourse should be postponed until after marriage.

c. Sexual conduct should be postponed until after marriage.

9. Does the church believe it is better to be single or married?

a. Married

b. Single

c. Either can be right

10. What does our church believe about masturbation?

a. Masturbation should be avoided.

b. Masturbation cannot be avoided.

c. Masturbation can be a good choice although sexuality should be shared.

11. What is our church's attitude toward divorce?

a. Divorce is the result of sin.

b. Divorce is immoral.

c. Divorce is legitimate, under some circumstances.

12. What is our church's understanding of abortion?

a.   Abortion is a woman's choice, and only she can determine the circumstances for choosing an abortion.

b.   Abortion is immoral.

c.   Abortion is permissible under some circumstances.

13. Should abortions be available for anyone?

a.   Yes, although we should not be required to finance them

b.   Yes, although minors should have parental support

c.   Yes

14. What is homophobia?

a.   Fear and hatred of people who are homosexual

b.   Fear of becoming homosexual

c.   Fear of people of the same sex

15. Are homosexuals welcome in the church?

a.   No

b.   Yes

c.   Yes, if they change or hide their behavior

Session 11

Building Blocks for Better Parent/Youth Communication

Purpose: This session promotes better communication by encouraging the expression of different viewpoints and by the sharing of information among youth, parents, and small-group leaders. Communication is a two-way street involving talking and listening. This session allows time for questions and responses in a safe, nonthreatening environment. The talking/listening is from parents to youth and from youth to parents, which provides building blocks for better communication in families.

Time: One hour and twenty-five minutes

Materials Needed

- Newsprint
- Felt-tipped markers
- Index cards
- Pens and pencils

Activities

Group Building	15 minutes
Fish Bowl	45 minutes
Evaluation of the Course	10 minutes
Closing Worship	15 minutes

Procedures

Group Building (15 minutes)

Do the "Name Tags" activity from Session 1 (p. 129 in this guide).

Fish Bowl (45 minutes)

Separate the group into two groups, with the parents in one group and the youth in the other. Appoint two small-group leaders for each group. Then instruct each group to go off by themselves and come up with ten questions that they, as a group, would like to ask the other group. Have them prioritize the questions by numbering which one they want to be asked first, second, third, and so on.

While the groups are away, rearrange the chairs in a large circle. Place four additional chairs in the center. When the parents and youth return, invite one parent, one youth, and one small-group leader to go to the chairs in "the fish bowl." (Make sure that there are both males and females in the center.) One chair will be left vacant.

Those in the fish bowl will begin discussing the first question from one of the lists. Everyone else will serve as observers (*listeners*). Only the people in the fish bowl are permitted to speak. Observers may move to the empty chair to ask a question, make a statement, or respond to something that has already been said, but they then must return to their place in the outside circle. When the first question has been answered, those people are thanked by the group and then they return to their chairs in the outer circle. Three more (one parent, one youth, and one small-group leader) are invited to volunteer to come forward. The first question from the other group is then read aloud and the process continues.

Some answers will be brief. Others, however, will take more time, especially those that are more value-oriented. Encourage all those who are in the fish bowl to share their feelings and, when appropriate, especially encourage parents to reflect on what it was like when they were teenagers dealing with these issues.

The leader should make sure that everyone is participating and communicating as well as listening.

After about forty-five minutes using this format, close off the discussion. Suggest that this group of parents and youth might get together again using the remaining questions as a means to continue the conversation.

Evaluation of the Course (10 minutes)

Ask youth and parents to fill out the appropriate course evaluation (on pp. 231–232 in this guide; p. 85 in the *Parent's Guide*; p. 75 in the *Older Youth Guide*).

Closing Worship (15 minutes)

Say to the group something like, "As this time together draws to a close, let us listen to God's Word as it has led us during this special time together." Have the following passages read by some youth and some parents: Gen. 1:26–27; Isa. 65:18; Eph. 2:19–22; Col. 3:12–17.

Then ask everyone to join in this litany (on p. 84 in the *Parent's Guide*; p. 74 in the *Older Youth Guide*):

> **Leader:** We are God's work of art created in Christ Jesus.
>
> **Participants:** In sovereign love, God created the world good and makes everyone equally in God's image, male and female, of every race and people, to live as one community ("A Brief Statement of Faith," lines 29–32).

> **Leader:** So God created humankind in God's own image, in the image of God was the human being created; male and female God created them. And God saw everything that was made, and behold it was very good.
>
> **Participants:** Life is a gift to be received with gratitude and a task to be pursued with courage (Confession of 1967, 9.17).
>
> **Leader:** Not only did God create us, but God created us in God's own image. All that we are, including our bodies, including our sexuality, is God's gift to us. We have been made to reflect God's goodness, wisdom, and love.
>
> **All:** Our sexuality is our way of being male and female in the world. Our sexuality is basic and affects our thoughts, feelings, and actions. Because our sexuality is called good by God, because it is God's gift to us, and because we are made in the image of God, we can feel good about our sexuality! Amen.

Next the leader reads Ex. 3:31–33 and Phil. 1:9–11. Then invite all those in the circle to name something that they are thankful for from this sexuality course, and afterward close with prayer.

Sexuality Course Evaluation

Older Youth

I would rate the sexuality education course as:

UNINTERESTING	SLIGHTLY INTERESTING	OK	GOOD	GREAT
❐	❐	❐	❐	❐

The most interesting part of the course was:

The thing I enjoyed most about the course was:

The thing I enjoyed least about the course was:

The part of the course most important to me was:

I wish there had been more:

Other comments:

Sexuality Course Evaluation

Parent

I would rate the sexuality education course as:

UNINTERESTING	SLIGHTLY INTERESTING	OK	GOOD	GREAT
❑	❑	❑	❑	❑

My perception of my teen's impression of the course is:

The aspect of the course most important to me was:

Because of this course, the lines of communication between me and my child about sexuality will:

IMPROVE	STAY THE SAME	BE DAMAGED
❑	❑	❑

I wish there had been more:

Other comments:

Notes

Notes

Notes

Notes

Notes

Notes